# web
## publisher's
# design
## guide
## for Windows

## Mary Jo Fahey

# CORIOLIS GROUP BOOKS

| Publisher: | Keith Weiskamp |
| Managing Editor: | Ron Pronk |
| Editor: | Jenni Aloi |
| Production: | Michelle Stroup |

Library of Congress Cataloging-in-Publication Data

Fahey, Mary Jo; Brown, Jeffrey W.

Web Publisher's Design Guide for Windows / Mary Jo Fahey and Jeffrey W. Brown

p. cm.

Includes Index

ISBN 1-883577-61-6 : $34.99

Printed in the United States of America

10 9 8 7 6 5 4 3 2 1

# Preface

Since the Fall of 1994, numerous books about the Internet have appeared on the market, but few approach the subject from an artist's point-of-view. Although Web publishing is distinctly different from traditional publishing, we've tried to present new information in a context that will be familiar to artists who presently work with Quark XPress and Photoshop. As Web pages become more and more popular, a whole new dimension will be added to graphic design. Web publishing is about to become an extensive new service that an artist can offer to his/her clients.

If you're an artist who's interested in creating Web pages, you're probably wondering how much there is to learn. Don't worry. HTML tagging is easy and the tricks you'll need to make small file sizes are in this book. You'll also find information about enhancing Web pages with color backgrounds, textures, image maps, sounds, movies and animation.

This book assumes you'll be designing for the Netscape browser. Although several other browsers exist, 70 percent of computer users who browse the Web use Netscape. It's easy to understand why Netscape is so popular since the other browsers can't see color backgrounds, color textures, inline JPEG images and CGI animation.

Artists can start creating Web pages on a computer hard drive with a copy of Netscape and a text processor (use the FTP function in America Online to download Netscape from ftp.netscape.com/pub/, or ask a friend who's on the Web to download a copy from the Netscape site at http://www.netscape.com). Get online as soon as possible since there's a lot to be learned from looking at other Web pages. The Web is also the best source of information about changes in HTML. Besides Netscape and a text processor, you'll need a modem (a 14.4 Kbps is a minimum speed but 28.8 Kbps is preferred), a phone line and a PPP or SLIP account from a local Internet provider.

Since many design organizations will want to run their own Web server, we've provided a thorough guide to setting up O'Reilly's WebSite software under Windows 95 or Windows NT. The software is an impressive, easy-to-use bundle, which O'Reilly & Associates offers free for sixty days. (Look for a fully functioning demo on the CD-ROM in the back of this book.)

For those who would prefer to lease space from an INternet provider, there are now hundreds of options nationwide.

One of the most interesting things about providing Web pages is the idea that the server can be anywhere. Geography doesn't matter on the Web. When you're ready to shop for a provider, look for a company that offers technical support and allows image maps (although most Web server software programs have image map capability, some providers are unwilling to support image maps). Rent space for one month to try out the relationship.

Since Web addresses change, we'll be providing readers with updates to the Web addresses published in this book (http://www.echonyc.com/~art/webdesign/webdesign.html). Please send email messages and let us know how you like the *Web Publisher's Design Guide* or if you discover any links that have changed.

Mary Jo Fahey

mjfahey@interport.net

Jeffrey W. Brown

pp002826@interramp.com

# Contents

# Chapter 10
# Setting up a Web server 291

# Appendix
# HTML 3 Reference Guide

# Using the Companion
# CD-ROM 393

# Index 417

# Acknowledgments

The *Web Publisher's Design Guide* was made possible thanks to a very large number of people who contributed their time and their talents. Special thanks to:

Brandee Amber Selck at IUMA for her great Web pages; Abigail Bowen at ECHO for her technical support and help with image maps; Thomas Boutell, author of Mapedit; Andrew Bulhak, author of Waveform Hold and Modify (WHAM); Peter Chowka for his many articles and URLs; Tom Cipolla for his advice on sound; Lisa Cresson for her help and encouragement; Frank DeCrescenzo for his beautiful graphics and hard work; Dwayne Davis, chairman of the NYPC Multimedia SIG; Diana DeLucia, owner of DeLucia Design for her creative ideas and sense of humor; Robert Denny for his WebSite software; Curtis Eberhardt for his insights into 3D graphics and animation; Frauke Ebinger at DeLucia Design for her beautiful graphics; Said Elbaqali of Key Computer for his help with QuickDraw 3D; Ron Elbert for reading the Photography chapter and his humorous email; Mark Elbert for his amazingly accurate vision and his kindness and clever graphics; Michael Erde at Interport for answering my questions about Unix; Merry and Guillermo Esparza for their many talents and dedication to beautiful graphics; John Farrar at DeLucia Design for his cover design; Gail Garcia, owner of Garcia Studio, for her stunning graphics, organization and funny sense of humor; Arch Garland owner of Flyleaf for his splash screen graphics; Beth Gilbrech for introducing me to the World Wide Web; Simon Higgs, author of Web Clock, for his clever Web pages; the Hot Dog development team for their outstanding HTML editor; Tim Hunter of Key Computer for his LexMark printer and 88 MB SyQuest drive; Grant Hurlbert at Pacific Coast Software for his stock photos; Joker for his thoughtful email; John A. Junod, author of Windows Sockets FTP Client Application (WS_FTP); Shirley Lew for her help and encouragement; Robert Liu at Best Business Solutions for his changes in the BBS Color Editor; Leonardo Haddad Loureiro, author of LVIEW Pro; Steve Margolis for his help with finding an Internet provider; Steven McGrew for responding to all my questions about video; Bill Murphy at The Webology Group for his help with CGI scripts; Patricia Pane at Adobe Systems for her help with Adobe Premiere; Alan Phillips, author of Programmer's File Editor; David Reinfurt at IDEO for his exceptional design and his introduction to Wayfinding; Christina Sun of Sun Studio for years and years of advice about art; Barbara Tanis at DeLucia Design for her art direction; Okey Nestor owner of Shankweiler Nestor for his art direction; Shrihari Pandit for help and advice; Alberto Ricci, author of SoundEffects, for his help with sound editing; Barry and Jackie Ryan for years of friendship and encouragement and Kleber Santos at Straightline International for his help with design ideas, his wonderful pages and JoJo.

Antonio Antiochia at Fry Multimedia; Antonio Arenas at The Image Bank; Elaine Arsenault; Don Barlow at The Image Bank; David Beach at IUMA; Brian Behlendorf; Gavin Bell; Josh Bevans at Strata; Gina Blaber at O'Reilly & Associates, Eileen Caetano at Silicon Graphics; Harry Chesley at Macromedia; Michael Clemens at Fry Multimedia; Daniel W. Connolly at the Laboratory for Computer Science at MIT; Katie Cotton at KillerApp Communications; Tom Cunniff at Fry Multimedia; Kevin Dowd at Atlantic; Betsy Ducey at Silicon Graphics; Juanita Dugdale at Society for Environmental Graphic Design; Kevin Ellis at Macromedia; Pat Fegan at Booz Allen & Hamilton; David Filo, founder of Yahoo; David Frerich at Silicon Graphics; David Fry, owner of Fry Multimedia; Bernard Furnival at Ken Hansen Imaging; Frank Gadegast at Technische Universitat in Berlin; Steven Garson at Fabulous Footage; Scott Geffert at Ken Hansen Imaging; Peter Geffert at Ken Hansen Imaging; Harrison Goldman at The Image Bank; Howard Goldstein at Ken Hansen Imaging; Sharon Gresh; Maynard Handley, author of Sparkle; Jason Held at Simon & Schuster; Patrick Hennessey, author of the Interactive Graphics Renderer; Donna Hoffman at Vanderbilt University; Stacy Horn, owner of ECHO; Kevin Hughes at EIT; Juvenile;Trevor Kaufman at Voyager; Duncan Kennedy at Apple Computer; Molly Ker at ECHO; Judy Kirkpatrick at Adobe Systems; Iva Kravitz at Two Twelve Associates; Cindy Krculic at DeLucia Design; Fred Krughoff at Rom Dog; Theresa LaGioia at The Image Bank; Fabrizio LaRocca at Random House; Robert Lord founder of IUMA; Luis; Roger Manco at Reach Marketing and Communications; Ed Manning at Cambium Development; Marcus; Charles Marelli at Modem Media; Peter Marx at Duet Corporation; Michael McGinn; Charles McGrew at Rutgers; Members of Mother Mary; Mesh Records; Raymond Meyer, owner of Raymond Meyer Studio; Eden Muir at Cybersites; Hass Murphy at Rom Dog; John Nardone at Modem Media; Pauline Neuwirth; Rory O'Neill at Cybersites; Tommy Oddo, founder of Oddo Design; Gabe Palacio; Tony Parisi; Jeff Patterson founder of IUMA; Lindsey Payne; Mark Pesce; Oliver Picker at Unisys; Berta Ponzo; Mark Rand at Oceana; Carlos Reynoso; Alicia Rockmore at Ragu; Manuel Ron; Sergio; Stephen Serwin at DeLucia Design; Sfuzzi; Alex Sherman at Modem Media; Scott Sindorf at Cybersites; Lily Smith at Shankweiler Nestor; The Staff at Cafe Mozart; Paul Strauss; John Tariot at FOOTAGE.net; David Theurer, author of DeBabelizer; Mark Trimishad at Silicon Graphics; Eric Twelker at KillerApp Communications; Two Twelve Associates; Umberto; Elizabeth Warren at The Image Bank; Robert Weideman; Heini Withagen at Eindhoven University, The Netherlands; Yale University Center for Advanced Instructional Media and Jerry Yang, founder of Yahoo.

**Artist featured in this chapter:**

*David Reinfurt is a multi-disciplinary graphic designer with a B.A. in Visual Communications from the University of North Carolina. David specializes in interaction design.*

*(reinfurt@ideo.com)*

# Chapter 1

# Planning

Although it's tempting to begin your Web page creations with graphics, in this chapter David Reinfurt makes us aware of key project elements to have in place before the graphics begin.

# The Reuters Web sites

*Summary:* In this chapter on planning, the Reuters sites provide an excellent Web site development model. Built by a professional graphic designer for a client who understands online information technology, this site represents perfect "Web craftsmanship."

*Note:* Two Twelve Associates is a multidisciplinary design firm specializing in environmental graphics, print and interactive design. The firm is located at:
596 Broadway, Suite 1212
New York, NY 10012-3234
212.925.6885.

Few people wander around the Web without a purpose. Travelers usually search and navigate with the help of signs, just as they do on the street.

For several decades, signs in architectural spaces have been designed by a group of graphic designers known as "environmental designers." Just as graphic design has evolved in the print medium, so have the visual aesthetics and formulas used in environmental graphics. For example, environmental designers have adopted the architect's phased approach to project development, which includes planning, schematics, design and production.

Environmental graphic designers now know a great deal about effective organization of space and use of environmental elements. In fact, one graphic design firm specializing in environmental graphics is uniquely positioned to offer advice on "planning a Web site." The underlying principles of helping people "find their way" are as appropriate for virtual spaces as they are for real spaces.

### Two Twelve Associates.
Using the principles of "wayfinding," the graphic designers at Two Twelve Associates have been designing spaces for almost twenty years. Wayfinding is the study of peoples' movements and their relationship to space. It's also the process of reaching a destination, which involves problem solving. Two Twelve Associates has used wayfinding design to plan spaces for clients such as the South Street Seaport, the Central Park Zoo, the Baltimore Light Rail Subway, the Baltimore Waterfront Promenade, the City of New York Department of Parks and Recreation and the Metropolitan Transportation Authority.

Recently, David Reinfurt, a graphic designer with Two Twelve, designed and built the two Web sites for Reuters, shown in this chapter. David's skill as an environmental

1.

graphic designer and his insight into how to plan a project will help Web designers organize their own sites.

## 1. Reuters News Machine.

For business people suffering from "information overload," Reuters "News Machine" (http://www.reuters.com) offers what might be called an electronic clipping service called "my.news." For a fixed monthly fee, a computer user can pre-define the categories of news they wish to receive, and Reuters will deliver all related stories. The service also offers general news, sports news, business news, offbeat news (alt.news) and an area called news.talk, dedicated to online discussions about current events.

a. **News content groups.** Up-to-the-minute reports from the Reuters bureaus around the world are organized into four "content" groups. Users can click on a category and then review a list of headline/synopsis items. Each news headline is a link to the full story. Content groups include:

- **news**, which contains general news items from around the world.

- **business**, which includes stories shaping the economic and business news.

- **sports**, which contains the latest sports stories.

- **alt.news**, which includes "offbeat" news.

1a.

[news.**search**]  [**my.news**]  [news.**talk**]

**1b.**

**2.**

***Tip:*** *The Reuters Business Information Products site has full-bleed images, which have been ghosted to a light gray and white and used to cover the background. This effect, which is specific to Netscape, is achieved with the <Body Background = "filename.gif" > tag at the top of the HTML document:*

```
<body background=
"filename.jpg"></body>
```

**b. News functions.** This consists of two unique "news tools" and a news discussion area where you can participate in news discussions with people around the world.

- **News.search** is a powerful search tool that responds to a keyword search gathering news items on any topic you choose.

- **My.news** is the Web equivalent of an electronic clipping service allowing you to pre-define news categories of interest. The news stories are automatically delivered to your computer several times a day.

- **News.talk** is an area containing news "threads," which are followed by people all over the world. Users exchange their views by posting messages to a particular thread in response to a news item.

## 2. Reuters Business Information Products.

Reuters Business Information site (http://www.reuters.com) was created to support two new Reuter's online business services: *Reuters Business Briefing* and *Reuters Business Alert.* These two online, user-definable news retrieval services offer news gathered from more than 2,000 sources and delivered up to 15 times a day to a subscriber's PC or server.

*Reuters Business Briefing* is a server-based product that can assemble news in one central location and distribute it on an enterprise-wide basis via Lotus Notes.

*Reuters Business Alert* is a smaller, workstation or LAN-based news-gathering service designed for PCs running Microsoft Windows.

**a. Products.** A mouse click on the Products button will take visitors to pages that describe both of the Reuters Business Information Products.

**(Products)**
Introducing Reuters Business Briefing and Reuters Business Alert Server—two new ways to help your company gain the competitive edge

**2a.**

*Tip:* Notice that the outline around buttons has been turned off. Netscape ordinarily displays a heavy blue line around an image that's a link (called an "active link") and a purple line if the link has been clicked (called a "visited link"). To turn off the outline, enter:

```
<img src="filename.gif"
align=top border=0>
```

**b. Sales Contacts.** The Sales Contacts button (Figure 2b1) will branch to a map of the United States. Clicking on a state (Figure 2b2) will bring up a silhouette image of the sales rep for that state (Figure 2b3), and, if the browser has a built-in sound player, the rep's "hello" will be heard.

**2b1.**

**2b2.**

**2b3.**

**c. Sources.** If visitors are interested in knowing the sources for news, a "Sources" button will branch to a section that will display the information onscreen.

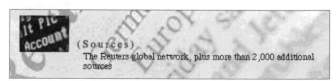

**2c.**

**d. Feedback.** The Feedback button (Figure 2d1) branches to a questionnaire. A multiple-choice format with check boxes makes the form (Figure 2d2) easy-to-use.

**2d1.**

**2d2.**

**e. The Network.** The Network button takes visitors to an area that changes most frequently. It includes product announcements and a "faq"—or frequently asked questions—section.

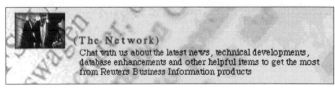

**2e.**

# David Reinfurt's tips on planning a Web site

*Summary: The essential early steps in the Web site development process do not involve graphics; they require the creation of an underlying structure.*

## 1. Assemble the team.

For a graphic design firm, the Web development team includes client members as well as members from the graphic design firm:

**a.** **A manager, client.** This person has the authority to make decisions and is most likely a member of the firm's marketing team. Ideally, this team member is very familiar with the Web and can be relied upon for content ideas.

**b.** **Writer/marketing specialist, client.** In Reuters' World Wide Web terminology, this person is known as an Editor. Analogous in some ways to a managing editor, this member contributes content ideas and has an ongoing role in the life of the Web project. Ideally, this team member is very familiar with the Web.

**c.** **A technical specialist, client.** This member is responsible for making the Web pages and the server work. The team might look to an Internet provider to fill this role. Ideally, this person is familiar with the IBM, Macintosh and Unix platforms.

**d.** **Graphic designers, graphic design firm.** Depending on the size of the project, two designers may be involved. A senior designer art directs and a junior designer is involved in production.

**e. Information Designer, graphic design firm.** This member has a writing background and will review the marketing content to see if it is appropriate for the Web. For example, marketing content created for print is often too wordy; an information designer will know how to edit the content for Web pages. This member should be very familiar with the Web.

## 2. Develop a concept.

Developing a concept usually involves a brainstorming session, which may last an entire week. At this stage, a rough content list consisting of bullets should be developed. This information will be refined and organized in a schematic process, outlined next. To help facilitate the flow of ideas in brainstorming sessions:

**a. Tour the Web.** Analyze what's possible and examine well implemented sites. Since the Web is large and changes frequently, each team member should have a connection and be able to search the Web independently.

**b. Consider sources for content.** Although a firm's existing collateral materials may be repurposed for a Web site, ideally the site should have new content.

**c. Develop a core channel or underlying paradigm or metaphor.**
One of the most important elements to consider during initial brainstorming sessions is the underlying paradigm:

- Is it a bookstore?
- Is it a record store?
- Is it a catalog?
- Is it a public relations vehicle?

The Reuters development team decided the News Machine site would be an online news source, somewhere between newspaper and television, and the Business Information Products site would be a public relations vehicle.

## 3. Develop a schematic (on paper).

While the writers develop copy, the graphic designers develop a minimal schematic. Copy, in the form of diagram labels, is used to identify the components of the Web site (Figure 3a):

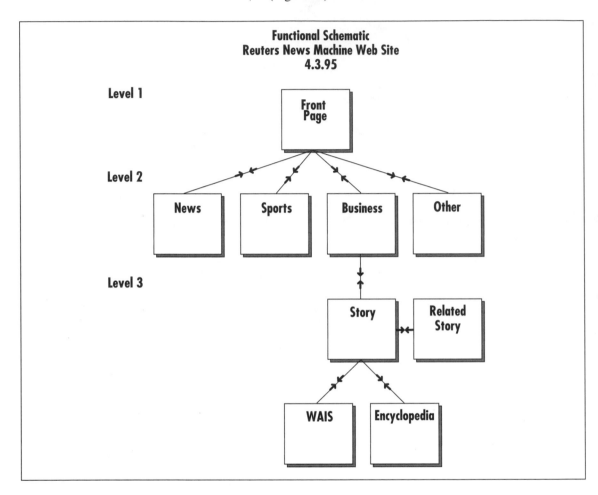

**3a.**

**3b.**

Level one contains the site's components as described in wayfinding design. (*See "'Wayfinding' principles in Web site design" later in this chapter.*) In this model, the components are the four news content areas and three news functions. Although these are not shown on the minimal schematic, they show up as text in the schematic prototype and as glyphs, or identifying icons, in the graphic design phase (Figure 3b).

Level two contains the destinations described in wayfinding design. In this model, destinations include types of news. (News, sports, business and other fields are page names, which were modified and rearranged later in the project.)

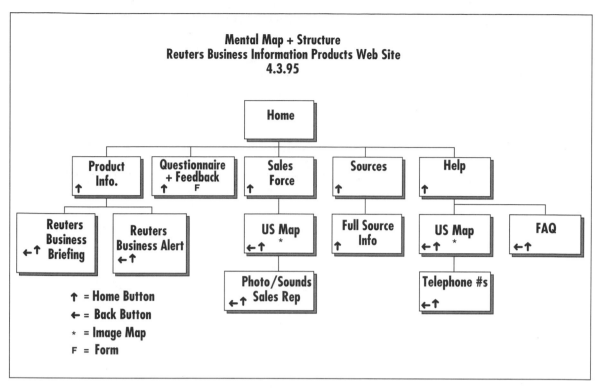

**Mental Map + Structure**
**Reuters Business Information Products Web Site**
**4.3.95**

- Home
  - Product Info. ↑
    - Reuters Business Briefing ←↑
    - Reuters Business Alert ←↑
  - Questionnaire + Feedback ↑ F
  - Sales Force ↑
    - US Map ←↑ *
      - Photo/Sounds Sales Rep ←↑
  - Sources ↑
    - Full Source Info ↑
  - Help ↑
    - US Map ←↑ *
      - Telephone #s ←↑
    - FAQ ←↑

↑ = Home Button
← = Back Button
* = Image Map
F = Form

**4a.**

## 4. Plan navigation.

The arrows on the schematic diagrams roughly describe navigation. Later, sets of "glyphs" are developed to help users navigate (represented schematically in Figure 4a and implemented in Figure 4b). Other navigation aids include a link to a help screen or a site map.

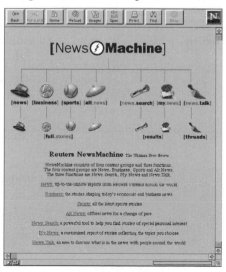

**4b.**

## 5. Create a schematic prototype (no graphics).

A schematic prototype consists of text-only Web pages. Although text is boring to look at, it focuses a team's attention on content before graphics are created. For the graphic design firm, a schematic prototype can be used to get client approval before moving on to the next phase. The prototype should follow the earlier schematic, and contain easy-to-read copy developed for quick consumption:

a. **Easy-to-read chunks.** The content should consist of plain language organized into chunks of from four to five items. For example, in the News Machine project, the graphic design elements on the Reuters "front page" evolved much later in the project. Early in the project, the front page was represented with text items:

- News

- Sports

- Business

- Other

b. **Analyze the information.** Carefully plan how information is presented. Web visitors should:

- **Understand where they are at all times.** At the prototype stage, locations were identified with text labels. Much later, matching graphic design elements were created as location identifiers on every page. In the Business Information pages, the page backgrounds identify a visitor's location.

- **Understand the "destinations" built into a site.** Although the decision to provide visitors with some facility to see all destinations at all times was made at the prototype stage, the tool bar did not take shape until later, in the graphic design stage. In the News Machine site, a toolbar on every page includes all the destinations available to a visitor.

- **Understand what action will take them to a destination.** At the prototype stage, text links were used as navigation links. Button and other graphic design elements were added later. For example, in the News

Machine site, a click on a small icon will give a larger icon at the top of the next page. This reinforces that the action is correct.

c. **Streamline the copy.** Since it is likely that Web visitors will do more scanning and glancing than reading from left to right, the content should be refined to contain essential information, conveyed in "keywords."

## 6. Begin the graphic design process.

If planning is phase one, then graphic design is phase two. During this second phase, the development team meets regularly to review the design direction. As in print, the design cycle is an interactive process. During this phase, the graphic designers carefully review the visual elements and constantly ask themselves, "How can I improve this?" "Does this work?" and "Are the visual elements easy to understand?"

The work that goes into the planning phase does not end when graphic design begins. During the graphic design phase, the designer must constantly look back at the planning work accomplished in phase one and ask "Does the project's design match the original project plan?" "Is it clear?" and "Are the ideas easy to understand?"

# "Wayfinding" principles in Web site design

***Summary:*** *Wayfinding principles, used to help people "find their way," offer important guidelines for Web site developers. These ideas will become even more valuable as Web sites develop into 3D spaces.*

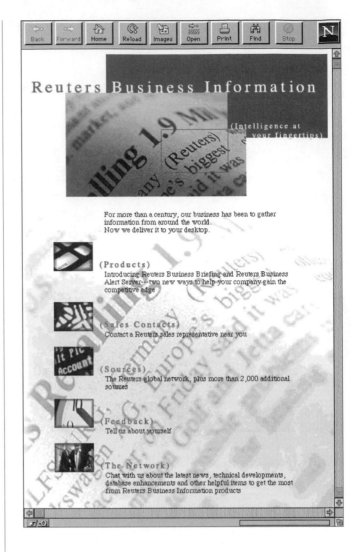

## 1. What is wayfinding?

Introduced to environmental design in the late 70s, the term "wayfinding" describes spatial behavior. It includes the decision making, decision execution and information processing involved in reaching a destination. Although the term initially referred to the process of reaching a physical destination, wayfinding principles may also be used for navigating Web sites. At the most basic level, wayfinding consists of "cognitive mapping" and "spatial problem solving," defined next.

  **a.** **Cognitive mapping.** The process of forming a mental image of a physical layout.

**2a.**

**2b.**

**b. Spatial problem solving.** Behavior, usually decision making, needed to make a journey or reach a destination.

## 2. Wayfinding decisions.

Wayfinding decisions are hierarchically structured in a "decision plan," which consists of one or more wayfinding decisions broken down into smaller decisions. For example:

**a. Decision to use Reuters news.search.** If the news.search page in the Reuters News Machine site is a destination, smaller wayfinding decisions required would include:

• Get on the Web.

• Use a bookmark or open the URL associated with the Reuters News Machine site.

• Select news.search from the Reuters home page. You would then see the screen shown in Figure 2a.

If news.search were not an option available on the Reuters home page, the list of decisions would include whatever actions would be necessary to get to the destination or the news.search page.

**b. Decision to contact a Reuters Sales Representative.** If the Sales Contacts page in the Reuters Business Information Products site is the destination, the smaller wayfinding decisions would be:

• Get on the Web.

• Use a bookmark or open the URL associated with the Reuters Business Information Products site.

• Select Sales Contacts from the Reuters home page.

• Scroll to the map of the United States.

• Click on a state.

• Record the name and phone number of the Reuters salesperson, as shown in Figure 2b.

## 3. Wayfinding conditions.

Wayfinding conditions result in a Web visitor's arrival at your site. Different visitors will have different reasons for viewing your site:

**4a.**

**4b.**

**4c.**

**a. The Web visitor is exploring.** The visitor has no particular goal or destination in mind.

**b. The Web visitor has an objective.** This Web visitor is seeking specific information.

## 4. The wayfinding design process.

Although wayfinding principles are applied throughout the entire planning and graphic design process, it is interesting to examine the details of the wayfinding design process:

**a. Identification of components.** In the News Machine project, identifying components was an essential part of the design process because it meant naming the four content areas and three functions. Identifying the types of news (news, business, sports and alt.news) took place in the planning phase and again in the design phase. Notice the change in the names from the schematic to the graphic design phase.

**b. Grouping of components into destinations.** In the News Machine site, Web visitors move from a front page to a destination page with news headlines and a news synopsis under each headline. Although it may contain further links, a page that contains news is considered a destination.

**c. Linking of components.** A toolbar with elements small enough to fit on every page means a Web visitor can branch to every section from every page.

## 5. Wayfinding design.

Wayfinding design involves themes that can be adapted and applied to Web site development:

**a. Decision diagram.** A decision diagram is a list of decisions a visitor has to make to navigate a site. Although this step was not used in the two Reuters projects, there was a conscious effort to review the number of steps a visitor needs to take to get to a destination. As in space planning for physical sites, visitors should take as few steps as possible to get to Web destinations.

**b. Graphics as landmarks.** Web site pages should have related graphics that act as a masthead, but multiple mastheads should not be identical. In the Reuters Business Information site, the masthead graphic varies slightly from page to page. The backgrounds also act as visual landmarks.

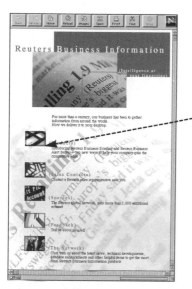

5b.

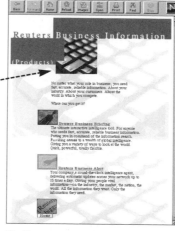

5b, 5c.

5c.

5c.

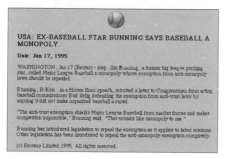

5c.

**c. Redundancy.** In the Reuters News Machine site, the "glyphs," or identifying icons, are repeated to remind Web visitors where they are at all times. Although the size varies, this reoccurring graphic assures that a Web visitor is not lost. In the Reuters Business Information Product example, notice how David repeated the identifying button image in the background graphic.

**d. Color.** Although color was not used as a landmark in either Reuters site, it can be used as an effective identifier to help a Web visitor navigate.

**e. Iteration.** Web designers should anticipate from 5 to 20 cycles of change in the development of a Web site. Focus groups, alpha testers, beta testers and a questionnaire on the Web site are all vehicles for gathering feedback from the people who travel the site.

## 6. Conclusion.

Although a planning phase can be rigorous, it represents a time-tested model that adds a solid foundation to a project. For example, experience has shown that the project model that included thorough planning withstands change much more than a project with little planning.

**Artist featured in this chapter:**

*Merry Esparza is an illustrator and painter who specializes in 3D computer illustration and interactive computer graphics.*

*mesparza@echonyc.com*

*http://www.echonyc.com/~art/merry/merry.html*

# Chapter 2

# Navigation

In this chapter on navigation, Merry Esparza introduces us to both 2D and 3D navigation on the Web. Although 3D "worlds" are relatively new, the technology does exist, and it's changing the way Web visitors move around. For example, text links and inline links on a "page" are replaced by new navigation controls in 3D space. The new 3D browsers include network anchors and node pointers that help Web travelers move by "hyperlinking" through 3D worlds.

# The Mobius Gallery

*Summary:* An art gallery in cyberspace provides a model for learning how to plan and develop navigation controls for your Web site.

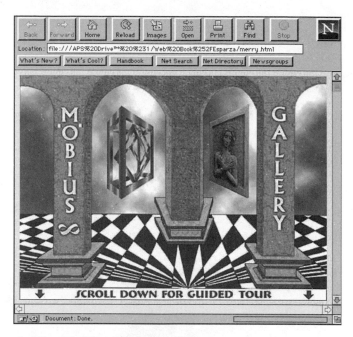

### 1. The Mobius Gallery Site.

Designed by computer artist Merry Esparza (mesparza@echonyc.com), the Mobius Gallery site (http://www.echonyc.com/~art/merry/merry.html) provides a showcase for Merry's artwork and Guillermo Esparza's paintings and sculpture. A Web site is a unique and advantageous space for artists to set up their own exhibit—it's international, art does not need to be physically transported and the site can be easily updated.

**a. Sculpture.** To display Guillermo's work, Merry photographed his paintings and sculpture and scanned the images into Photoshop. "La Magdalena," shown on this page, is a cast stone high-relief figure, created by Guillermo in 1994. The original is in The National Museum of Catholic Art and History in New York City.

**b. Painting.** Although images of Guillermo Esparza's paintings can be seen on the Web, electronic duplicates can never totally reflect his original work, which can be found inside many New York City churches. His projects have included wall murals, domes, sanctuary paintings and sanctuary statues. Geographically spread out, they can be easily brought together in only one place—a Web site.

**Above:** Merry Esparza's splash screen for the Mobius Gallery site. **Below:** Merry created a 3D cube for her logo.

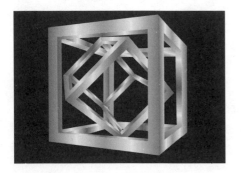

**Below:** Three dimensional mural created for "Empyrean," an interactive computer strategy game.

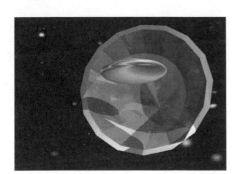

**c. Graphics** is the section of the Web site containing Merry's computer illustration. One of her specialties is optical illusion art, reflected in the site's splash screen. Merry explains that the Mobius Gallery's opening screen is designed to "reflect the relationship between the viewer and the work of art." In the image, Merry superimposes "inverted perspective" on "linear perspective." Linear perspective establishes depth by using actual or suggested lines that intersect in the background. This creates a space where objects diminish in size relative to distance from the viewer's eye. Combined are elements of inverted perspective, a concept used in Byzantine art. In inverted perspective, objects that are "farthest away" appear larger than elements in the foreground.

Merry's work in three dimensional art has also led to a series of murals she created for "Empyrean," her computer strategy game. Merry built a prototype game in Macromedia Director and is currently talking with game developers about building an interactive game for the Web. As Merry explains, "by 1996, cable modems will provide enough bandwidth for game developers to by-pass CD-ROMs and develop exclusively for the Web."

## 2. Future 3D graphics on the Mobius site.

Merry's work in 3D graphics overlaps new developments in Web technology. As a result, she sees the Mobius Gallery as a test site for interesting new software programs. Examples include:

**a. VRML and 3DMF.** Merry plans to develop a 3D version of the Mobius Gallery, which Web visitors could navigate with 3D browsers such as Intervista's WorldView browser (see Figure 2a). Three dimensional spaces also have the potential for typed conversation between visitors or between Guillermo, Merry and visitors. On the Internet, typed conversations are known as "Internet Relay Chat" or "IRC." The WebFX VRML 3D browser from Paper Software (http://www.paperinc.com) embeds itself into Web browsers and supports 3D space.

**2a.**

*Above: Intervista's WorldView browser is a VRML software application that allows you to navigate 3D objects and walk about in 3D worlds.*

*Tip: AdHoc Software has created a utility to convert Autodesk 3DStudio files to VRML (the utility is available on the CD-ROM in the back of this book).*

3D "walkthrough" environments can be built with Strata's *Studio Pro Blitz for Windows* (*available in December '95*) and a growing number of other 3D application software programs. The developments that make "walkthrough" worlds on the Web possible are two new cross-platform 3D file formats with built-in features designed for Web travel. VRML (*Virtual Reality Modeling Language*), sponsored by Silicon Graphics and 3DMF (*3D Meta File*) from Apple Computer will soon become as familiar to Web artists as GIF and JPEG.

Software application programs that are VRML- and 3DMF-savvy will have a selection on the File menu for saving a 3D image as a VRML or 3DMF file. Applications will also have built-in features that enable artists to specify the location of a "network anchor" or "hot spot." Network anchors are clickable spots in a 3D world that hold URL information. When clicked, the Web visitor hyperlinks or travels to a related Web site. (*Note: See "Following WWW anchors in VRML with the WorldView browser" in the Animation chapter.*)

**b. Apple's QuickTime VR.** For Web visitors to see Gallery "rooms" from a 360-degree perspective, Merry is planning QuickTime VR (virtual reality) movies for the Mobius site. 3D panels can be rendered for a 360-degree panoramic image and stitched together using Apple's QuickTime VR Authoring Tools Suite. Using Apple's QuickTime VR Player for Windows, visitors can twist, turn, twirl, zoom, and pick up 3D objects in a 3D environment. In the future, the QuickTime VR experience will include music and hyperlinks to other Web sites; Apple has only just begun to develop the QuickTime VR format.

**c. Animated 3D graphics for the Director Internet Player.** Merry sees potential for animated tours with music, sound effects and interactivity using Macromedia's new Director Internet Player technology. The player's "streaming" characteristic makes Macromedia's new development very attractive for Web visitors because it means there's no waiting for Director files to download.

# Principles of Web site navigation

**Summary:** *For the past few decades, print, radio and television have been considered the three mass market media. Recently, the Web has been described as the fourth mass market medium. This very different new medium allows viewers to interact and "navigate."*

Graphic designers who have started to design Web pages have the privilege of shaping the newest media—the media that are predicted to influence the way we work, play, think and learn. Because of its rapid growth, the Web will evolve in ways we cannot anticipate. Although many changes are expected to occur in the next few years, there are several underlying principles that are likely to remain:

## 1. Hypermedia.

The Web is a hypermedia system developed in 1989 by Tim Berners-Lee, a software engineer at the Center for European Particle Physics. Hypermedia is interactive information that has no beginning and no end. Although "home pages" are starting points, Web pages should be thought of as non-linear. Links found on each page jump to other Web pages, providing a random sequencing of information. Viewers can choose to "navigate" through an information base in a variety of ways, depending on the links they follow—and the information base can be spread out all over the world. Hypermedia is a term invented in the 1970s, but the concept dates back to 1945. Read on for a bit of history:

a. **Vannevar Bush and the "Memex" system.** In 1945, thirty years before anyone thought of a personal computer, computer scientist Vannevar Bush described a "Memex," a system that provided "associative indexing," or the ability to string together information meaningful to an individual user. Bush envisioned a system with text and graphics that could be viewed either sequentially or by following a user's trail of associative thinking.

b. **Ted Nelson and the word "hypermedia."** In the 1970s, Ted Nelson, author of Dream Machines, introduced the term "hypermedia." He saw hypermedia as a two-way medium in which computer users are creators as much as they are consumers. Apple Computer has promoted this idea since their 1987 introduction of HyperCard, a user-friendly hypermedia "authoring" toolkit for Macs.

c. **Two-way communication is attracting big business.** Although CD-ROMs and kiosks have hypermedia characteristics, most are read-only. The potential for two-way communication is much stronger on the World Wide Web. As a result, commercial interests are focused on the Web's marketing potential. From a marketing point of view, tomorrow's virtual worlds can attract the curious Web explorers, and "dynamic" database engines can measure and track a visitor's every response.

## 2. Active explorer vs. passive observer.

An underlying theme in every form of hypermedia is the viewer as an active explorer. As a traveling "participant" in the media, the viewer is given the option of deciding where to go and how to get there. Viewers move around to navigate and interact with an information base.

a. **Two-dimensional HTML.** The two-dimensional Web page formed from HTML tags is becoming less of a page and more of a "background" for multimedia player windows and new animation technologies built into the browser's page. Examples include the Director Internet Player, the new 3D browsers and Hot Java, an interactive 3D animation technology that can enhance a browser page with multimedia presentations or launch small "applets" in the form of interactive floating windows. All of these new developments have been built with viewer participation in mind.

**b. Three dimensional VRML and 3DMF.** In VRML and 3DMF "worlds," there are no passive observers. "Navigation" in 3D implies moving through a space or handling objects. Software engineers involved in the development of 3D worlds have invented built-in "anchors," or "hot spots." This means a click on an object in a 3D world will "hyperlink" a Web visitor to another "world."

## 3. The home page.

Regardless of how a Web site is organized or how many pages a site has, the starting point is referred to as the "home page." Although Web visitors can travel directly to any page on a Web site, it's the home page address that usually gets published or promoted.

## 4. Navigating with URLs.

URLs, or Uniform Resource Locators, are addresses used to locate information on the Web. URLs can be used to locate Web documents, FTP files, Gopher files, news files or other Web resources as they're developed. Navigation on the Web means opening a link that contains a URL. This can be accomplished by using a browser's Open command and typing in the URL or by clicking on a link that contains a URL. A URL stores information in three ways:

**a. Protocol information** is the first part of the URL. For example, Microsoft has a Web site and an FTP site. To access the FTP site, type the following FTP protocol into the Open Command's dialog box:

```
ftp://ftp.microsoft.com
```

*Tip: Browser software programs can "download" a file from an FTP site with a click on an ftp link on a Web page. However, browser software cannot "Upload." John A. Junod's Windows Sockets FTP Client Application is a Windows shareware FTP utility that can be used to transfer files to and from file servers on the Internet. Look for WS FTP on the CD-ROM in the back of this book.*

To access the Web site, type the following http protocol into the Open Command's dialog box::

```
http://www.microsoft.com
```

The protocol provides a clue concerning what type of information request is sent from the "client" (*browser software*) to a server (*any computer on the Internet*). HTTP (*Hypertext Transfer Protocol*) is the most common protocol found on the Web because it is used to request Web documents from HTTP servers. FTP (*File Transfer Protocol*) is used to access files on an FTP server.

**b.** **Domain name information** is the part of the URL that follows the protocol. For example, the Yahoo search engine created by David Filo and Jerry Yang can be found at:

```
http://www.yahoo.com
```

where www.yahoo.com is the domain name.

Early Internet addressing assigned addresses to machines or "hosts." Later, Domain Name Service (DNS) addressing was implemented and addresses now refer to "domains" and not physical machines. A domain is considered to be an entity that can be a person or an organization.

Although it's implied that the domain name reflects the name of the organization managing the physical Web "server" or "host," many Internet providers allow their clients to use their own domain names on server space they lease. On behalf of a client, a provider can apply to InterNIC, an organization that registers and maintains a database of domain names used on the Internet (http://ds.internic.net/ds). InterNIC is the result of a cooperative agreement with the National Science Foundation, AT&T and Network Solutions, Inc. The registration process takes about a week and the application procedure is handled through email (http://rs/internic.net/templates.html). Once InterNIC approves a domain name, the provider receives a notification via email.

**c. Directory and file name information** follows the domain name and provides additional information about the location of a file or directory. If a file name is present in a URL, it has a three or four letter extension and will occur in the position furthest to the right. The names to the left of the file name, separated by slashes, are directory names. For example, a text file containing information about a Microsoft office product may be found on the Microsoft ftp site at:

```
ftp://ftp.microsoft.com/deskapps/office/kb/
    Q122/3/31.txt
```

deskapps, office, kb, Q122 and 3 are directory names. In contrast, the Web page devoted to Microsoft PowerPoint may be found at:

```
http://www.microsoft.com/MSPowerPoint/default.htm
```

where MSPowerPoint is the name of a directory and default.html is the name of a document.

## 5. 2D navigational structures.

**a. Linear "slide shows."** The simplest Web sites are developed as linear slide shows in which one page is equivalent to the next, without a top-down structure.

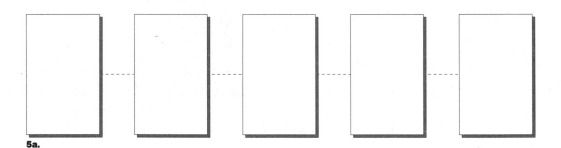

**5a.**

For example, small sites with one or two dozen pages can be arranged with simple navigation buttons to move ahead or back.

**b. Hierarchical tree.** Large sites should be organized into "branches," or grouped "areas." Visitors can choose to follow a branch that interests them, which may bring them to a "fork" and then to a related group of pages. However, hypermedia experts have known for some time that when allowed to cross from one branch to another without first going back "up the tree," viewers get lost. In Figure 5b, notice there are no interconnecting lines between branches. In order to navigate from one major branch to another, a visitor must follow a branch back to the starting point.

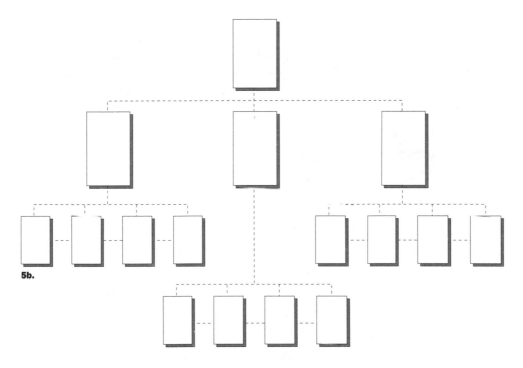

5b.

## 6. 2D navigation controls.

**a. Text links.** Text links are the most common form of links on a browser page. The color of the text link indicates the type of link:

- **Link text** is blue by default in the Netscape browser, indicating that a different Web page can be accessed with a click on the highlighted text. Link text is not necessarily underlined because viewers may turn underlining on or off in the Preferences dialog box.

Sculpture

*Merry Esparza's button link with a border.*

**6b1.**

*The same graphic with the border turned off.*

**6b2.**

The color of text links can be changed on Netscape browser pages with a hexadecimal HTML code added to the BODY tag. (*Note: See "Convert a Pantone RGB value to a Web page color code with the BBS Color Editor" in the Online Tools chapter.*)

- **Visited link text** is purple by default in the Netscape browser, indicating that the link has been followed.

- **Active link text** is red by default in the Netscape browser, indicating that the link is open.

**b.** **Inline graphics as links (buttons or arrows).** Inline graphics are graphics that are loaded on the browser page along with text. When inline images are defined as links, the Netscape browser outlines the graphic with a border coded with the same colors as text links (Figure 6b1). A blue border indicates the link has not been followed, purple indicates the link has been followed, and red indicates the link is open. This border can be turned off with a Border=0 attribute added to the image <IMG> tag (Figure 6b2). For example:

```
<IMG SRC="button1.gif" border=0>
```

### 7. Creating 2D navigation controls with HTML.

HTML text links and inline graphic links are both created with the HTML link tag <A>...</A>. Inside the link tag, you'll need:

**a.** **The name of a file or URL to link, which will be specified with the HREF attribute inside the link.**
For example:

```
<A HREF="toc.html">
```

**b.** **The text or graphic that will act as the "hot spot."**
Examples:

```
<A HREF="toc.html">Sculpture
<A HREF="toc.html"><IMG SRC="optica.gif">
```

**c.** **An ending link tag.**

Some examples:

```
<A HREF="toc.html">Sculpture</A>
<A HREF="toc.html"><IMG SRC="optica.gif"></A>
```

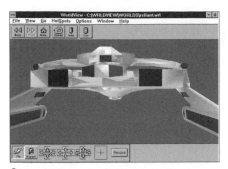

**8a.**

**8b.**

**8c1.**

**8c2.**

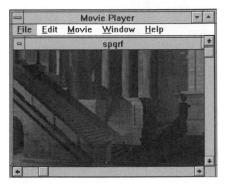

**8c3.**

## 8. 3D navigation controls.

**a.** **VRML's "network anchors"** are encountered in a VRML 3D browser window when the viewer's mouse passes over a link which, when clicked, will "hyperlink" the viewer to another Web site. (*Note: When the mouse pointer passes over a link, the pointer will change from an arrow to a pointer hand. For more infomation, see "Following WWW anchors in VRML with the WorldView browser" in the Animation chapter.*)

**b.** **WorldView's navigation controls** were invented by Intervista when they built their VRML browser. The controls provide a means to move and control navigation. Web visitors can either use the arrow controls or pass their mouse over the crosshair to navigate.

**c.** **QuickTime VR's "node pointers"** are encountered in a QuickTime VR movie player window when the viewer's mouse passes over a link which, when clicked, will move the viewer to another movie "node."

**d.** **QuickTime VR's navigation controls** are encountered in a QuickTime VR movie player window. Viewers use the Shift and Control keys on their computer keyboards to Zoom in and out.

## 9. Creating 3D navigation controls with VRML and 3DMF.

Since VRML and 3DMF are both file formats, 3D software applications that support VRML and 3DMF export or save 3D rendered images as VRML or 3DMF files.

An "extra" feature that will be important for creating 3D worlds is the ability to add network anchors in a VRML or 3DMF file. These are in the form of URLs, which, when clicked, will hyperlink a Web visitor to another part of the Web.

# Information design and Web site "map making"

*Summary:* *Preliminary structural sketches are an important part of the hypermedia development process.*

*Above:* *3D murals created for "Empyrean," Merry Esparza's interactive computer strategy game.*

## 1. Flowcharting.

Flowcharts, or program maps, are essential to the hypermedia design process. Merry used a sketch book to create ideas for her interactive computer game. Sketches can lead to new ideas, which the information designer or illustrator can refer to in the schematic.

## 2. Interactive storyboarding.

For large projects with production teams, storyboards provide a convenient means to communicate development ideas to an entire team. Some companies find it helpful to create wall maps, which show the function and approximate layout of all the graphic components.

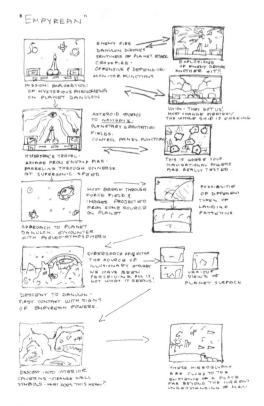

2.

# Create a table with HTML to hold navigation buttons and text links

*Summary:* *Tables created with HTML tags form an "invisible grid" that can hold text or graphics.*

Table tags are an important part of the "Netscape Extensions to HTML." Table cells can be used to form columns of text, which are otherwise impossible to create with HTML. For the Mobius Gallery home page, Merry discovered that a table offers a convenient way to line up button graphics and text links—each is in a separate table cell with the borders turned off.

## 1. Use Photoshop to crop button graphics.

Since the button graphics will occupy table cells, crop them into identical-sized rectangles, using Photoshop's Info palette:

**a.** Open Photoshop and select Open from the File pull-down menu.

| File | Edit | Mode | Image | Filter | Select |
|---|---|---|---|---|---|
| New... | | | | | Ctrl+N |
| Open... | | | | | Ctrl+O |
| Open As... | | | | | |
| Place... | | | | | |
| Close | | | | | Ctrl+W |
| Save | | | | | Ctrl+S |
| Save As... | | | | | |
| Save a Copy... | | | | | |
| Revert... | | | | | |
| Acquire | | | | | ▶ |
| Export | | | | | ▶ |
| File Info... | | | | | |
| Page Setup... | | | | | |
| Print... | | | | | Ctrl+P |
| Preferences | | | | | ▶ |
| Exit | | | | | Ctrl+Q |

**1a.**

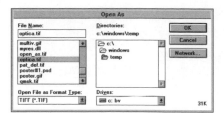

**1b.**

**b.** Select a graphic in the dialog box that appears and click on OK.

**c.** Select Show Info from the Window|Palettes pull-down menu.

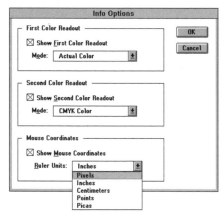

**1c.**

**d.** The Info Palette will appear as a floating palette in the Photoshop work area. Click on the Info Palette's pop-up menu to select Palette Options.

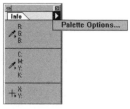

**1d.**

**e.** Click on the Mouse Coordinates Ruler Units pop-up menu to select Pixels. Click on OK.

**1e.**

**1f.**

**1g.**

**f.** Select the rectangle marquee in the Photoshop Toolbox.

**g.** Drag a selection rectangle around your graphic.

**h.** Note the Width and Height measurements in the Info Palette—you'll need these measurements to crop your other button graphics.

**1h.**

```
Edit   Mode   Image
Undo Marquee  Ctrl+Z

Cut           Ctrl+X
Copy          Ctrl+C
Paste         Ctrl+V
Paste Into
Paste Layer...
Clear
Fill...
Stroke...
Crop

Define Pattern
Take Snapshot
```

**1i.**

```
File   Edit   Mode   Image   Filter   Select
New...                               Ctrl+N
Open...                              Ctrl+O
Open As...
Place...

Close                               Ctrl+W
Save                                Ctrl+S
Save As...
Save a Copy...
Revert...

Acquire                                   ▶
Export                                    ▶

File Info...

Page Setup...
Print...                            Ctrl+P

Preferences                               ▶

Exit                                Ctrl+Q
```

**2a.**

**i.** When you're satisfied with the selection rectangle, select Crop from the Edit pull-down menu.

**j.** You will need to repeat these steps for all of your button graphics.

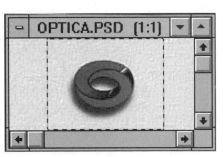

**1j.**

## 2. Save the graphic.

**a.** Select Save As from the File pull-down menu.

**b.** Type in a file name.

**c.** Press on the Format pop-up box and select CompuServe GIF. A GIF extension will be added to the file name. Click on OK.

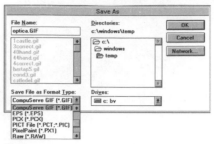

**2b, 2c.**

### 3. Open a Text File Editor.

Use Notepad or a word processor. If you use a word processor, be sure to save the document as Text Only.

### 4. Create a new HTML document.

Start a new document with the following markup tags:

```
<HTML>
<HEAD>
<TITLE>Mobius Gallery</TITLE>
</HEAD>
```

### 5. Add a Body Background tag.

Merry used a small tile with a paper texture for the Mobius Gallery background. When you list a GIF or JPEG image in the BODY tag with a Background attribute, Netscape will automatically tile it to fill the background:

```
<HTML>
<HEAD>
<TITLE>Mobius Gallery</TITLE>
</HEAD>
<BODY BACKGROUND="paper.jpeg">
</BODY>
</HTML>
```

**5.**

6.

## 6. Add an Image tag.

The IMG tag contains a "source," or SRC parameter, which contains the name of an image file. In this example, the image is the splash screen that Merry designed for the Mobius Gallery (Figure 6).

```
<HTML>
<HEAD>
<TITLE>Mobius Gallery</TITLE>
</HEAD>
<BODY BACKGROUND="paper.jpeg">
<IMG SRC="Gallery3.jpeg">
</BODY>
</HTML>
```

## 7. Add a Table tag.

The <TABLE>...</TABLE> tag is the principle tag used to begin and end a table:

```
<HTML>
<HEAD>
<TITLE>Mobius Gallery</TITLE>
</HEAD>
<BODY BACKGROUND="paper.jpeg">
<IMG SRC="Gallery3.jpeg">
<TABLE>
</BODY>
</HTML>
```

## 8. Add a Table Row tag.

Use a table row tag <TR> each time you define a new row. (*Note: Merry used this tag twice in her HTML document since her table has two rows.*)

```
<HTML>
<HEAD>
<TITLE>Mobius Gallery</TITLE>
</HEAD>
<BODY BACKGROUND="paper.jpeg">
<IMG SRC="Gallery3.jpeg">
<TABLE>
<TR>
</BODY>
</HTML>
```

*Tip: An HTML specification is currently under development that will add typo-graphic controls to HTML with style sheets. For more information, stay tuned to the following page:*

`http://www.w3.org/hypertext/WWW/Arena/style.html`

## 9. Add a Table Header tags.

The Table Header tag <TH>…</TH> is used to define text or graphics that will appear in data cells. In this sample, Merry used the table header tag to define a row of images followed by a row of text. (*Note: The Table Header tag <TH>…</TH> is very similar to the Table Data tag <TD>…</TD>. Although both function the same, the Table Header tag has a default BOLD FONT and a default ALIGN=CENTER, which was useful in this sample.*)

```
<HTML>
<HEAD>
<TITLE>Mobius Gallery</TITLE>
</HEAD>
<BODY BACKGROUND="paper.jpeg">
<IMG SRC="Gallery3.jpeg">
<TABLE>
<TR>
<TH><A HREF="toc.html"><IMG SRC="optical.gif"></A></TH>
<TH ><A HREF="toc2.html">
      <IMG SRC="optica2.gif"></A></TH>
<TH><A HREF="toc3.html"l><IMG SRC="optica3.gif">
</A></TH>
</TR>
<TR>
<TH><A HREF="toc.html">Sculpture</A></TH>
<TH><A HREF="toc2.html">Paintings</A></TH>
<TH><A HREF="toc3.html">Graphics</A></TH>
</TABLE>
</BODY>
</HTML>
```

## 10. Use the WIDTH attribute to widen cells.

The default width of each of the table cells caused the entire table to look too narrow (Figure 10a). By experimenting with the Width attribute in the Table Header tag, Merry was able to center the table on the page (Figure 10b).

```
<HTML>
<HEAD>
<TITLE>Mobius Gallery</TITLE>
</HEAD>
<BODY BACKGROUND="paper.jpeg">
<IMG SRC="Gallery3.jpeg">
<TABLE>
<TR>
<TH width=160><A HREF="toc.html">
     <IMG SRC="optical.gif"></A></TH>
<TH width-160><A HREF="toc2.html">
     <IMG SRC="optica2.gif"></A></TH>
<TH width=160><A HREF="toc3.html">
     <IMG SRC="optica3.gif"></A></TH>
</TR>
<TR>
<TH width=160><A HREF="toc.html">Sculpture</A></TH>
<TH width=160><A HREF="toc2.html">Paintings</A></TH>
<TH width-160><A HREF="toc3.html"l>Graphics</A></TH>
</TR>
</TABLE>
</BODY>
</HTML>
```

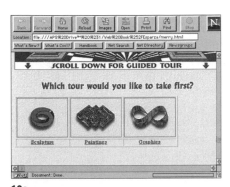

**10a.**

**10b.**

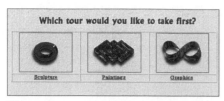

**11a.**

**11b.**

## 11. Use the Border attribute to turn borders off.

By default, the table data tag and the image tag add borders
that Merry needed to turn off (Figure 11a). Use the Border
attribute in both tags to make the borders disappear
(Figure 11b).

```
<HTML>
<HEAD>
<TITLE>Mobius Gallery</TITLE>
</HEAD>
<BODY BACKGROUND="paper.jpeg">
<IMG SRC="Gallery3.jpeg">
<TABLE BORDER=0>
<TR>
<TH width=150><A HREF="toc.html">
      <IMG SRC="optical.gif" BORDER=0></A></TH>
<TH width=150><A HREF="toc2.html">
      <IMG SRC="optica2.gif" BORDER=0></A></TH>
<TH width=150><A HREF="toc3.html">
      <IMG SRC="optica3.gif" BORDER=0></A></TH>
</TR>
<TR>
<TH width=150><A HREF="toc.html">Sculpture</A></TH>
<TH width=150><A HREF="toc2.html">Paintings</A></TH>
<TH width=150><A HREF="toc3.html">Graphics</A></TH>
</TR>
</TABLE>
</BODY>
</HTML>
```

## 12. Add line breaks.

The Line Break tag <BR> adds space below the table.

```
<HTML>
<HEAD>
<TITLE>Mobius Gallery</TITLE>
</HEAD>
<BODY BACKGROUND="paper.jpeg">
      <IMG SRC="Gallery3.jpeg">
<TABLE BORDER=0>
<TR>
<TH width=150><A HREF="toc.html">
<IMG SRC="optical.gif" BORDER=0></A></TH>
<TH width=150><A HREF="toc2.html">
      <IMG SRC="optica2.gif" BORDER=0></A></TH>
<TH width=150><A HREF="toc3.html">
      <IMG SRC="optica3.gif" BORDER=0></A></TH>
</TR>
<TR>
<TH width=150><A HREF="toc.html">Sculpture</A></TH>
<TH width=150><A HREF="toc2.html">Paintings</A></TH>
<TH width=150><A HREF="toc3.html">
Graphics</A></TH>
</TR>
</TABLE>
<BR>
<BR>
</BODY>
</HTML>
```

*Tip: Providing a signature area aids in interactive design by encouraging viewers to send comments, questions or suggestions about your Web site. By adding a mailto URL to the HREF attribute, viewers get an empty mail form to fill out.*

## 13. Add the signature area.

It's customary to add a signature area at the bottom of each Web page. This area contains contact information, separated from the rest of the page with a horizontal rule (<HR>).

```
<HTML>
<HEAD>
<TITLE>Mobius Gallery</TITLE>
</HEAD>
<BODY BACKGROUND="paper.jpeg">
      <IMG SRC="Gallery3.jpeg">
<TABLE BORDER=0>
<TR>
<TH width=150><A HREF="toc.html">
<IMG SRC="optical.gif" BORDER=0></A></TH>
<TH width=150><A HREF="toc2.html">
      <IMG SRC="optica2.gif" BORDER=0></A></TH>
<TH width=150><A HREF="toc3.html">
      <IMG SRC="optica3.gif" BORDER=0></A></TH>
</TR>
<TR>
<TH width=150><A HREF="toc.html">Sculpture</A></TH>
<TH width=150><A HREF="toc2.html">Paintings</A></TH>
<TH width=150><A HREF="toc3.html">Graphics</A></TH>
</TR>
</TABLE>
<BR>
<BR>
<HR>
<ADDRESS>
Merry Esparza can be contacted at:<BR>
Merry Esparza Design<BR>
</ADDRESS>
<A HREF="mailto:webmaster@ref.com">
      webmaster@ref.com</A>
</BODY>
</HTML>
```

## 14. Summary of HTML tags used in this section.

The tags you see in this list (in alphabetical order) reflect the HTML3 specification:

### \<A\>...\</A\>

Referred to as an "anchor," this tag uses the HREF attribute to link to an external file or "anchor." For example:

```
<A HREF="toc.html">Sculpture</A>
```

*Note: The HTML file name must include the path name if the file is located in another directory.*

### \<ADDRESS\>...\</ADDRESS\>

The address tag provides a means of "signing" your Web page. The information inside provides Web visitors with information about who created the page and who they can contact. This tag occurs at the bottom of a Web page, in a section known as the "signature."

*(Note: It is customary to add an email address to the signature and to use a mailto URL. By building a link with an email address and by adding the mailto URL to the HREF attribute, viewers get an empty email form with the address already filled out whenever they click on the link.)*

### \<BODY\>...\</BODY\>

A tag used to open and close the body of a document.

### \<BR\>...\</BR\>

A tag used to break a line.

### \<HEAD\>...\</HEAD\>

A tag used to open and close the header portion of a document.

### \<HTML\>...\</HTML\>

A tag used to open and close a HTML document.

### \<HR\>

A tag used to create a horizontal rule. This tag does not require an ending tag.

*Tip: Such features as tables can only be viewed by Netscape 1.0 and higher and some other advanced browsers. If you will be including tables, forms or other "Netscape extensions" in your Web pages, it's a good idea to tell viewers that some features will not appear correctly without the use of a browser that supports those features.*

**<IMG>**

Used to refer to an inline image, this tag uses the SRC="…" attribute, which represents the the URL (location) of the image.

For example:

```
<IMG SRC = "optica3.gif">
```

This tag also uses the BORDER attribute, which can be used to turn off the border around an inline graphic used in a link.

For example:

```
<IMG SRC="optica3.gif BORDER=0>
```

**<TABLE>...</TABLE>**

A tag used to describes the beginning and end of a table. This tag uses the BORDER attribute to control the width of the border.

For example:

```
<TABLE BORDER=0> or
<TABLE BORDER=1>
```

**<TD>...</TD>**

A tag used to describe the contents of a table cell. *(Note: the contents of the Table Data cell are ALIGN=LEFT.)*

**<TH>...</TH>**

A tag used to describe the contents of a header table cell. (*Note: The contents of the Table Header cell are BOLD FONT and ALIGN=CENTER.*) Both the Table Data <TD> and the Table Header <TH> tags use the WIDTH attribute:

For example:

```
<TD WIDTH=160>
<TH WIDTH=160>
```

**<TITLE>...</TITLE>**

A tag used to describe the title of a document, which shows up inside a document's title bar.

**<TR>...</TR>**

A tag used to describe a table row.

# Chapter 3

**Artist featured in this chapter:**

*Gail Garcia is a graphic designer/art director based in New York City. Her projects include conference brochures, conference catalogs, consumer product brochures, promotional materials, signage, logos, book design, annual reports and corporate newsletters.*

*gjgarcia@interport.net*

*http://www.echonyc.com/ ~art/arsenault/arsenault. html*

# Page Layout Tools

For graphic designers, Quark XPress and Photoshop have become as common as the Schaedler Rule and the Pantone color book. In this chapter, Gail Garcia offers tips on how to use Quark XPress and Photoshop as tools to design Web pages.

# The Arsenault Designs handbag catalog

**Summary:** *In this chapter on layout tools, graphic designer Gail Garcia (gjgarcia@interport.net) demonstrates how to use popular page layout tools to create Web pages.*

G ail Garcia feels her previous design work in print influenced her design of the Arsenault handbag catalog (http:// www.echonyc.com/~art/arsenault/arsenault.html). However, the Web pages Gail designed required visual characteristics that were selected specifically for viewing onscreen:

## 1. Developing the concept.

a. **Organizing principles.** In a print catalog, Gail would have mixed handbag styles on the pages. For the Web pages, however, she felt there was a need to visually organize the products together according to distinct styles. Gail helped her client define three product groups: shopping bags, zipper bags and miscellaneous specialty items, grouped in a category called Sample Sale.

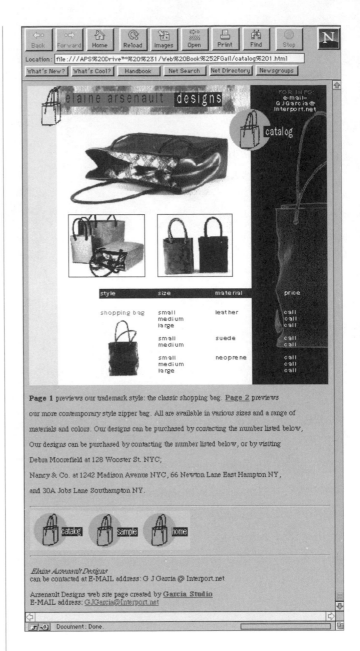

**b. Existing photography.** Gail has photographed her client's handbags for a previous printed catalog. She used the same images for the Web project, but used Photoshop to create a high-contrast look. Gail used shadows and shading on each of the products to create a three-dimensional quality.

**c. Color.** Although Gail found colors she liked for the Web pages, she admits she would never use the selected colors in print. The bags, hand-made and rather expensive, would need softer shades on a printed brochure. For the Web, Gail felt the colors should convey a strong, straightforward image that could be better achieved with bright colors.

## 2. Planning the site.

On paper, Gail created a sketch of the entire Web site. On what looked like an inverted tree, Gail drew three priniciple branches from the home page including:

**a. A Shopping Bag page.** This would branch to the shopping bag styles. These large, open tote-bags would need the largest images in order to show product detail and color selections.

**b. A Zipper Bag page.** This branches to several types of zipper bags including Elaine Arsenault's original zipper bag and her more recent miniature zipper bag, popular for evening.

**c. A Sample Sale page.** This branches to pages with eye-glass cases, cosmetic bags and small purses.

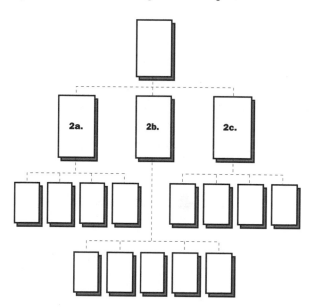

## 3. Designing the site.

**a.** **Splash screens or page banners**. Gail discovered she could open Quark XPress EPS pages in Photoshop 3.0 as EPS TIFF Preview images. By saving the art as GIF or JPEG, the images are ready for Web pages. (*Note: Gail recommends reducing bit-depth in LView Pro or Photoshop to create the smallest possible files for downloading.*)

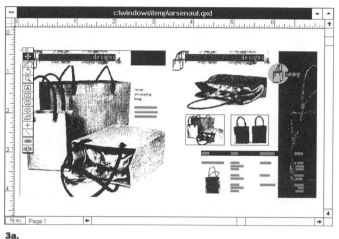

**3a.**

**3b.**

**b.** **Image maps inside the splash screens.** Gail wanted handbags and buttons inside the splash screens to be clickable "hot spots." This meant her splash screens needed image maps. Clicking on a "hot spot" transports a viewer to another Web document. In this case, a click on a handbag or button branches to a product page.

Before creating the image map "hot spots" on her splash screens, Gail spoke to Internet provider/consultant Bill Murphy of the Webology Group (http://www.webology.com). Since image maps require cgi (common gateway interface) scripts to run, you'll need to gather information from your Internet provider, unless you're planning to run your own server. A cgi script (imagemap) comes standard with most Web servers; it will reside on the Web server and will need to be referenced in your HTML document. The map file describes the coordinates of the clickable "hot spots."

*Tip:* To learn about the information you'll need for your HTML documents with image maps, ask your provider for an address that contains an image map. If you're using the Netscape browser, select Source from the View pull-down menu. Look for anchor tags <A> with the HREF attribute and <IMG> tags with the ISMAP attribute. The format will give you clues about path name requirements for your Web document. You'll still need a sample map file from your provider, which you can use as a model for your map file.

*Tip:* For information and instructions on how to upload files to your Internet provider's service, see the chapter on image maps.

Bill Murphy explains, "with a variety of new Web server software programs arriving on the market, it's hard to predict what your provider's software will see in a map file or inside your Web document. The situation will also vary depending on the amount of server space you're renting. For example, companies that rent a dedicated space may be able to set up their own map directories." For Web designers, Bill recommends the following:

• **Use Thomas Boutell's *Mapedit*** to draw the object primitives (rectangles, circles, ovals, polygons and points) on a GIF image, set the URLs for each area and export the marker definitions or object coordinates into a map file. For example, a map file's text might contain:

```
circle (115, 428) 41 /~art/arsenault/catalog.html
circle (269, 435) 37 /~art/arsenault/sample.html
default /~art/arsenault/arsenault.html
```

• **For a Netscape server**, create a link in your Web document using the following format:

```
<A HREF="dirname/filename.map><IMG SRC="image.gif" ISMAP></A>
```

• **For a CERN server**, create a link in your Web document using the following format:

```
<A HREF=". . /cgi-bin/htimage/dirname/filename.map><IMG SRC="image.gif" ISMAP></A>
```

• **For a NCSA server**, create a link in your Web document using the following format:

```
<A HREF=". . /cgi-bin/imagemap/dirname/filename.map>
<IMG SRC="image.gif" ISMAP></A>
```

**c. Double-spaced HTML text with text links.** Gail improvised to create double-spaced paragraph text. Since there is no HTML tag to achieve double spacing, Gail added extra line spacing with the paragraph tag <p> (Figure 3c1). She also used traditional HTML text links within the paragraphs (Figure 3c2).

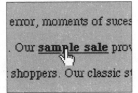

and apply them to bags for every occasion...for all people. We start our creative process with thoughtful experimentation and the use of our own style development systems. This process involves lots of trail and error, moments of sucess and failure, and millions of fabulous and not so fabulous samples. Our **sample sale** provides a preview of the fabulous sucesses for the more daring discount shoppers. Our classic styles can be viewed by

**3c1.**

error, moments of suces

. Our **sample sale** pro

shoppers. Our classic st

**3o2.**

**d. Inline Transparent GIF images as buttons.** At the bottom of each page, Gail created a row of inline transparent GIF images, which she used as links to the principle locations on the Web site. Gail used Leonardo Haddad Loureiro's *LView Pro* to create transparent GIF images. (*Note: LView Pro can be found on the CD-ROM in the back of this book.*)

**e. Customer Inquiries/Feedback.** Gail used the Mailto URL in the signature portion of her documents to accomodate Web visitors who want to send email. By building a link with an email address (Figure 3e1) and adding the Mailto URL to the HREF attribute, viewers get an empty email form (Figure 3e2) with the address already filled out whenever they click on the link. (*Note: See Create an HTML document, in this chapter.*)

**3d.**

GJGarcia@Interport.net

**3e1.**

**3e2.**

# Use Quark XPress to design a Web page

**Summary:** *Since type and images are so easy to handle in Quark XPress, Gail Garcia found a way to use this favorite page layout program to design Web pages.*

S ince Gail likes to design in "spreads," Quark XPress provides a familiar medium that's easy to use. A page can be converted to a PICT and then a GIF image by saving the page as an EPS image in Quark XPress, opening the image in Photoshop and then resaving the image in Photoshop. Because of bandwidth limitations, Gail kept the Quark XPress page small. The procedure is outlined below.

### 1. Open a Quark XPress document.

**a.** Open Quark XPress and select New|Document from the File pull-down menu.

**b.** Gail chose a page size of 6.5 inches wide by 4.5 inches tall, typed these dimensions into the width and height boxes and clicked on OK.

**1a.**

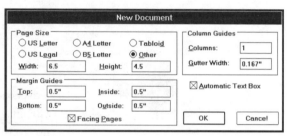

**1b.**

**c.** Gail built her pages with scanned photographs imported into picture boxes, and text boxes containing Franklin Gothic type.

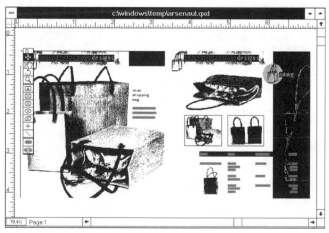

**1c.**

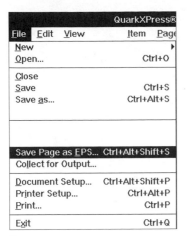

**2a.**

## 2. Save pages as EPS images.

**a.** When the spreads were complete, Gail chose Save Pages as EPS from the File pull-down menu.

**b.** Next, Gail typed a file name in the Save Page as EPS dialog box and clicked on OK.

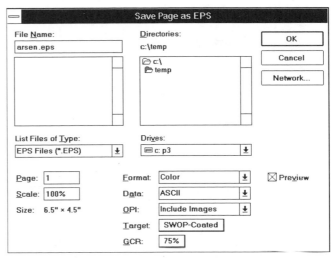

**2b.**

## 3. Open EPS images in Photoshop.

**a.** Gail opened Photoshop and selected Open from the File pull-down menu.

**b.** The file open dialog box in Photoshop 3.0 will "see" the Quark XPress EPS images as "EPS TIFF Preview."

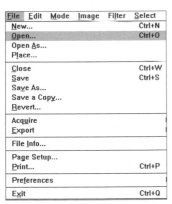

**3a.**

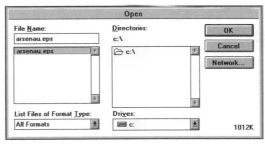

**3b.**

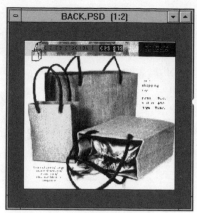

**3c.**

**c.** Click on Open. The image will be displayed in a Photoshop window.

**d.** With the eps image open, Gail chose Save As from the File pull-down menu.

**e.** Gail saved the image with a GIF extension.

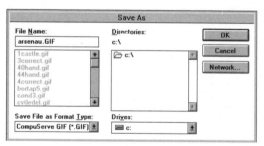

**3d.**

**3e.**

# Use LView Pro or Photoshop to reduce bit-depth

*Summary:* Since bandwidth is related to the time it takes to download an image, Gail reduces file size by reducing bit-depth.

**1a.**

**3e.**

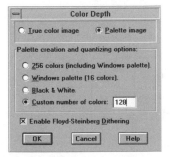

**2b, 2c, 2d, 2e.**

G raphic designers who design for electronic mediums will become accustomed to reducing bit-depth to "optimize" the file sizes of their images.

### 1. Open a GIF image in LView Pro.
**a.** Open LView and select Open from the File pull-down menu.

**b.** Select an image from the dialog box and click on Open.

**c.** The image will open in an LView window.

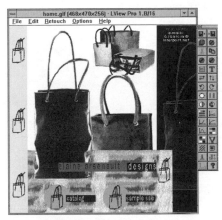

**1c.**

### 2. Reduce the color depth.
**a.** Select Color Depth from the Retouch pull-down menu. A dialog box will be displayed.

**b.** Select "Palette Image."

**c.** Type 128 into the box labeled "Custom number of colors."

**d.** Make sure there is an "X" in the box labeled "Enable Floyd-Steinberg Dithering."

**e.** Click OK.

### 3. Save the image.
Choose Save As from the File menu, type a file name, and click on OK.

# Use LView Pro to create a transparent GIF image

*Summary:* Use LView Pro to assign a transparent shade to an image's background color.

**1a.**

To make the color around the buttons transparent, Gail used Leonardo Haddad Loreiro's LView Pro. (*Note: LView Pro is a shareware software program available on the CD-ROM in the back of this book.*)

LView Pro
1.B/16

### 1. Open a GIF image in LVIEW Pro.

**a.** Open LView and select Open from the File pull-down menu.

**b.** Select an image from the dialog box and click on Open.

**c.** The image will open in a LView window.

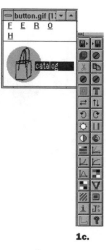

**1c.**

### 2. Select a background color.

The background color you select will be saved as a transparent shade.

**a.** Select Background color from the Options pull-down menu.

**2a.**

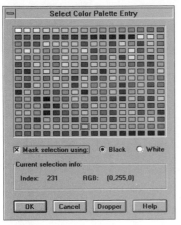

2b.

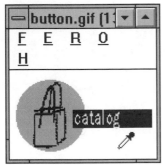

2d.

**b.** Select Color Palette Entry will appear as a floating palette in the LVIEW work area.

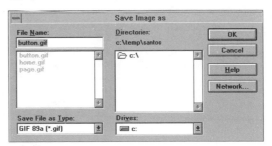

2c.

**c.** Click on the Dropper button at the base of the palette.

**d.** Position the eyedropper over the area you would like transparent and click your left mouse button.

## 3. Save the image as a transparent GIF.

**a.** With the image open, choose Save as from the File pull-down menu.

**b.** GIF 89a will be displayed in the Format pop-up menu. This is the abbreviation for transparent GIF.

**c.** Enter a file name and use the GIF extension.

**d.** Click on OK.

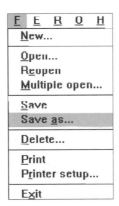

3a.

3b, 3c, 3d.

# Finding marker definitions for a map file with Mapedit

*Summary: Use Mapedit to draw object primitives over your hot spots, set URLs, and save the marker definitions into a map file. Unless you're running your own server, you'll need to find out if your Internet provider is using the CERN or NCSA server. You will need this information to export your map file from Mapedit.*

Mapedit

## 1. Open Mapedit and a GIF image.

**a.** Open Mapedit and select Open/Create from the File pull-down menu.

**1a.**

**b.** Type a map file name and a GIF file name in the dialog box that follows. If you're not sure of the file name or the directory, use the browse button to locate the file(s).

**c.** Select NCSA or CERN as the map file format (you will need to obtain this information from your provider).

**d.** If you're creating a new map file, Mapedit will recognize the map file does not exist and a dialog box will be displayed. Click on OK.

**e.** Your GIF image will be displayed in a window.

**1b, 1c.**

**1d.**

**1e.**

2a.

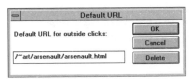

2b.

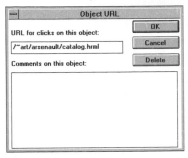

2c.

4a.

4b.

5a.

5b.

6.

## 2. Draw an object primitive on your image.

**a.** Select an object primitive tool from the Tools pull down menu.

**b.** Draw a shape on the GIF image.

**c.** When you have completed the shape, click the right mouse button. A dialog box will be displayed.

## 3. Enter an object URL.

Type in a URL which includes the name of the page to be diaplayed when a viewer clicks on the region you've defined. Click on OK.

## 4. Add a default URL.

The default URL refers to the page that will be displayed if a web visitor clicks outside of the regions you've defined.

**a.** Select Edit Default URL from the File pull-down menu. A dialog box will be displayed.

**b.** Enter a URL. Click on OK.

## 5. Save the map file.

**a.** Select Save As from the File pull-down menu.

**b.** Enter a map file name and select a format. Click on OK.

**c.** A confirmation message will be displayed.

5c.

## 6. Check your map file in a text editor.

Open your map file in Programmer's File Editor or another text editor.

# Create an HTML document

*Summary: Once Gail had developed a plan for the entire site, the individual Web pages were easy to assemble.*

## 1. Open a Text File Editor.

Use Notepad or a word processor. If you use a word processor, be sure to save the document as Text Only.

## 2. Create a new HTML document.

Every HTML document consists of a HEAD and a BODY. Start a new document with the following markup tags:

```
<HTML>
<HEAD>
<TITLE>arsenault design</TITLE>
</HEAD>
<BODY>
```

## 3. Add an Image tag.

The IMG tag contains a "source" or SRC parameter, which contains the name of the image file:

```
<HTML>
<HEAD>
<TITLE>arsenault design</TITLE>
</HEAD>
<BODY>
<IMG SRC="page1-new.jpeg">
</BODY>
</HTML>
```

## 4. Add double-spaced text after the image.

Since HTML does not have a tag for double-spaced paragraph text, Gail used the paragraph tag after each line to open up the line spacing:

```
<HTML>
<HEAD>
<TITLE>arsenault design</TITLE>
</HEAD>
<BODY>
<IMG SRC="page1-new.jpeg">
<P>
<P>
```

*Tip: For information and instructions on how to upload files to your Internet provider's server, see the chapter on image maps.*

```
<P> Our design applications take already familiar,
functional carrying concepts, <P>and apply them to bags
for every occasion...for all people. We start our cre-
ative process<P> with thoughtful experimentation and
the use of our own style development systems.  <P>This
process involves lots of trial and error, moments of
success and failure, and millions of  <P>fabulous and
not so fabulous samples.
</BODY>
</HTML>
```

## 5. Add a link within a paragraph.

A link within a paragraph should occur naturally in the text. In this example, Gail uses the words "sample sale" to act as a link to the sample sale Web page:

```
<HTML>
<HEAD>
<TITLE>arsenault design</TITLE>
</HEAD>
<BODY>
<IMG SRC="page1-new.jpeg">
<P>
<P>
<P> Our design applications take already familiar, func-
tional carrying concepts, <P>and apply them to bags for
every occasion...for all people. We start our creative
process<P> with thoughtful experimentation and the use
of our own style development systems.  <P>This process
involves lots of trial and error, moments of success and
failure, and millions of  <P>fabulous and not so fabu-
lous samples. Our <A HREF="online-sample 1.html">
<B>sample sale</B></A> provides a preview of the fabu-
lous<P> successes for the more daring discount shoppers.
</BODY>
</HTML>
```

## 6. Create a rule and add navigation buttons.

Gail built a uniform button area at the bottom of each page. She created horizontal rules above and below the button area using the horizontal rule tag <HR> :

```
<HTML>
<HEAD>
<TITLE>arsenault design</TITLE>
</HEAD>
<BODY>
<IMG SRC="page1-new.jpeg">
<P>
<P>
<P> Our design applications take already familiar,
functional carrying concepts, <P>and apply them to bags
for every occasion...for all people. We start our cre-
ative process<P> with thoughtful experimentation and
the use of our own style development systems. <P>This
process involves lots of trial and error, moments of
success and failure, and millions of <P>fabulous and
not so fabulous samples. Our <A HREF="online-sample
1.html">
<B>sample sale</B></A> provides a preview of the fabu-
lous<P> successes for the more daring discount shop-
pers.
<P>
<HR>
<A HREF="online-catalog 1.html">
<img border=0 img src=".catalog.gif">
<A HREF="online-sample 1.html">
<img border=0 img src=".sample.gif">
<A HREF="online-e-home pg.html">
<img border=0 img src=".homepg.gif"></A>
<HR>
</BODY>
</HTML>
```

## 7. Add the signature area.

```
<HTML>
<HEAD>
<TITLE>arsenault design</TITLE>
</HEAD>
<BODY>
<IMG SRC="page1-new.jpeg">
<P>
<P>
<P> Our design applications take already familiar, func-
tional carrying concepts, <P>and apply them to bags for
every occasion...for all people. We start our creative
process<P> with thoughtful experimentation and the use
of our own style development systems.  <P>This process
involves lots of trial and error, moments of success and
failure, and millions of  <P>fabulous and not so fabu-
lous samples. Our <A HREF="online-sample 1.html">
<B>sample sale</B></A> provides a preview of the fabu-
lous<P> successes for the more daring discount shoppers.
<P> .
<HR>
<A HREF="online-catalog 1.html"><img border=0 img
src=".catalog.gif">
<A HREF="online-sample 1.html"><img border=0 img
src=".sample.gif">
<A HREF="online-e-home pg.html"><img border=0 img
src=".homepg.gif"></A>
<HR>
<P>
<ADDRESS>
Elaine Arsenault Designs </ADDRESS>
can be contacted at E-MAIL address:
        GJGarcia@Interport.net
<P>
```

```
Arsenault Designs web site page created by
<A HREF="online-garcia.html"><B>Garcia
Studio</B></A><br>  E-MAIL address:
<A HREF="mailto:GJGarcia@Interport.net">
GJGarcia@Interport.net</A>
</BODY>
</HTML>
```

## 8. Summary of HTML tags used in this section.

The tags you see in this list (in alphabetical order) reflect the HTML3 specification:

### <A>...</A>

Referred to as an "anchor," this tag uses the HREF attribute to link to an external sound file or "anchor." For example:

```
<A HREF="online-sample1.html"><B>sample sale</B></A>
```

*Note: The HTML file name must include the path name if the file is located in another directory.*

### <ADDRESS>...</ADDRESS>

The address tag provides a means of "signing" your Web page. The information inside provides Web visitors with information about who created the page and who they can contact. This tag occurs at the bottom of a Web page in a section known as the "signature."

### <B>...</B>

A tag used to apply bold-facing to text.

### <BODY>...</BODY>

A tag used to open and close the body of a document.

### <HEAD>...</HEAD>

A tag used to open and close the header portion of a document.

### <HTML>...</HTML>

A tag used to open and close an HTML document.

**\<HR>**

A tag used to create a horizontal rule. This tag does not require an ending tag.

**\<IMG>**

Used to refer to an inline image, this tag uses the SRC="..." attribute, which represents the URL (location) of the image. For example:

```
<IMG SRC = "page1-new.jpeg">
```

**\<P>**

A tag used to indicate a new paragraph. This tag does not require an ending tag.

**\<TITLE>...\</TITLE>**

A tag used to describe the title of a document, which shows up inside a document's title bar.

# Chapter 4

# Online Tools

Online tools are an exciting precursor to "software-over-the-Web," which is predicted to be the future of computing. Better Business Solution's Color Editor, Patrick Hennessey's Interactive Graphics Renderer, and the Yahoo Search engine are all highly interactive programs from pioneers who have initiated that vision today.

Although not all of the tools in this chapter are quite so interactive, they are all valuable resources for the Web artist who uses the Web as a current and convenient source of information. The chapter begins with a color editor tool from a company in Houston called Better Business Solutions (BBS). Web artists who need hexadecimal codes for their HTML tags to color a background or text can use this editor as a translation tool. Patrick Hennessey's 3D rendering tool creates small, antialiased images that are available for downloading, and Steven McGrew's Gizmo Gallery holds buttons, icons, images, sounds and movies that he's made available for Web artists.

For an excellent online Web page design guide, take a look at Yale University's Center for Advanced Instructional Media. Yahoo Search is a popular tool to find information on the Web, and even Netscape's own pages hold vital information about changes in HTML, helper applications, and other Web resources for artists.

# Convert a Pantone RGB value to a Web page color code with the BBS Color Editor

***Summary:*** *Visit Better Business Solutions' Web page, enter the RGB value of a desired Pantone shade (gathered from Photoshop) and watch the BBS Color Editor display the color and generate the required HTML code for your Web page.*

Adobe Photoshop™ 3.0

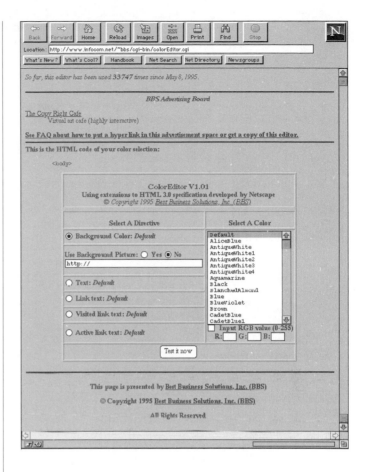

**B**etter Business Solutions' Web page is an essential tool for graphic designers who want to add color to a Web page. You can access the tool, called the BBS Color Editor, at:

`http://www.infocom.net/~bbs/cgi-bin/colorEditor.cgi`.

Adding color to a Netscape background or text requires placing a "hexadecimal red-green-blue triplet" in an HTML document tag. For example, to color a background white, the tag would appear like this:

`<Body bgcolor="#ffffff">`

The BBS Color Editor has an extensive list of color names that were created by BBS. When I wrote and asked them if RGB color information (Photoshop, 0-255) could be translated into the HTML hexadecimal triplets needed for the HTML tags, they wrote back and said they had added an RGB field to their Color Editor! Graphic designers can obtain an RGB

**1a.**

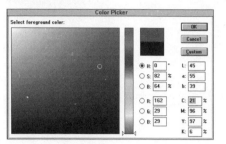

**1b.**

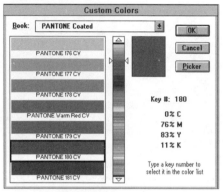

**1d.**

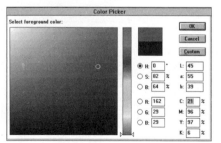

**1e.**

value for any shade they use in Photoshop (Pantone, Toyo, Trumatch), type the RGB values into the Color Editor, and the Editor displays the desired shade on screen and generates the hex code for an HTML document shown in the following table:

The Pantone shades used in this example are:

| Item | Pantone # | RGB Value | Hex Code |
|---|---|---|---|
| Background | 3935CV | R=255<br>G=248<br>B=84 | #fff854 |
| Text | 302 | R=0<br>G=56<br>B=80 | #003850 |
| Linked text | 1685CV | R=114<br>G=41<br>B=22 | #722916 |
| Visited link text | 172CV | R=246<br>G=37<br>B=0 | #f62500 |
| Active link text | 355 | R=0<br>G=140<br>B=60 | #008c3c |

*(Note: At this time, the HTML codes used to add color to a background and text are referred to as the "Netscape Extensions to HTML" and work only with the Netscape browser.)*

## 1. Find desired shade(s) in Photoshop.

Decide which Pantone you'd like to use for the Background, Text, Link text, Visited link text and Active link text. Locate the RGB values of these shades:

**a.** Click on the Foreground color swatch in the Toolbox.

**b.** Click on Custom.

**c.** Click on the pop-up box in the Custom Colors dialog box to select a color model.

**d.** Scroll to select a shade.

**e.** Click on Picker to display the window shown in Figure 1e.

○ R: 162
○ G: 29
○ B: 29

2.

○ Background Color: *Default*

3a.

☐ Input RGB value (0-255)

3b.

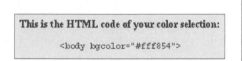

R: ☐  G: ☐  B: ☐

3c.

Test it now

3d.

This is the HTML code of your color selection:

&lt;body bgcolor="#fff854"&gt;

3e.

○ Text: *Default*

4a.

This is the HTML code of your color selection:

&lt;body bgcolor="#fff854" text="#003850"

4e.

○ Link text: *Default*

5a.

## 2. Record the RGB value of your color(s).

The Color Picker dialog box will display RGB values of the color you choose. Record this information.

## 3. Find the hex code for Background Color.

**a.** On the BBS Color Editor Web page, make sure the radio dial next to Background Color is selected.

**b.** Click to enter an "X" in the Input RGB value field.

**c.** Enter the RGB values you recorded from Photoshop.

**d.** Click on the Test it now button.

**e.** The BBS Color Editor will change the background to your desired color and the hexadecimal HTML code will be displayed at the top of the Editor *(in this example, body bgcolor="#fff854")*.

## 4. Find the hex code for Text.

**a.** On the BBS Color Editor Web page, make sure the radio dial next to Text is selected.

**b.** Click to enter an "X" in the Input RGB value field.

**c.** Enter the RGB values you recorded from Photoshop.

**d.** Click on the Test it now button.

**e.** The BBS Color Editor will change the text to your desired color and the hexadecimal HTML code will be displayed at the top of the Editor *(in this example, text="#003850")*.

## 5. Find the hex code for Link text.

*(Note: Link text refers to highlighted text that is activated with a mouse click.)*

**a.** On the BBS Color Editor Web page, make sure the radio dial next to Link text is selected.

**b.** Click to enter an "X" in the Input RGB value field.

**c.** Enter the RGB values you recorded from Photoshop.

**d.** Click on the Test it now button.

○ Visited link text: *Default*

**6a.**

○ Active link text: *Default*

**7a.**

**e.** The BBS Color Editor will change the text to your
desired color and the hexadecimal HTML code will be
displayed at the top of the Editor *(in this example,
link="#722916")*.

This is the HTML code of your color selection:

```
<body bgcolor="#fff854" text="#003850" link="#722916">
```

**5e.**

## 6. Find the hex code for Visited link text.

*(Note: Visited link text refers to a link that's already been
followed.)*

    **a.** On the BBS Color Editor Web page, make sure the radio
dial next to Visited link text is selected.

    **b.** Click to enter an "X" in the Input RGB value field.

    **c.** Enter the RGB values you recorded from Photoshop.

    **d.** Click on the Test it now button.

    **e.** The BBS Color Editor will change the text to your
desired color and the hexadecimal HTML code will be
displayed at the top of the Editor *(in this example,
vlink="#f62500")*.

This is the HTML code of your color selection:

```
<body bgcolor="#fff854" text="#003850" link="#722916"
vlink="#f62500" alink="#008c3c">
```

## 7. Find the hex code for Active link text.

*(Note: Active link text refers to a link that's currently active
or a link with a mouse button held down.)*

    **a.** On the BBS Color Editor Web page, make sure the radio
dial next to Active link text is selected.

    **b.** Click to enter an "X" in the Input RGB value field.

    **c.** Enter the RGB values you recorded from Photoshop.

    **d.** Click on the Test it now button.

    **e.** The BBS Color Editor will change the text to your
desired color and the hexadecimal HTML code will be
displayed at the top of the Editor *(in this example,
alink="#008c3c")*.

## 8. Try creating a new HTML document.

To test your color tags, create an HTML document on your hard drive and open it in Netscape:

**a.** Open Notepad or a word processor.

**b.** Create a new document.

**c.** Begin a new document with the following markup tags:

```
<HTML>
<HEAD>
<TITLE>New Colors</TITLE>
</HEAD>
```

## 9. Add the color tags.

```
<HTML>
<HEAD>
<TITLE>New Colors</TITLE>
</HEAD>
<BODY BGCOLOR="#fff854" text="#003850"
      link="#722916" vlink="#f62500" alink=#008c3c">
</BODY>
```

## 10. Test a Background picture.

The Color Editor can test any picture available on any server as a background image. All you need is the correct URL (Uniform Resource Locator). If the image is smaller than the Netscape window, Netscape will *tile*, or repeat the image to form a wallpaper effect.

Netscape's server has background samples (Figure 10a) available to you for download (http://home .netscape.com/assist/net_sites/bg/backgrounds.html). The Color Editor can display a swatch as a test background:

**a.** Go to Netscape's "Background Samples" page at http://home.netscape.com/ assist/net_sites/bg/back-grounds.html.

**b.** Record the file names of any samples you'd like to test.

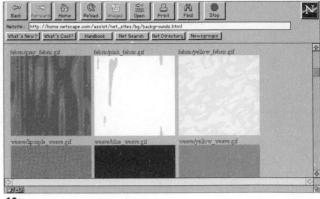

**10a.**

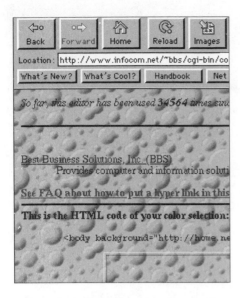

Use Background Picture: ⦿ Yes ○ No
http://home.netscape.com/assist/net_site

**10c.**

*Tip: To replace a file name in the URL field, click in the text and use the right arrow key to move the cursor all the way to the right. Press the Delete key until the file name is deleted, then re-type another name.*

**c.** Click on Yes in the Use Background Picture field on the Color Editor page.

**d.** Enter:

```
http://home.netscape.com/assist/net_sites/bg/fabric/
    yellow_fabric.gif
```

**e.** Try a few of your selections by substituting another file name in place of fabric/yellow_fabric.gif.

## 11. Create a new HTML document.

To test your background picture, create an HTML document on your hard drive and open it in Netscape. *(Note: Example #12 requires that your SLIP or PPP connection be open; however, you can test example #14 on your hard drive.)*

**a.** Open SimpleText.

**b.** Create a new document.

**c.** Add the following markup tags:

```
<HTML>
<HEAD>
<TITLE>New Colors</TITLE>
</HEAD>
```

## 12. Add the BODY tag.

```
<HTML>
<HEAD>
<TITLE>New Colors</TITLE>
</HEAD>
<BODY BACKGROUND=http://home.netscape
      .com/assist/net_sites/bg/fabric/yellow_fabric.gif>
</BODY>
```

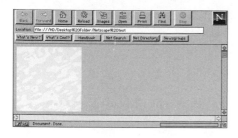

*Tip: Try using the URL for a Netscape background sample in the <IMG> tag. Instead of tiling the swatch as a background, only one swatch will appear on the page.*

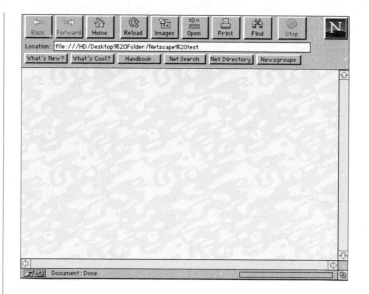

## 13. Copy a background sample (optional).

Copy a sample to your hard drive and use the file name in your BODY tag:

**a.** Go to Netscape's "Background Samples" page

```
http://home.netscape.com/ assist/net_sites/bg/
backgrounds.html
```

**b.** Press and hold down the mouse pointer on a sample.

**c.** Select Save this image as.

**d.** Use the default name or type in a file name.

**e.** Click on Save.

## 14. Create a new BODY tag (optional).

*(Note: the file name you create for your tag may vary depending on where the image is located. This example assumes the file yellowfabric.gif is is in the same directory as the HTML document. The file name together with one or more directory names is referred to as the path. )*

```
<HTML>
<HEAD>
<TITLE>New Colors</TITLE>
</HEAD>
<BODY BACKGROUND="yellow_fabric.gif">
</BODY>
```

## 11. Summary of HTML tags used in this section.

The tags you see in this list (in alphabetical order) reflect the HTML3 specification:

### \<BODY>...\</BODY>

A tag used to open and close the body of a document. This tag uses the following attributes:

**Background** specifies a URL to point to a background image that will tile to the full document image area. For example:

```
<Body Background="yellow_fabric.gif">
```

**bgcolor** controls the color of the background. For example:

```
<Body Bgcolor="#fff854">
```

**text** controls the color of normal text. For example:

```
<Body text="#003850">
```

**link** controls the color of link text. For example:

```
<Body link="#722916">
```

**vlink** controls the color of visited link text.

```
<Body vlink="#f62500">
```

**alink** controls the color of active link text.

```
<Body alink="#008c3c">
```

### \<HEAD>...\</HEAD>

A tag used to open and close the header portion of a document.

### \<HTML>...\</HTML>

A tag used to open and close an HTML document.

### \<TITLE>...\</TITLE>

Used inside the head, this tag describes the title of a document, which shows up inside a document's title bar.

# 3D Rendering on the Web

*Summary:* *Visit Patrick Hennessey's Interactive Graphics Renderer and generate your own custom 3D images for your home page.*

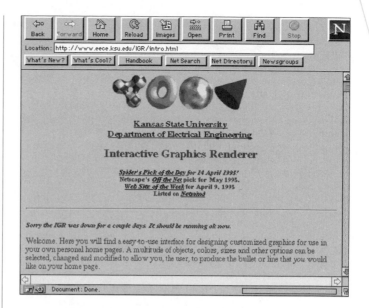

The Interactive Graphics Renderer (IGR) (http://www.eece.ksu.edu/IGR/), written by Patrick Hennessey, is an extraordinary example of how Web pages can be built to be interactive. Patrick's "renderer" creates small, high-quality, antialiased 3D images based on choices a Web visitor inputs in an online form. (*Note: Antialiasing is the smoothing of "jaggies" in digitized images.*)

Patrick, who is a student at Kansas State University, wrote the 3D rendering program in C on an IBM 386/40 running Linux 1.1.50. He permits free use of the 3D images for personal or not-for-profit reasons. For any other use, contact Patrick at: spectre@ksu.ksu.edu.

Patrick has upgraded his site since the time of this writing, so the following steps may vary slightly.

### 1. Getting started.
Click on the I've read the license. Let's GO! button.

> **I've read the license. Let's GO!**

1.

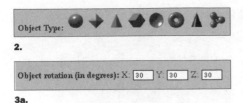

**2.**

**3a.**

**3b.**

| 32 color |
|---|
| 16 color |
| 32 color |
| 50 color |
| 256 color |

**4a.**

| Small |
|---|
| Tiny |
| Small |
| Medium |
| Large |
| Huge |
| Gigantic |

**4b.**

**5a.**

## 2. Choose an object type.

**a.** Choose a sphere, diamond, pyramid, cube, dent, torus, cone, or blob.

**c.** The object you choose will appear at the top of the page labeled "current graphic." *(Note: This type of selection, called an* image map*, causes the object to be re-drawn immediately when it is selected with the mouse.)*

## 3. Choose an object rotation.

**a.** Fill in the X,Y and Z boxes with a numbers to rotate the object. (e.g. 30, 30, 30).

**b.** Click on the Render with these options button.

## 4. Choose rendering options.

Click on each of the pop-up boxes next to Rendering Options:

**a.** Select the number of colors to be used to render.

**b.** Choose the size of the object to be rendered. *(Note: Gigantic is still small since these are all small graphics.)*

**c.** Click on the Render with these options button.

## 5. Choose color.

**a.** Click on the pop-up box Base Color and select a color.

**b.** Click on the pop-up box Mix Color and select a color.

**c.** Click on the Render with these options button.

**5b.**

**7a.**

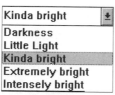

**8a.**

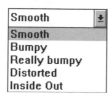

**8b.**

**9a.**

## 6. Choose Mix Type.

Click on one of the objects that displays how rendered paint will turn out.

**6.**

## 7. Choose a light source.

**a.** Click on the pop-up box labeled Light Source Location and select a location.

**b.** Click on the Render with these options button.

## 8. Choose a surface property.

**a.** Click on the pop-up box labeled Smooth and select a surface property from the list.

**b.** Click on the pop-up box labeled Kinda bright and select a surface property from the list.

**c.** Click on the Render with these options button.

## 9. Download the image.

**a.** Click on Gimme!

**b.** Select a location on your hard drive.

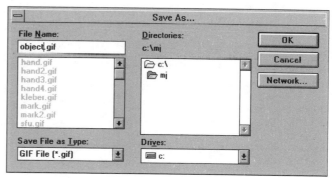

**9b.**

**torus**

**blob**

**sphere**

**cone**

**c.** Accept the default file name or type in another name.

**d.** Click on Save. *(Note: The GIF file you save will have a text file icon.)*

### 10. View the graphic (optional).

Since the GIF file you download has a text file icon instead of an image file icon, you may want to satisfy your curiosity by opening the image in Photoshop.

**a.** Open Photoshop.

**b.** Select Open from the File pull-down menu. *(Note: Select Open As from the File pull-down menu in version 2.5.1. Choose GIF file from the pop-up menu and open the file.)*

**c.** Open the GIF file.

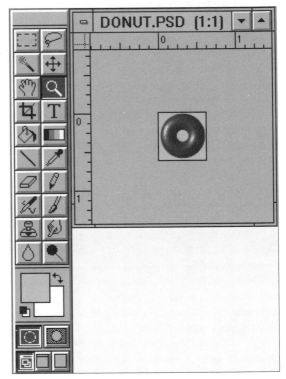

**10c.**

# Steven McGrew's WWW Resource Guide

*Summary:* *Visit Steven McGrew's home page, where he invites visitors to copy graphics from an area he calls Graphical GiZMo's.*

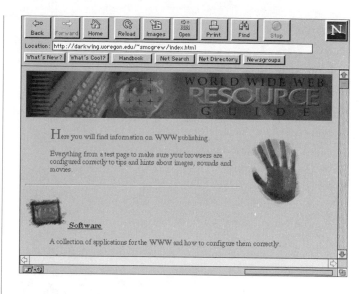

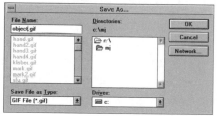

**2b.**

**2c.**

S teven McGrew of the University of Oregon has built a home page he calls "WWW Resource Guide," which is located at http://darkwing.uoregon.edu/~smcgrew/. He invites Web visitors to copy his icons, buttons, images, sounds, animations and VRML datasets, but asks for an email message if his artwork is used. Send your email to smcgrew@theskye.uoregon.edu.

The page where visitors can copy images is called Graphical GiZMo's. Netscape has a built-in save function that can be used to copy or download the images to a hard drive.

## 1. Select a Gizmo.
Scroll the Web page to select a gizmo.

## 2. Copy an image.
**a.** Press and hold down the mouse pointer on an image.

**b.** Select Save this image as.

**c.** Use the default file name or type in a new file name.

**d.** Click on OK.

# Searching the Web on Yahoo Search

***Summary:*** *Looking for links that complement your page? Doing research? Just browsing the Web? Try using the search engine at http://www.yahoo.com.*

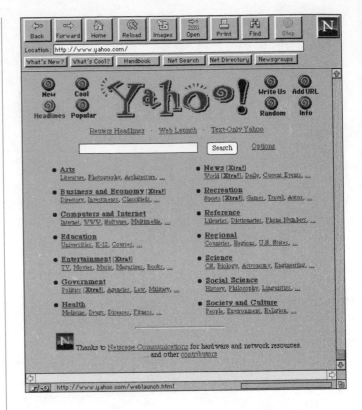

If you've never used a search engine, you'll be amazed at the power of this tool, which will search the Web for a topic of your choice. There are several such "search engines" or "robots" on the Web, and Yahoo (http://www.yahoo.com) is one of the most popular.

Yahoo was created by David Filo and Jerry Yang, both Electrical Engineering students at Stanford University, where this tool was housed for the first nine months of operation. Yahoo is now off-campus; it's an independent company, and the "robot" runs on three Silicon Graphics Indy machines. For speed reasons, complex searches are not allowed. Although the engine supports a simple Boolean "and" search, an optional fill-in form allows a visitor to specify a number of matches through a pop-up box on the form.

## 1. Select a topic from Yahoo's "top-level."

The simplest way to use Yahoo is to select from among the categories organized on the home page. Each has links that will lead you to related home pages.

**a.** Select one of the topics organized into "top-level" categories on the Yahoo Home page.

**b.** Click on a link.

**1b.**

**c.** The link will take you to pages of other links and related Web pages.

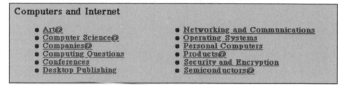

**1c.**

## 2. Use the Yahoo search form.

**a.** Type in any topic on the Yahoo home page.

**b.** Click on the Search button.

**c.** A page of related links will be displayed for you to explore.

**2a, 2b.**

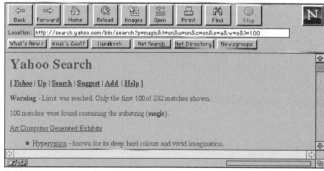

**2c.**

# WWW Style Manual from Yale University

*Summary: Visit Yale's C/AIM site (Center for Advanced Instructional Media) to learn about Web site development from the award-winning Yale faculty.*

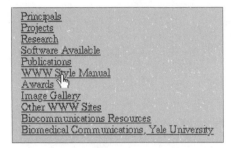

When you want to set up your own Web site, go to Yale's WWW Style Manual home page (http://info.med.yale.edu /caim/C_HOME.HTML). Here you will find much of the information you need.

Topics are divided into three categories: Interface Design in WWW Systems, WWW Page Design and Optimizing Performance in WWW Pages. One of the most valuable topics in the Yale pages is navigation, which includes schematics. For Web artists who are learning about links, these schematics provide a clear image of how to design a "system" of Web pages. (An example is shown below.)

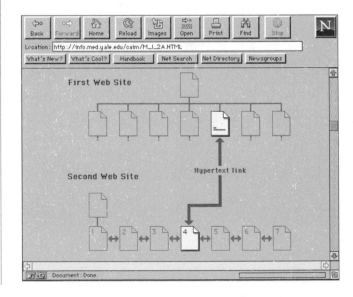

# Net Site assistance from Netscape

*Summary:* *Visit Netscape's home page to download helper applications and updated reference material on changes in HTML.*

**1.**

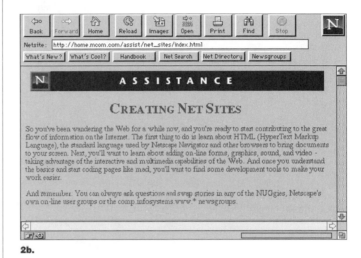

**2a.**

*Tip:* *If you're not currently online, it is possible to load Netscape on your hard drive and compose HTML documents locally. Create the HTML documents using Programmer's File Editor located on the CD-ROM in the back of this book.*

*For updates to HTML, get a friend who is online to download current reference materials on HTML.*

Netscape's own Web site (http://home.mcom.com /home/welcome.html) is a valuable resource for downloading helper applications and current reference materials on HTML:

## 1. Click on Home.

Click on the Home button at the top of your browser window to go to the Netscape home page.

**2b.**

## 2. Create Net Sites.

Scroll down and then click on Creating Net Sites (Figure 2a). This page contains documents that you can read online or save to your hard drive.

Topics on the Assistance page (Figure 2b) include:

### Authoring Documents

Look for the latest reference materials on HTML. (For example, this section provides *A Beginner's Guide to HTML, Composing Good HTML, Extensions to HTML* and *Guides to Writing HTML Documents.*)

### Adding Functionality

Look for *Off the Web*, a newsletter published monthly by Chris Tacy, and additional directory listings of mailing lists and newsgroups to assist Web developers.

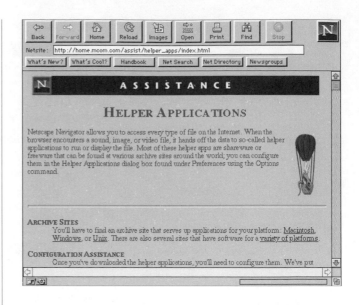

**Developer Tools**

Look for utility software programs to download, such as LView Pro, Programmer's File Editor, Mapedit and HTML Editors.

## 2. Save a document.

**a.** To save, click on the *A Beginner's Guide to HTML document* link.

**b.** Select Save As from the File pull-down menu.

**c.** Select Plain Text from the Format pop-up box.

**d.** Click on Save.

*(Note: You can open amd print the text you have saved from within your text file.)*

## 3. Prepare to download a Helper App.

Go back to the Netscape home page by clicking on either Home or Back.

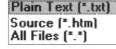

**2c.**

## 4. Click on Helper Apps.

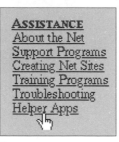

**4.**

ations for your platform: Macintosh, Windows, or U:
f platforms.

**5a.**

● ftp://ftp.cica.indiana.edu

**5b.**

**The Indiana Archive**

EMWAC contains a mirror of the largest ftp site for Windows public domain software at Indiana ftp.cica.indiana.edu. Some useful information and index files have been processed here.

First, there are some text files to give general information, some of which are **big**.

- *Overall Index*
- *Readme file*
- *List of mirror sites*
- *Notice to mirror sites*

Next, there are the individual indexes. These have hypertext links in them to the real files. If you select one of the indexes, toggle your Web reader to save the file to disk, and then select the link, you should be able to retrieve the file. Alternatively, you may find that your Web reader is smart enough to know that it is getting a binary file and automatically try to save it to disk.

**5c.**

- *Program/ftp index*
- *Vbasic index*
- *Sdl index*
- *Sounds index*
- *Sndxamp index*
- *Toolbook index*
- *Util index*
- *Winsock index*
- *Winword index*
- *Wpwin index*
- *Wrk index*

**5d.**

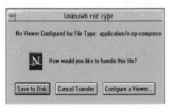

**sounds index**

- *121human.zip* 940831 Wave files from the CD - "Still The 13th Man" [1.32m]
- *14-wave.zip* 920714 14 WAV Files for Windows 3.1
- *18tons.zip* 941024 Plays WAV & MIDI files that are dropped on it
- *86wave.zip* 920416 86 WAV Files for Windows 3.1
- *abcd30.zip* 950719 A-B-CD: Super CD-ROM player and Jb (16/32bit)
- *acdr.zip* 921205 Audio CD player, Also Catalogs CDs in Paradox format
- *actrpel.zip* 950502 Sit wave ( WAV) files from The MONOLITH CD
- *adlibhw.zip* 920616 Play WAVE files through the adlib sound card
- *alab11d.zip* 940223 Audio Lab V1.1d sample editor for Windows 3.1
- *aladdin.zip* 940728 Small sound bites from the Disney film [1.2mb]
- *alarmc.zip* 930814 Alarm clock plays your favorite WAV file

**5e, 5f.**

Unknown File Type

No Viewer Configured for File Type: application/x-zip-compress

N    How would you like to handle this file?

[ Save to Disk ]   [ Cancel Transfer ]   [ Configure a Viewer... ]

**5g.**

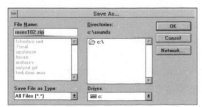

Save As...

File Name:
roses102.zip

Directories:
c:\sounds

[ OK ]
[ Cancel ]
[ Network... ]

Save File as Type:           Drives:
[ All Files (*.*) ]          [ c: ]

**5h.**

---

Topics on the Helper Applications page include:

**Archive Sites**

Lists sites where you can download helper applications.

**Configurations Assistance**

Provides assistance with configuring your helper applications to work with your browser.

**For the Experts**

Contains C software to implement JPEG image compression and a FAQ (Frequently Asked Questions) page devoted to advanced graphics.

## 5. Download a Helper App.

**a.** Click on a platform under "Archive sites." (For example, click on the Windows link.)

**b.** Click on an archive site in the list that follows (For example, click on ftp://ftp.cica.indiana.edu.)

**c.** Scroll to locate a category.

**d.** Click on a category. (For example, click on Sound.)

**e.** Scroll to locate the utility of your choice.

**f.** Click on a link to download the software

**g.** A dialog box will be displayed which will ask you if you want to save the file. Click on Save to Disk.

**h.** Select a "destination directory" to save the software to your hard drive.

# PC software archives

**Summary:** *The PC software archives maintained at university sites have extensive collections of the latest freeware and shareware. Learn how to "point" your Netscape browser to download the latest version of a PC software program.*

**Note:** *Because of the load on these public sites, it may be easier to reach the "mirror" sites listed in the next section.*

**1.**

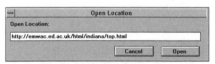

**2.**

**3.**

Wondering if your software is outdated? Check the software archives at the SimTel Coast-to-Coast Software Repository (http://www.coast.net/SimTel/), the OAK Software Repository (http://www.acs.oakland.edu/oak/) or the Unofficial Windows 95 Software Archives (http://www.netex.net/w95/index.html). Each of these archives contains a huge collection of freeware and shareware programs that you can download through Netscape.

## 1. Open a location.
Click on the Open button in the Netscape window.

## 2. Enter a URL.
URLs (Uniform Resource Locators) point to data on the World Wide Web. The data could be in the form of a Web document (HTML or SGML), a file on an FTP or Gopher server or Usenet "news" from an NNTP server.

   **a.** To locate the SimTel Coast-to-Coast Software Repository type:

```
http://www.coast.net/SimTel/
```

## 3. Scroll the SimTel home page.
Use the up and down scroll arrows on your Netscape window to scroll down the SimTel home page.

**4.**

**5.**

**6.**

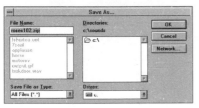

**7a.**

**7b.**

**8.**

## 4. Pick a category.

Select a PC software category from the table on the SimTel home page.

## 5. Pick an action.

Click on a link to browse or search the archive.

## 6. Scroll the directory.

Use the up and down scroll arrows on your Netscape window to scroll the directory.

## 7. Start a download.

**a.** To download a text file or a program, click on the name of the file in the directory.

**b.** A dialog box will be diplayed which will ask if you want to save the file. Click on Save to Disk.

## 8. Select a destination directory.

When the download is complete, a dialog box displays prompting you to select a directory for saving. Use the file list window to select a directory.

# SimTel archive mirror sites

*Summary: The "mirror" sites listed hold the same contents as the main SimTel archive.*

SimTel, the Coast to Coast Software Repository™, is located on SimTel.Coast.NET.

Files are available by anonymous FTP in directories /SimTel/msdos, /SimTel/win3, /SimTel/win95,/SimTel/nt, and /SimTel/vendors on SimTel's primary mirror site FTP.Coast.NET and from these secondary mirror sites:

### Canberra, Australia
```
archie.au (139.130.23.2)
        /micros/pc/SimTel
```

### Sao Paulo, Brazil
```
ftp.unicamp.br (143.106.10.54)
        /pub/simtel
```

### Beijing, China
```
ftp.pku.edu.cn (162.105.129.30)
        /pub/simtel
```

### Prague, Czech Republic
```
pub.vse.cz (146.102.16.9)
        /pub/simtel
```

*Tip:* If a mirror site located in your time zone is busy, try a site in a distant time zone, where net traffic is experiencing a slow period. For instance, mirror sites in the U.S. are often busy during U.S. business hours, but a site like FUNET is frequently available during U.S. business hours because low-use hours in Finland correspond with peak hours in the U.S.

## Lancaster, England

```
micros.hensa.ac.uk (194.80.32.51)
      /mirrors/simtel
```

## London, England

```
src.doc.ic.ac.uk (155.198.1.40)
      /pub/packages/simtel
      /pub/packages/simtel-win3
```

## London, England

```
ftp.demon.co.uk (158.152.1.44)
      /pub/mirrors/simtel
```

## Espoo, Finland

```
ftp.funet.fi (128.214.248.6)
      /mirrors/simtel.coast.net/Simtel
```

## Neuilly, France

```
ftp.grolier.fr (194.51.174.67)
      /pub/pc/SimTel
```

## Paris, France

```
ftp.ibp.fr (132.227.60.2)
      /pub/pc/SimTel
```

## Bochum, Germany

```
ftp.ruhr-uni-bochum.de (134.147.32.42)
      /mirrors/simtel.coast.net/SimTel
```

## Chemnitz, Germany

```
ftp.tu-chemnitz.de (134.109.2.13)
      /pub/simtel
```

## Mainz, Germany

```
ftp.uni-mainz.de (134.93.8.129)
      /pub/pc/mirrors/simtel
```

## Paderborn, Germany

```
ftp.uni-paderborn.de (131.234.10.42)
      /SimTel
```

### Tuebingen, Germany

```
ftp.uni-tuebingen.de (134.2.2.60)
    /pub/simtel
```

### Hong Kong

```
ftp.cs.cuhk.hk (137.189.4.110)
    /pub/simtel
```

### Hong Kong

```
ftp.hkstar.com (202.82.0.48)
    /pub/simtel
```

### Haifa, Israel

```
ftp.technion.ac.il (132.68.7.8)
    /pub/unsupported/simtel
```

### Pisa, Italy

```
cnuce-arch.cnr.it (131.114.1.10)
    /pub/msdos/simtel
```

### Saitama, Japan

```
ftp.saitama-u.ac.jp (133.38.200.1)
    /pub/simtel
```

### Saitama, Japan

```
ftp.riken.go.jp (134.160.41.2)
    /pub/SimTel
```

### Tokyo, Japan

```
ftp.crl.go.jp (133.243.18.20)
    /pub/pc/archives/simtel
```

### Seoul, Korea

```
ftp.kornet.nm.kr (168.126.63.7)
    /pub/SimTel
```

### Seoul, Korea

```
ftp.nuri.net (203.255.112.4)
    /pub/Simtel
```

## Netherlands

```
ftp.nic.surfnet.nl (192.87.46.3)
        /mirror-archive/software/simtel-msdos
        /mirror-archive/software/simtel-win3
```

## Wellington, New Zealand

```
ftp.vuw.ac.nz (130.195.2.193)
        /pub/simtel
```

## Krakow, Poland

```
ftp.cyf-kr.edu.pl (149.156.1.8)
        /pub/mirror/simtel
```

## Warsaw, Poland

```
ftp.icm.edu.pl (148.81.209.3)
        /pub/simtel
```

## Aveiro, Portuga

```
ftp.ua.pt (193.136.80.6)
        /pub/simtel
```

## South Africa

```
ftp.sun.ac.za (146.232.212.21)
        /pub/simtel
```

## Slovak Republic

```
ftp.uakom.sk (192.108.131.12)
        /pub/SimTel
```

## Slovenia

```
ftp.arnes.si (193.2.1.72)
        /software/SimTel
```

## Stockholm, Sweden

```
ftp.sunet.se (130.238.127.3)
        /pub/pc/mirror/SimTel
```

## Zurich, Switzerland

```
ftp.switch.ch (130.59.1.40)
        /mirror/simtel
```

## Taipei, Taiwan

NCTUCCCA.edu.tw (140.111.1.10)

    /PC/simtel

    /PC/windows/simtel

## Nonthaburi, Thailand

ftp.nectec.or.th (192.150.251.33)

    /pub/mirrors/SimTel

## Ankara, Turkey

ftp.metu.edu.tr (144.122.1.101)

    /pub/mirrors/simtel

## Concord, CA, USA

ftp.cdrom.com (192.216.191.11)

    /pub/simtel

## Urbana, IL, USA

uiarchive.cso.uiuc.edu (128.174.5.14)

    /pub/systems/pc/simtel

## Rochester, MI, USA

OAK.Oakland.Edu (141.210.10.117)

    /SimTel

## St. Louis, MO, USA

wuarchive.wustl.edu (128.252.135.4)

    /systems/ibmpc/simtel

## Norman, OK, USA

ftp.uoknor.edu (129.15.2.20)

    /mirrors/SimTel

## Corvallis, OR, USA

ftp.orst.edu (128.193.4.2)

    /pub/mirrors/simtel

## Salt Lake City, UT, USA

ftp.pht.com (198.60.59.5)

    /pub/mirrors/simtel

*Mark Elbert* *is a graphic*
*artist and a musician who*
*graduated from Pratt*
*Institute with a degree*
*in industrial design. Mark*
*has created Web pages*
*for* **Mother Mary***, a*
*New York-based*
*alternative rock band.*

*(mother@interport.net)*

http://www.echonyc.com
/~art/mesh/mesh.html

# Chapter 5

# Photography

Images are the most popular "multimedia" elements on the Web.
Because of bandwidth limitations—the objective is to keep graphics
files to a minimum.

To introduce readers to ideas about file size, Mark Elbert's notes on
Web graphics summarize details such as Web page size, color scanning, bit-depth, file naming conventions and advice on testing a Web
page before it's "launched" into cyberspace.

Mark's Web projects will give readers clues about how to assemble
their own pages. And, in a section on digital photography, the digital
imaging experts at Ken Hansen Imaging in New York offer tips on
using digital photography. Included are details about filmless digital
cameras and QuickTime VR movies, a new technology from Apple
Computer that stitches still images together to form an interactive
panoramic movie.

# Mark Elbert's notes on Web graphics

*Summary:* *Mark Elbert relays tips on Web page size, color palettes, dithering and file formats.*

Graphic designers can leverage everything they know about print and often reuse graphics that have been created for print. In this section, Mark Elbert's notes on graphics will help graphic designers make a transition from print to Web graphics.

## 1. Plan the size of your images.

Since most microcomputer color monitors are 14-inch color screens, you should plan your graphics to fit this average-sized window. Here's the available space in a single Netscape window (resized to fill the screen) on an average monitor:

| Dimension | Pixels (or pts) | Picas | Inches |
|---|---|---|---|
| Horizontal measure | 604 | 50.33 | 8.38 |
| Vertical measure | 304 | 25.33 | 4.22 |

When planning the height of your graphic, decide whether you'd like the average visitor to experience the graphic in "pages," or if you want the graphic to fit within the first viewable window. Set a graphic's height to 304 pixels to limit the graphic to one screen. Although Netscape's default window has an inside vertical dimension of 320 pixels, there will be an offset of 8 pixels along the top of the browser window.

## 2. Color scanning: the transition from print.

The 24- and 30-bit scanners that graphic designers use for print provide information for the printed page, far in excess of what you'll need or want for Web graphics.

The 24-bit image you edit in Photoshop should be reduced to a second, smaller image of 8 bits or fewer. Half of your image manipulation steps will be to reduce file size because file size

*Tip: Digital cameras capture 24-bit images that provide more than enough data for Web images. For more information, see "Digital cameras and QuickTime VR" in this chapter.*

*Tip: Before resampling or changing the bit-depth in your image, make a duplicate of the image. Select Duplicate from the Image pull-down menu in Photoshop and give it an alternate name.*

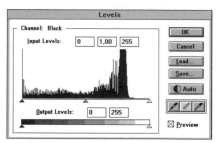

**3a.**

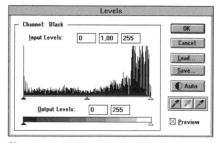

**3b.**

is critical on a Web page. Look for examples in this chapter that demonstrate how to reduce bit-depth in Photoshop. *(Note: LView Pro is also an image editor that can be used to reduce bit-depth. It is available on the CD-ROM in the back of this book and it's described later in this chapter.)*

**a. Scan to a particular size.** Most scanning software programs allow you to scan to a particular size. Rather than resizing the image in Photoshop, it's best to scan to your desired size on the scanner, as resizing in Photoshop causes blurriness.

**b. Scan to a larger resolution.** In spite of the fact that you will ultimately not need more than 72 pixels per inch, graphic designers generally agree that the best images are those that are "oversampled" or scanned at a higher resolution and then resampled.

### 3. Correct the color of your image.

Improve the color in an image by redistributing the color tones. This can be accomplished by "setting the white point and black point" or by manually selecting the lightest and darkest areas in a scanned photo. *(Note: See "Creating a 'banner graphic' or 'splash screen'" in this chapter for steps on how to set the white point and black point.)*

**a. Histogram before color correction.** A histogram from Photoshop reflects the tonal distibution in an image or the brightness and darkness values. Note that the x-axis reflects the colors from darkest (left) to brightest (right). The y axis reflects the number of pixels with each value.

**b. Histogram after color correction.** After setting the white point and black point to color-correct the image, the color is more evenly distributed.

### 4. Changing the bit-depth.

By reducing bit-depth, you reduce file size. Conversion to a smaller bit-depth is accomplished through a Mode change in Photoshop. When converting from RGB Mode to Indexed Color Mode, a dialog box will appear and allow you to select a bit depth and a dithering option.

*Tip: Figure 5a, 5c and 7 are available on the CD-ROM in the back of this book. Open the photos on a PC with a color monitor to see the differences in bit-depths.*

**5a.**

**5b.**

**5c.**

By reducing the bit-depth in an image, you also reduce the number of colors. When you convert an RGB image to Indexed color in Photoshop, the program builds a color table or palette for the image. Although an RGB image can contain 16.7 million colors, an indexed color image contains 256 colors. Photoshop simulates a larger RGB palette using the available 256 colors. *(Note: For more information and examples, see the secton on bit-depth in this chapter.)*

Photoshop allows you to control the following "palette types" when you convert to Indexed Color Mode:

- *Exact Palette.* Photoshop uses the same 256 colors present in the original RGB image.

- *Uniform Palette.* Photoshop uses the default color table. Dithering is an option.

- *Adaptive Palette.* Photoshop creates a color table of colors more commonly used in the image. *(Note: When converting to Indexed Color Mode in Photoshop, the Adaptive Palette is the best option.)*

- *Custom Palette.* Photoshop displays a Color Table dialog box, allowing you to edit the color table using the Color Picker. The palette can be saved for later use.

- *Previous Palette.* Photoshop makes this option available when you have already converted an image using the Custom or Adaptive Palette option.

## 5. Dithering.

Dithering adjusts the color of adjacent pixels to fool the eye into thinking there is a third color present. Greg Marr, a color manipulation expert at Equilibrium, recommends selecting dithering whenever it is an option.

- **a. 24 bits, millions of colors, no dithering.** A 24-bit image on an 8-bit monitor has some dithering.

- **b. 4-bits, 16 colors, dithering.** Photoshop's dithering applied in a Mode change from RGB to Index Color Mode camouflages a reduction in the number of colors.

- **c. 4-bits, 16 colors, no dithering.** Without dithering, there are too few colors in a 4-bit image to approximate skin coloring.

**7.**

### 6. Add type after reducing the bit-depth.

Don't subject the type in your image to "dithering." Add type after you have settled on a bit-depth that you like.

### 7. Color duotone and grayscale options.

Color duotone and grayscale images look better at smaller bit-depths than do full color images. For instructions on how to create a duotone, see "Creating a duotone from a grayscale image" later in this chapter.

| Image | Color | Duotone | Grayscale |
|---|---|---|---|
| 8-bit, GIF | 160 K | 148K | 144K |
| 8-bit, JPEG (med.) | 60 K | 44K | 52K |
| 4-bit, GIF | 92 K | 100K | 80K |
| 4-bit, JPEG (med.) | 32 K | 48K | 52K |

### 8. File naming conventions.

Your Web documents should have proper "extensions," which help the Web server identify the file type:

| Format | Extension |
|---|---|
| HTML | .html(Unix), .htm (DOS) |
| GIF | .gif |
| JPEG | .jpg, .jpeg |

Use very short file names without spaces (8 characters or less) and avoid using the following characters in file names:

| Character | Name |
|---|---|
| < > | angle brackets |
| \ | backslash |
| \| | vertical bar |
| [ ] | brackets |

*continued*

*Tip: Browsers are constantly evolving like other software programs. Try to stay familiar with new developments by downloading new versions occasionally. Current information about updates to HTML can be obtained within Netscape's own system of home pages at:*
*http://www.netscape.com*

*Once you're on the Netscape home page, scroll down to "Assistance" and click on "Creating Net Sites." This will take you to a page of HTML reference materials. Danial W. Connolly, who's on staff at the World Wide Web Consortium in the Laboratory for Computer Science at MIT, also maintains a Web site filled with information about HTML at:*
*http://www.w3.org/hypertext/www/markup/markup.html*

*Tip: The Cyber Cafe at 273 Lafayette Street in New York City (corner of Prince) is an example of a growing trend that began in the San Francisco Bay area in 1991 (212.334.5140).*

*Owned by Michael Youmans, Thomas Wise and Evan Galbraith III, the Cyber Cafe is SoHo's newest "hot spot" where cafe patrons can order coffee and a sandwich while they browse the Web, send e-mail or take lessons from cafe experts.*

| Character | Name |
|-----------|------|
| : | colon |
| , | comma |
| = | equals |
| / | forward slash |
| + | plus sign |
| " | quotation mark |
| ; | semicolon |

## 9. Test the download speed of your Web page.

HTML documents may be built on your hard drive using a text editor such as Notepad. Use Netscape off-line to check your work. However, the download speed you'll experience when you load a file from your hard drive will be much faster than the average Web visitor's 14.4 Kbps modem.

As soon as you've developed a large graphic for your Web page, you should test the download speed over a 14.4 Kbps modem. If the graphics are slow to load, you'll have trouble attracting Web visitors. Web visitors will be reluctant to return if they have to wait several seconds for downloads.

## 10. Test the Web page on other browsers.

"Netscape-specific" features on a Web page include features such as color backgrounds, color type and inline jpeg images. To see what your page looks like with another browser, you may want to consider looking at your HTML file locally (on your hard drive) with the Windows 95 Web explorer or one of the browsers used by popular online services.

If you have access to a server site early in the development cycle, place your files on the server and try to look at your page with America Online, CompuServe, or Prodigy.

## 11. Test your Web page on other platforms.

If your firm does not own an IBM PC, consider getting on the Web through another platform at a public computer rental facility, which rents time on the Internet by the hour.

# Pixel-depth

*Summary*: Learn how "pixel-depth" or "bit-depth," a critical color characteristic, will affect the performance of your Web pages with graphics.

*Tip: Equilibrium, the company that created DeBabelizer, is continually adding functionality to their software. Recent additions include "readers" and "writers" for Alias, Electric Image, the Avid OMF Interchange format, QuickTime, the Tiff Group 4 (fax) format and SoftImage. New readers include PhotoCD and Photoshop 3.0, and new writers include DP Anim and JPEG. (Note: Although a JPEG writer existed before, the new JPEG writer includes support for grayscale.) Equilibrium's Web site is located at http://www.equil.com*

Graphic designers who have worked with Photoshop to produce artwork for print may not be acquainted with "pixel depth" or "bit depth." Bit-depth is defined as the number of bits used to make up a color pixel:

| Bit depth | Number of Colors |
|-----------|------------------|
| 2 bits | 4 colors |
| 3 bits | 8 colors |
| 4 bits | 16 colors |
| 5 bits | 32 colors |
| 6 bits | 64 colors |
| 7 bits | 128 colors |
| 8 bits | 256 colors |
| 16 bits | 65,536 colors |
| 24 bits | 16 million colors |

For print graphics, the objective is to increase the bit depth; for Web graphics, as in game software development, the objective is to reduce bit depth.

The critical objective for a Web page artist is the same objective shared by game developers: combine what looks like the largest amount of color and the smallest possible file size. Web pages have a critical performance issue. Web visitors will grow impatient and won't want to return to a Web page if there's a long delay while images download.

## 1. Plan "target" size and physical dimensions.
Spend time traveling the Web and get acquainted with the file sizes and physical dimensions of the graphics you see.

**1b.**

**1c.**

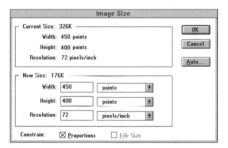

**1d.**

The images you see that download quickly will be the ones you'll want to examine closely. You can discover a file's format, the file size and the physical dimensions by downloading the image to your hard drive:

**a.** Position your mouse pointer on a Web page graphic.

**b.** Hold down the mouse button and select Save this Image as.

**c.** Let go of the mouse button, select a folder or your desktop for saving, enter the name of your file, and click on OK. The file name extension will tell you if the image is a GIF or a JPEG file.

**d.** Open the image in Photoshop and select Image Size from the Image pull-down menu. Note the image resolution and the physical dimensions.

## 2. Compare image file sizes.

**a.** **40 K, JPEG.** At 40 K, the Condé Nast image downloads very quickly.

**b.** **108 K, GIF.** At 108 K, the Disney MoviePlex image downloads rather slowly.

**2a.**

**2b.**

**4a.**

**4b.**

**4c.**

### 3. Browsers have a 256 color "per page" total.

The palette you plan for one image may affect the palettes of other images on the page because browsers limit the total number of colors to 256 per page.

### 4. Experiment with lower bit depth.

Images respond differently when you lower the bit depth. For example, an image with a large variety of colors will not respond well to a lower bit depth because colors get "used up" quickly.

**a. 8 bits, 256 colors, dithered GIF.** This image of children waiting to climb into a school bus has a wide variety of colors. This image begins to look "patchy" even at 8 bit. (Note the little girl's back pack and the head lights of the bus.) As a 200K GIF file, this image will download slowly.

**b. 7 bits, 128 colors, dithered GIF.** The image of a teacher and student starts to look patchy at 7 bits. As a 112K GIF file this image will download slowly.

**c. 4 bits, 16 colors, dithered GIF.** The image of the teacher and student holds up well in grayscale at a lower bit-depth. As a 28K GIF file, this image will download faster than the full color version.

Both images look superior and download faster when saved as JPEG. However, there are tradeoffs. For a comparison of GIF versus JPEG, see the next section in this chapter. *Note: Figure 4a, 4b and 4c are available on the CD-ROM in the back of this book. Open the photos on a PC with a color monitor to see the differences in bit-depths.*

# Saving your image: GIF or JPEG?

**Summary**: *Learn about the differences between GIF and JPEG, two popular graphics file formats found on the Web.*

*Tip: Many graphic designers and their clients have decided to create Web pages with elements that can only be seen with a Netscape browser. Most base this decision on the fact that from 70 to 80 percent of computer users on the Web are using the Netscape browser.*

*The "browser extras" are referred to as the "Netscape Extensions to HTML" and offer a graphic designer more control over graphics than any other browser. It is thought that other browsers will eventually add similar features.*

The decision to save an image as GIF or JPEG may depend on the image. Although GIF images are popular because of the special effects that can be used, detailed images and flesh tones often look better when saved as JPEG:

## 1. GIFs are read by more browsers.

GIF is the predominant image file format used by Web page designers because it can be read by more browser programs as an "inline" image. Inline images appear on the browser page with text. "External" images are those that must be loaded and displayed with an add-on viewer program, referred to as a "helper application."

Netscape can read JPEG images as inline graphics, but most other browser programs will ignore JPEGs tagged as inline images. A JPEG image referenced with a link will be displayed in a viewer application's floating window when the link launches the viewer software.

## 2. GIFs can be used for special effects.

GIF images are 8-bit images that may also be stored as "transparent GIFs." This type of GIF is popular for special effects such as fading and silhouettes. "Interlaced GIFs" are another popular option because they appear to download faster than "non-interlaced GIFs." The image is quickly drawn in low resolution and then gradually fills in with pixels as the image is downloaded.

## 3. GIF images sometimes have "banding."

Because GIF images are 8 bit, the image may contain "banding," or look posterized. This is due to the way the browser reads the image and usually occurs with blends and flesh tones. An image with a large amount of detail will look better if saved as a JPEG image. Banding, which will often be seen in an 8-bit

*Tip: Equilibrium, the company that created DeBabelizer, also makes a DeBabelizer "Lite" product. Unlike the full package, which supports scripting and batch processing, DeBabelizer Lite is a translation tool that contains a large number of "readers and writers." (Note: Animation file formats such as QuickTime, FLC and FLI are not supported in the Lite version of DeBabelizer.) Keep in mind that DeBabelizer is only available for the Macintosh. I've presented it in this book because it is a very useful image processing tool.*

GIF, will be smoothed in the JPEG format with some dithering. A summary of file format characteristics:

| Format | Plus/Minus |
|--------|------------|
| GIF | **Plus** The GIF files can be read by a majority of browsers as an "inline" image. |
| | **Plus** GIF images can be saved as "interlaced GIF," a format that *appears* to download faster than "non-interlaced" GIF. The image is quickly drawn in low resolution and is gradually filled in with pixels. |
| | **Plus** GIF images can be saved as a "transparent GIF." This GIF drops out whatever color is assigned as transparent. (*This may be accomplished with Leonardo Haddad Loreiro's LView Pro available on the CD-ROM in the back of this book.*) |
| | **Minus** GIF images may appear "posterized" in some browsers. (See next page.) |
| JPEG | **Plus** Photographs do not appear "posterized." |
| | **Minus** JPEG files look somewhat dithered and are not read as inline images by many browsers. |

## 4. JPEG was designed for 24-bit color.

The JPEG compression algorithm (invented by the Joint Photographic Experts Group) is really intended for 24- or 32-bit color. When an image is compressed, this "lossy" algorithm throws information away.

Should a Web designer reduce an image to 8 bits and then save it as JPEG? Since most of the color monitors used on the Web are 8-bit color, 24-bit color images on Web pages are unnecessarily large and a waste of color information. An 8-bit JPEG image stores what appears to be a lot more than 8-bits of information and although the loss of data may be visible on a printed page, it is not visible on screen. *(Note: do not save a JPEG image twice as JPEG, or your image will be noticeably "pixelated." )* Reduce your Web graphic to 8 bit, save it as a JPEG, but store an original 24-bit RGB image for future editing.

*Tip:* *"Posterization" is a term that refers to a "flattening" of the brightness values in an image (Note: The image on this page is from the Pacific Coast Software collection of stock photography at:* `http://www.pacific-coast.com/`)

The differences between GIF and JPEG images is most obvious in skin tones, where the posterization that occurs is very pronounced. Notice the difference in the two photos on this page. The top photo is a JPEG image and the photo below is a GIF image.

# GIF and the LZW compression patent

**Summary:** *Even though there have been rumors that the GIF file format may disappear due to the legal dispute between Unisys and CompuServe, the 8-bit file format, which may someday be upgraded to 24-bit, is not going away.*

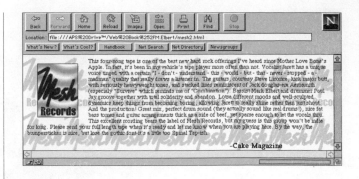

Graphic designers who develop Web pages appreciate the GIF file format for the "transparent gif" that makes silhouettes possible and the "interlaced gif," which appears to download quickly to the browser screen in "waves." Although the JPEG file format is superior to GIF for displaying color detail, a JPEG image can't be saved with a "transparent" background, nor can it be interlaced.

### Unisys and the compression patent.

The GIF file format, owned by CompuServe, uses LZW compression. LZW (Lempel, Ziv, Welch) is a lossless, 8-bit compression-decompression scheme that was originally developed by the Lempel-Ziv team, but later improved by Terry Welch when he worked for the Sperry Corporation. Unisys took over the LZW patent when Sperry became part of Unisys in 1986. The LZW scheme, unlike a "lossy" compression schme, doesn't throw away information when it compresses. Ever since Unisys took over the patent, they have been licensing the compression algorithm to online services and modem manufacturers. They have also been quietly enforcing the patent in the software market, as the scheme is popular among companies who make image editing software programs.

### "Grandfathering" the license.

In pursuing their right to the patent, Unisys "grandfathered" the license to any software product that used LZW compression prior to January 1995. However, as of January 1st, any new product, or any software product update, requires a license.

# The moveable grid for pictures and text

*Summary*: *Can a graphic designer develop a grid for a Web page? Not really. HTML tags describe how elements should be placed in relationship to each other. Placement is not described in relationship to the page, because the page size can change.*

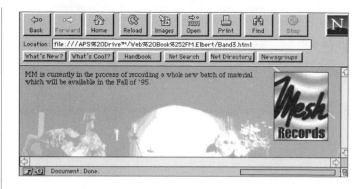

When a graphic designer uses page layout software, he or she has a tool that offers very precise page geometry for a printed page.

Since a Web page can be resized, page elements need to be described in relationship to each other, and not the page. In the sample shown on this page, the Mesh Records image has been tagged with an **ALIGN=RIGHT** attribute tag, which will align the image on the right side of the text regardless of how the browser window gets resized. Note there is a small amount of horizontal spacing on either side of the image to push the text away from the edge, which is the result of an HTML "attribute" called HSPACE shown later in this chapter.

If horizontal space does get added, you will not be able to control the space on one side and not the other. This page offset around the edge appears to be 8 points or pixels.

# Using HTML to move page elements horizontally

*Summary*: In the absence of a grid, it's valuable to understand how HTML can be used to move elements horizontally or vertically. In page layout software these commands would be referred to as paragraph-based.

*Tip:* Most HTML tags "place" images in relationship to the left margin. Very few tags are available that place images on the right or anywhere in between. The examples on the next few pages demonstrate a few tags that can be used like tabs to move elements "varying" distances across the page.

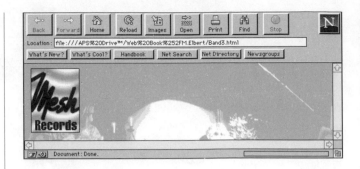

Images and text that are "tagged" into place horizontally on a Web page maintain their position relative to other elements when the page is resized.

## 1. Open a text file.

Use Notepad or a word processor. If you use a word processor, be sure to save the document as Text Only.

## 2. Create a new HTML document.

Start a new document with the following markup tags:

```
<HTML>
<HEAD>
<TITLE>New Side Band</TITLE>
</HEAD>
<BODY>
```

## 3. Add the name of a GIF file to the BODY tag.

Background images can be used in Netscape. Add the name of the GIF file that you'd like to use as the background image to the BODY tag:

```
<HTML>
<HEAD>
<TITLE>New Side Band</TITLE>
</HEAD>
<Body Background ="New_Band.gif">
```

**4.**

## 4. Add an Image tag.

The IMG tag contains a "source" or SRC parameter, which contains the name of the image file:

```
<HTML>
<HEAD>
<TITLE>New Side Band</TITLE>
</HEAD>
<Body Background ="New_Band.gif">
<IMG SRC="Mesh Wave.gif">
</BODY>
</HTML>
```

The result is shown in Figure 4.

## 5. Add text after the image.

Unless the browser is instructed how to handle text, it will flow the text immediately after the image:

```
<HTML>
<HEAD>
<TITLE>New Side Band</TITLE>
</HEAD>
<Body Background ="New_Band.gif">
<IMG SRC="Mesh Wave.gif">MM is currently in the process
of recording a whole new batch of material which will be
available in the Fall of '95.
</BODY>
</HTML>
```

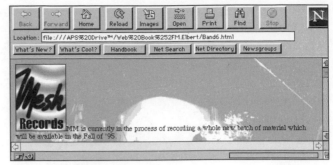

5.

## 6. Add a paragraph tag after the image (optional).

A paragraph tag <p> will flow the text on the line below the image and open up paragraph spacing.

```
<HTML>
<HEAD>
<TITLE>New Side Band</TITLE>
</HEAD>
<Body Background ="New_Band.gif">
<IMG SRC="Mesh Wave.gif"><p>MM is currently in the
process of recording...
</BODY>
</HTML>
```

6.

*Tip: Although the Definition List <DL> tag is intended for glossary text, it can be used to indent text or images incrementally across a page.*

## 7. Use the ALIGN attribute to move an image.

The ALIGN attribute, which is part of the IMG tag, is the simplest way to move an image across the page.

Use the ALIGN=RIGHT attribute in an IMG tag:

```
<HTML>
<HEAD>
<TITLE>New Side Band</TITLE>
</HEAD>
<Body Background ="New_Band.gif">
<IMG SRC="Mesh Wave.gif"ALIGN=RIGHT>
</BODY>
</HTML>
```

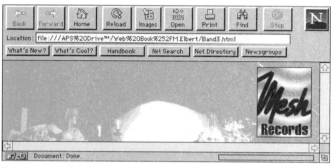

**7.**

## 8. Use the <DL> tag to move an image or text.

Since the <DL> tag formats an "indented" list, nesting several <DL> tags works to further indent pictures, text or both across the page.

**a. Nest two <DL> tags with text and the ALIGN=LEFT attribute in the IMG tag** *(Note: The <DL> tag works to move an image):*

```
<HTML>
<HEAD>
<TITLE>New Side Band</TITLE>
</HEAD>
<Body Background ="New_Band.gif">
<DL><DL><IMG SRC="Mesh Wave.gif"ALIGN=LEFT></DL></DL>
MM is currently in the process of recording a whole new
batch of material which will be available in the Fall of
'95.
```

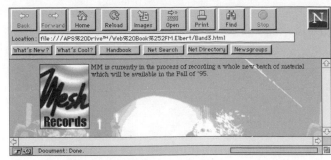

**8a.**

**b.** Nest four <DL> tags with text and the ALIGN=LEFT attribute in the IMG tag:

```
<HTML>
<HEAD>
<TITLE>New Side Band</TITLE>
</HEAD>
<Body Background ="New_Band.gif">
<DL><DL><DL><DL><IMG SRC="Mesh
Wave.gif"ALIGN=LEFT></DL></DL></DL></DL> MM is current-
ly in the process of recording a whole
new batch of material…
```

## 9. Add space around an image with HSPACE.

The HSPACE attribute added to the Image tag will push the text away from the image but it will add space on both sides of the image at once.

Using the HSPACE attribute may be a problem if you're trying to line up the left edge of the image with text further down the page. If this is the case, text offset may be created with extra Canvas in Photoshop which you can then make transparent with LView Pro.

**8b.**

*Tip:* HSPACE adds space on either side of an image and VSPACE adds space above and below.

**9.**

Nest four <DL> tags (with text) and add HSPACE:

```
<HTML>
<HEAD>
<TITLE>New Side Band</TITLE>
</HEAD>
<Body Background ="New_Band.gif">
<DL><DL><DL><DL>
<IMG SRC="Mesh Wave.gif"ALIGN=LEFT HSPACE =20 >
</DL></DL></DL></DL>MM is currently…
```

## 10. Use BLOCKQUOTE to move page elements.

The BLOCKQUOTE tag will indent an image or text the same amount as two nested <DL> tags.

### Use the BLOCKQUOTE tag:

```
<HTML>
<HEAD>
<TITLE>New Side Band</TITLE>
</HEAD>
<Body Background ="New_Band.gif">
<BLOCKQUOTE>
<IMG SRC="Mesh Wave.gif"ALIGN=LEFT>
MM is currently in the process of recording a whole new batch
of material which will be available in the Fall of '95.
</BLOCKQUOTE>
</BODY>
</HTML>
```

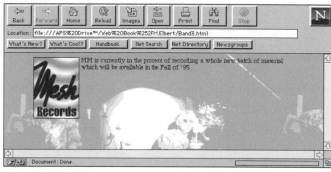

**10.**

*Tip: The <CENTER>...</CENTER> tag can also be used to move page elements horizontally. See the Image Map chapter for an example of how to use this tag.*

11.

## 11. Use BLOCKQUOTE to move a column.

Depending on where you place the tag, the BLOCKQUOTE tag will indent an image and several paragraphs.

### Use the BLOCKQUOTE tag:

```
<HTML>
<HEAD>
<TITLE>New Side Band</TITLE>
</HEAD>
<Body Background ="New_Band.gif">
<BLOCKQUOTE>
<IMG SRC="Mesh Wave.gif"><p>
<Font Size=+2>Clubs, New York</Font><p>
<b>Chelsea</b><p>
Tramps<BR>
51 West 21st Street<BR>
727.7788<BR><p>
<b>East Village</b><p>
Brownies<BR>
169 Avenue A<BR>
420.8392<BR>
CBGBs<BR>
315 Bowery<BR>
982.4052<p></BLOCKQUOTE>
```

## 12. Use the <BR> tag to add line breaks.

In the example in Step 11, notice how the <BR> tag adds a line break.

# Using HTML to move page elements vertically

*Summary*: *HTML tags that move page elements vertically are very few in number. Absent are the sophisticated paragraph-based commands present in page layout software that add precise spacing before or after a paragraph.*

**1.**

Integrating pictures and text "inline" is challenging. For example, "align" does not refer to text alignment, as in word processing. Here, align refers to the position of an image.

### 1. ALIGN=BOTTOM.

In this example, ALIGN=BOTTOM lines the text up with the bottom of the image.

Use the ALIGN=BOTTOM attribute in an IMG tag. *(Note: The <Font Size=+2> tag has been used to make the words "Clubs, New York" slightly larger than the body type. The value can be a number from 1 to 7. The number 3 is considered the "basefont" or the default size):*

```
<HTML>
<HEAD>
<TITLE>New Side Band</TITLE>
</HEAD>
<Body Background ="New_Band.gif">
<BLOCKQUOTE>
<IMG SRC="Mesh Wave.gif" ALIGN=BOTTOM>
<Font Size=+2>Clubs, New York</Font><p>
<b>Chelsea</b><p>
<b>East Village</b><p>
Brownies<BR>
169 Avenue A<BR>
```

**2.**

## 2. ALIGN=TOP.

In this example, ALIGN=TOP really doesn't line up the image with the top of the text.

**Use the ALIGN=TOP attribute in an IMG tag:**

```
<HTML>
<HEAD>
<TITLE>New Side Band</TITLE>
</HEAD>
<Body Background ="New_Band.gif">
<BR>
<BLOCKQUOTE>
<IMG SRC="Mesh Wave.gif" ALIGN=TOP>
<Font Size=+2>Clubs, New York</Font><p>
<b>Chelsea</b><p>
Tramps<BR>
51 West 21st Street<BR>
727.7788<p>
```

```
420.8392<p>
CBGBs<BR>
315 Bowery<BR>
982.4052<p></BLOCKQUOTE>
```

### 3. The <BR> and <p> tags.

In the previous example, the break line tag, or <BR>, breaks the line but does not add extra line spacing.

The paragraph tag or <p>, also breaks the line but adds paragraph or line spacing.

### 4. The VSPACE attribute.

The VSPACE attribute will push the text further from the image, but will add space on both sides of the image at once.

```
<HTML>
<HEAD>
<TITLE>New Side Band</TITLE>
</HEAD>
<Body Background ="New_Band.gif">
<BR>
<BLOCKQUOTE>
<IMG SRC="Mesh Wave.gif" ALIGN=BOTTOM VSPACE=25>
```

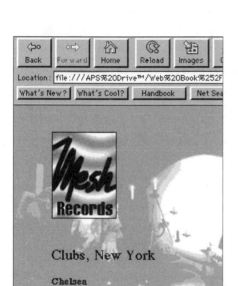

**4.**

*Tip: For information and instructions on how to upload files to your Internet provider's server, see the Image Map chapter.*

## 5. HTML tags used in the two previous sections.

The tags you see in this list (in alphabetical order) reflect the HTML 3 specification:

**<B>...</B>**

A tag used to apply bold-facing to text.

**<BLOCKQUOTE>...</BLOCKQUOTE>**

A tag used to create a paragraph indent on one or more paragraphs.

**<BODY>...</BODY>**

A tag used to open and close the body of a document. This tag can be used to refer to a background image in the form:

```
<Body background"New_Band.gif">
```

**<BR>**

A tag used to insert a line break.

**<DL>...</DL>**

The "Definition List" tag is usually used for definitions or short paragraphs with no bullets or numbering. In this section, this tag is nested several times, to indent the Mesh Records logo. For example:

```
<DL><DL><DL><DL><DL><DL><DL><IMG SRC="Mesh
Wave.gif"></DL>
</DL></DL></DL></DL></DL></DL>
```

**<FONT SIZE=VALUE>...</FONT>**

A tag used to change the default font size. The value can be any number from 1 to7 or it can be represented +- any value from 1 to 7. The value 3 is considered the "basefont" or the default font size.

**<HTML>...</HTML>**

A tag used to open and close a HTML document.

**<HEAD>...</HEAD>**

A tag used to open and close the header portion of a document.

**<IMG>**

Used to refer to an inline image, this tag uses the SRC="…" attribute, which represents the the URL (location) of the image. For example:

```
<IMG SRC = "Mesh Wave.gif">
```

This tag uses the ALIGN attribute (or parameter) to indicate the placement of an "inline" image. Options include TOP, BOTTOM, LEFT and RIGHT. For example:

```
<IMG SRC = "Mesh Wave.gif" ALIGN=LEFT>
```

This tag also uses the HSPACE attribute which adds space on either side of an image. For example:

```
<IMG SRC = "Mesh Wave.gif" ALIGN=LEFT HSPACE=20>
```

**<p>**

A tag used to indicate a new paragraph. This tag does not require an ending tag.

**<TITLE>…</TITLE>**

A tag used to describes the title of a document, which shows up inside a document's title bar.

# Creating a "banner graphic" or "splash screen"

*Summary*: *Learn how to create a banner graphic or splash screen, the first image Web visitors will see when they visit your Web page.*

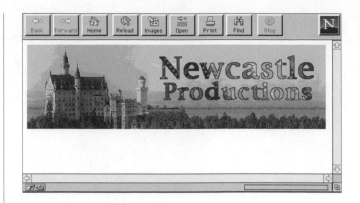

With the preparation of a banner graphic, Mark Elbert demonstrates how to size, scan, edit and adjust the palette of a banner image. *(See "Convert a Pantone RGB value to a Web Page Color" code in the Online Tools chapter for steps on how to assign color to the browser background and text.)*

## 1. Plan the size of your banner.

Rather than fill the entire screen, Mark chose 504 pixels for the width of his banner, 100 pixels less than the maximum measurement. The height he chose was 144 pixels.

## 2. Scan your artwork.

Using a 24-bit flatbed scanner, Mark scanned more information than he needed (higher resolution), but to the exact dimensions. After opening the image in Photoshop, he resampled the image to 72 pixels per inch and used the Unsharp Mask filter to correct the slight fuzziness that results when Photoshop interpolates pixel information. To duplicate Mark's methods, follow these steps:

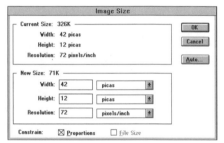

**2b, 2c.**

  **a.** Select Image Size... from the Image pull-down menu.

  **b.** Type 72 in the Resolution field. Select pixels/inch.

  **c.** Click on OK.

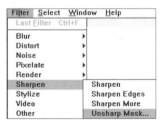

**2d.**

  **d.** Select Filter|Sharpen|Unsharp Mask.

  **e.** With Preview selected, Photoshop will display what the filter will do to your image. Choose an Amount of 25%, a Radius value of 1.0 pixels and a Threshold value of 0.

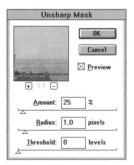

**2e.**

Click on OK, the result is shown at the top of the next page.

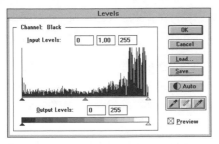

3a.

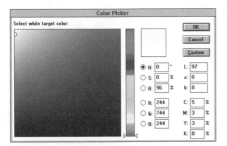

3b.

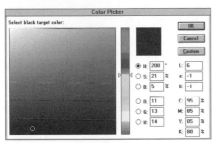

3c.

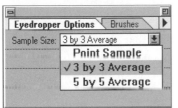

3d.

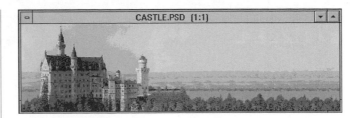

## 3. Correct the color.

After color scanning, Mark checked to see how the brightness and darkness tones were distributed. By mapping the lightest and darkest parts of the image to a target white and a target black, Mark corrected the color, which made a significant visible difference in the image.

**a.** Select Adjust|Levels from the Image pull-down menu.

**b.** Set a "target white" by double clicking on the white eye dropper and type in 5,3,3 in the C, M, Y boxes. *(Note: Use 7,3,3 for images that have more dark values than light.)* Then click on OK.

**c.** Set a "target black" by double clicking on the black eye dropper and type in 95, 85, 85 and 80 in the C, M, Y, K boxes. Click on OK.

**d.** Set the eyedropper tool at a 3-pixel sample. Double click the eyedropper and select 3 by 3 Average from the pop-up menu.

**e.** Map the "target" white on the area that appears to be the lightest portion of your image by selecting the white eye dropper and clicking on that area.

**f.** Map the "target" black on the area that appears to be the darkest portion of your image by selecting the black eye dropper and clicking on that area.

**g.** You'll notice a change in most scanned images immediately. The castle photo that results is shown at the top of the next page.

**4b.**

**4c.**

**5a.**

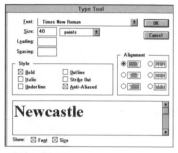

**5b, 5c, 5d, 5e.**

**5f.**

## 4. Create a separate layer for type.

By creating a separate layer for type, you will ensure the type's pixels do not get mixed in with your image.

**a.** Select Show Layers from the Window/Palettes pull-down menu.

**b.** Select New Layer from the palette's pop-up menu. A New Layer dialog box will appear.

**c.** Create a name for your new layer and click OK.

## 5. Create type in the new layer.

**a.** Select the Text tool.

**b.** Click on your image. A dialog box will appear.

**c.** Select a font and a type size.

**d.** Type your text into the box at the base of the dialog box.

**e.** Click on OK. Figure 5f shows the results.

## 6. Adjust the position of your type.

You can move your type as long as it is selected. A flashing dotted outline around your type will indicate that it is still selected. If you click your mouse button, you'll drop the selection which may be re-selected with the following techniques:

**a.** Select the Magic Wand tool, click on one of the letters, and select Similar from the Select pull-down menu (6a2).

**b.** Select the Magic Wand tool, click on one of the letters, hold down the Shift key, and continue to click on the remaining letters.

**c.** Select All from the Select pull-down menu.

```
Select   Window   Help
All              Ctrl+A
```

**6c.**

```
Select   Window   Help
All              Ctrl+A
None             Ctrl+D
Inverse
Float            Ctrl+J
Color Range...
Feather...
Modify                  ▶
Matting                 ▶
Grow             Ctrl+G
Similar
Hide Edges       Ctrl+H
Load Selection...
Save Selection...
```

**6a2.**

**7a1.**

**7a2.**

**7b.**

**7c.**

**8a.**

## 7. Copy an image and paste it into the type.

**a.** Leaving the banner art open, Mark opened another image of filmstrip art and copied the entire image to the clipboard.

**b.** Mark returned to the banner artwork and with the type still selected, he chose Paste Into from the Edit pull-down menu.

**c.** Mark positioned the filmstrip art inside the type by dragging the selection with the mouse. The filmstrip art moved inside the type each time he dragged the mouse. To drop the selection, he selected None from the Select pull-down menu.

## 8. Add an outline to the type.

**a.** With the type still selected, Mark selected Stroke from the Edit pull-down menu.

**b.** With Black selected as a Foreground color, he selected a width of 1 pixel, to be centered on the type selection at 100% Opacity and Normal Mode.

**c.** Mark found the combination of Stroke settings through trial and error. By selecting Undo from the Edit pull-down menu, he was able to try alternate paint colors in the outline and vary the location.

**8b.**

**9a.**

**9b.**

*Tip: The following technique is provided for Web designers who have access to a Macintosh.*

## 9. Reduce pixel depth (using Photoshop).

When Mark finished editing the image in RGB Mode, he experimented with Photoshop's Indexed Color Mode to see how far he could reduce the pixel depth without altering the color. (*Note: If you have access to a Macintosh, see the next section for instructions on how to reduce the bit-depth in DeBabelizer. DeBabelizer, by Equilibrium Software, is an advanced color manipulation tool written by game industry expert David Theurer.*)

**a.** Select Indexed Color from the Mode pull-down menu.

**b.** Experiment by selecting smaller bit depths with and without dithering to see how the color in your image holds up. Each time you try a selection, select Edit|Undo if you do not like the color.

Mark was able to reduce the image to a 6-bit color depth (Figure 9b) without a noticeable change in the color. This made a significant change in the file size:

| Bit depth | File Size |
| --- | --- |
| 8-bit | 71K |
| 6-bit | 44K |
| 6-bit | 33K (DeBabelizer) |

## 10. Reduce pixel depth (using DeBabelizer).

**a.** Open your RGB image in DeBabelizer.

**b.** Select Change Pixel Depth from the Palette pull-down menu. Equilibrium Technologies recommends that you always select dithering when you reduce the number of colors. Although you can change the amount of dithering by selecting Options|Dithering Options & Background Color from the Palette pull-down menu, DeBabelizer's default setting is the amount Equilibrium has determined to be the best amount.

Start by reducing your image to 128 colors and look at the image. If you don't like the change, select Undo from the Edit pull-down menu. Keep stepping down to fewer colors to determine when the color change becomes visible. Mark was able to reduce the palette to 64 colors without a noticeable change in the image.

### 11. Save the Image.

**a.** Select Save As from the File pull-down menu *(in Photoshop or DeBabelizer)*.

**b.** Select Compuserve GIF or JPEG from the pop-up menu.

*(Note: Photoshop 3.0 does not add interlacing to GIF images. Interlacing gives the Web visitor the impression of a faster download by quickly painting the image in low resolution and gradually filling it in.)*

To add interlacing to a Photoshop GIF image, you'll need *LView Pro* by Leonardo Haddad Loreiro. DeBabelizer also has an option to save a file as an Interlaced GIF. *(Note: LView Pro is available on the CD-ROM in the back of this book)*.

**c.** Give your image a name and try to keep your file name to a minimum of eight characters (no spaces) with a file extension such as .gif, .jpg or .jpeg. *(Note: File extensions must be limited to three characters on the DOS/IBM platform.)* Removing vowels from the file name helps to reduce the number of characters. Mark used DeBabelizer and chose "interlaced GIF" as the file format for saving.

### 12. Create an HTML file to test your image.

**a. Open a text file editor.** Use Notepad or your word processor. If you use a word processor, be sure to save the document as Text Only.

**b. Create a new HTML document.** Start a new document with the following markup tags.

```
<HTML>
<HEAD>
<TITLE>Newcastle Productions</TITLE>
</HEAD>
<BODY>
```

**c.** **Add the Image tag.** Reference your GIF (or JPEG) image with the addition of an <IMG> tag:

```
<HTML>
<HEAD>
<TITLE>Newcastle Productions</TITLE>
</HEAD>
<BODY>
<IMG SRC ="Newcstle.gif">
```

**d.** **Close with an ending BODY and HTML tag and save the file.** Save the document. If you're using a word processor, save the text as ASCII or Text Only. Give the file a name and add an .html extension (.htm if the Web server you're using is a Windows 3.1 machine).

**e.** **Test the HTML document in Netscape.** Open Netscape and then open your document by selecting Open File... from the File pull-down menu. Make sure your GIF image and your HTML document are in the same directory.

To test a number of alternate images, create several HTML files and save them under different file names or open Programmer's File Editor and Netscape at the same time and vary between the two applications. Each time you edit your HTML document, save it and click on "Reload" in Netscape's Toolbar to retest.

# Linking a thumbnail GIF to an external JPEG

*Summary: By creating a small GIF thumbnail on your Web page, your image can be viewed with most browsers. The thumbnail loads quickly and a larger, JPEG image download can be optional (a JPEG viewer "helper application" will be required with browsers other than Netscape).*

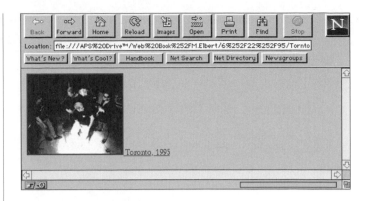

**1.**

B y reducing an image to a thumbnail-size GIF and making the thumbnail a link to a larger, JPEG version of the same image, Mark Elbert created a Web page that can be viewed by most browsers. At the same time, he also provided an optional image format for a detailed photo.

## 1. Save an original image in Photoshop.

**a.** When you have finished editing your image in RGB Mode, select Indexed Color from the Mode pull-down menu. Select Adaptive palette and Diffusion Dither. Try selecting smaller bit-depths until you notice an unsatisfactory change in the image. (Select Undo from the Edit pull-down menu if you're unhappy with a selection.)

**b.** Select Save As from the File pull-down menu.

**c.** Choose JPEG from the Format pop-up box.

**d.** Choose an image quality.

**e.** Name the file. Add .jpg as a file extension at the end of the name.

## 2. Reduce your photo to "thumbnail size."

**a.** Open your original RGB image (without the .jpeg extension) in Photoshop.

**b.** Select Image Size… from the Image pull-down menu.

**c.** Type in a small number for the width value (such as 2 inches) and Photoshop will proportionally size the height for you. *(Note: Record what the height and width values are in pixels as you will need this information for your IMG tag.)* Click on OK.

*Tip: For information and instructions on how to upload files to your Internet provider's server, see the Image Map chapter.*

**d.** Select Filter|Sharpen/UnSharp Mask to correct the fuzziness that results when you resize an image. Use 25%, 1.0 Radius value and a Threshold of 0.

### 3. Save the "thumbnail."

**a.** Select Save As from the File pull-down menu.

**b.** Choose Compuserve GIF from the Format pop-up box.

**c.** Name the file to eight characters with no spaces. Add .gif as a file extension at the end of the name.

### 4. Create a HTML document.

**a. Open a text editor.** Use Notepad or your word processor. If you use a word processor, be sure to save the document as Text Only.

**b. Create a new HTML document.** Every HTML document consists of a HEAD and a BODY. Start a new document with the following markup tags:

```
<HTML>
<HEAD>
<TITLE>Toronto</TITLE>
<BODY>
```

**c. Add an Image tag.**

In this example, the thumbnail GIF image as well as the text, "Toronto, 1995," will be a link to the external JPEG image listed inside the anchor tag <AHREF></A>:

```
<HTML>
<HEAD>
<TITLE>Toronto</TITLE>
</HEAD>
<BODY>
<A HREF = "toronto.jpg"><IMG SRC="Tor_sm.gif">
Toronto, 1995</A>
</BODY>
</HTML>
```

**4d.**

**4h.**

**d.** Add image sizing to your image tag (optional). Image sizing is a Netscape feature that adds speed to the downloading of images. When Netscape encounters an inline image, it builds a bounding box to display the image. With the height and width information in the IMG tag, the bounding box can be built without delay.

The height and width in pixels can be obtained from the Image Size… dialog box in Photoshop. In this example, the width is 144 pixels and the height is 123 pixels:

```
<A HREF = "toronto.jpg"><IMG SRC="Tor_sm.gif"
WIDTH=144 HEIGHT=123> Toronto, 1995</A>
```

**e. Control the width of the image border (optional).** When you make an image an "anchor" or a link, the browser will display a colored border to act as a clue for visitors. For menu buttons that are obvious links, the border can be turned off by adding Border=0 to your IMG tag. In this example, this would be written:

```
<A HREF = "toronto.jpg"><IMG SRC="Tor_sm.gif"
WIDTH=144 HEIGHT=123 BORDER=0> Toronto, 1995</A>
```

*(Note: For the formatting requirements of this book, the lines are broken. In an HTML document, breaks should only occur where there are spaces or new lines).*

**f. Save the file.** Save the document. If you're using a word processor, save the text as ASCII or Text Only. Give the file a name and add a .html extension (.htm if the Web server you're using is a DOS machine).

**g. Test the HTML document in Netscape.** Open Netscape and then open your document by selecting Open File… from the File pull-down menu. Make sure your GIF image, your JPEG image and your HTML document are in the same directory.

**h. Test the HTML document in other browsers.** In browsers other than Netscape, a JPEG viewer will be launched when you click on either the thumbnail or the text link. The JPEG image will be displayed in a separate floating window.

## 6. Summary of HTML tags used in this section.

The tags you see in this list (in alphabetical order) reflect the HTML3 specification:

### <A>...</A>

Referred to as an "anchor," this tag uses the HREF attribute to link to an external sound file or "anchor." For example:

```
<A HREF="Toronto.jpg">Toronto, 1985</A>
```

*Note: The movie file name must include the path name if the file is located in another directory.*

### <BODY>...</BODY>

A tag used to open and close the body of a document.

### <HTML>...</HTML>

A tag used to open and close a HTML document.

### <HEAD>...</HEAD>

A tag used to open and close the header portion of a document.

### <IMG>

Used to refer to an inline image, this tag uses the SRC="..." attribute that represents the the URL (location) of the image. For example:

```
<IMG SRC = "Tor_sm.gif">
```

In this section, image sizing was added to the Image tag with the WIDTH and HEIGHT attributes.

For example:

```
<IMG SRC="Tor_sm.gif" WIDTH=144 HEIGHT=12>
```

To turn off the image border, the BORDER=0 attribute can be used in the Image tag. For example:

```
<IMG SRC="Tor_sm.gif" WIDTH=144 HEIGHT=123
BORDER=0>
```

### <TITLE>...</TITLE>

A tag used to describe the title of a document that shows up inside a document's title bar.

# Wrapping text around a photo

***Summary:*** *Prepare a Photoshop image with extra background to simulate a text offset for a text "runaround." Use an IMG statement in an HTML document with an ALIGN attribute to get the text to wrap.*

LView Pro
1.B/16

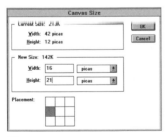

**1a.**

**1b.**

Although space can be created around an image with the HSPACE attribute, which is used with the IMG tag, Mark didn't want the browser to add horizontal spacing on both sides of the image he planned for his Web page.

Mark created additional background and filled it with a gray that matches *most* browser backgrounds. He then used software that assigned the background a transparent value.

## 1. Create a text "offset."

A text offset distance is the distance between an image and the text. Add a background equal to your desired offset distance with the Image|Canvas Size command in Photoshop. This "extra" edge around the photo can be assigned a transparent value in *LView Pro by* Leonardo Haddad Loreiro (*available on the CD-ROM in the back of this book*).

**a.** Working in RGB Mode, select Canvas Size from the Image pull-down menu.

**b.** In the Canvas Size dialog box, click on the box-map to indicate where your image should go when you add canvas. Add background by increasing the values in the width or height box.

**2a1.**

**2a2.**

**2b1.**

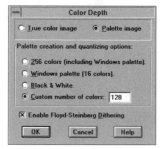

**2b2, 2d, 2e.**

**c.** Before you save, select Indexed Color from the Mode pull-down menu. Experiment to see how much you can reduce the bit-depth without altering the image. Always select "Adaptive Palette, Diffusion Dither."

When you're satisfied with the dimensions of the background, choose Save As from the File menu and select CompuServe GIF from the Format pop-up box.

**d.** Before you open your file in a program that can write a Transparent GIF file, color the background a shade that is not in the photo.

Mark chose a blue-gray *(Note: Pick a shade that has a color and tonal value close to the background)*.

## 2. Make the background transparent.

Follow these steps to use *LView Pro*:

**a.** Use the Open command in the *LView Pro* software to open the GIF file.

**b.** Select Color Depth from the pull-down menu labeled "R." A dialog box will be displayed.

**c** Select "Palette Image."

**d.** Use the chart in the "Bit-Depth" section of this chapter to select identify a bit-depth you would like to try. Type this number into the box labeled "Custom number of colors."

**e.** Make sure there is an "X" in the box labeled "Enable Floyd-Steinberg Dithering."

**f.** Click on OK.

**g.** Choose Save As from the File menu, type a file name, and click on OK.

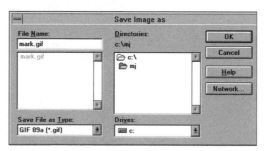

**2g.**

**3.** Follow these steps for *DeBabelizer* (Macintosh):

**a.** Use the File|Open command in DeBabilizer software to open the GIF file.

**b.** Select Options|Dithering and Background Color from the Palette pull-down menu.

**c.** Click the RGB radio value dial or button at the bottom of the screen.

**d.** Use the Eyedropper tool to select the background shade you'd like to be transparent.

**e.** Choose Save As from the File pull-down menu.

**f.** Select GIF|Interlaced & Transparency from the pop-up box.

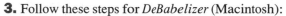

**3d.**

| Non-interlaced | GIF |
| Interlaced | Dr. Halo CUT |
| Non-interlaced & Transparency | IMG |
| ✓Interlaced & Transparency | JPEG, JFIF |

**3f.**

**g.** DeBabelizer will give your file name a GIF extension. Save the file. Click on Save.

## 2. Create an HTML file.

**a. Open a text editor.** Use Notepad or your word processor. If you use a word processor, be sure to save the document as Text Only.

**b. Create a new HTML document.** Start a new document with the following markup tags:

```
<HTML>
<HEAD>
<TITLE>Wrapping Text</TITLE>
</HEAD>
<BODY>
```

**c. Add an Image tag.**

```
<HTML>
<HEAD>
<TITLE>Wrapping Text</TITLE>
</HEAD>
<BODY>
```

**d. Add an ALIGN attribute to your IMG tag.**
The ALIGN attribute in an IMG tag controls the way the image aligns with text. In this next example, ALIGN=LEFT moves the image to the left edge of the page and the text wraps around on the right.

```
<IMG SRC = "MarkT.gif" ALIGN=LEFT>
```

**e. Add headlines and HTML "headline" tags.** The HTML tags for headlines range from <H1>…</H1> to <H6>…</H6>. <H1> is the largest headline size available and <H6> is the smallest. The actual size of this type will be relative to whatever the Web visitor has set as a default font size in his or her browser. For example, if a Web visitor has never altered the font size in Netscape's Preferences dialog box, the default size for body text will be 12 points.

All of the headline or Title sizes will be relative to this "Basefont" size. In this example, Mark Elbert and Bassist have been tagged with headline or title tags <H2> and <H3>. *(Note: See item "f" for a tag to control the font size).*

```
<HTML>
<HEAD>
<TITLE>Wrapping Text</TITLE>
</HEAD>
<BODY>
<IMG SRC = "MarkT.gif" ALIGN=LEFT>
<H2>Mark Elbert></H2><p>
<H3>Bassist</H3><p>
```

**f. Use the Font Size tag (optional).** Font size can be controlled with the <Font Size=value> tag where values range from 1 to 7. In this system, the "Basefont" has a value of 3.

This tag can also be written with a preceding + or - to indicate a size that is relative to the "Basefont." In this example, the entire headline or just the "initial" capital can be controlled, depending on the placement of the tags.

**Mark Elbert**

Bassist

**Mark Elbert**

Bassist

Notice the tag is placed inside the headline tag and the ending </Font> tag is required:

```
<H2><Font Size=+3>Mark Elbert</Font></H2><p>
<H3><Font Size=+3>Bassist</Font></H3><p>
```

In this example, the Font Size tag is used to make the initial capital larger:

```
<H2><Font Size=+3>M</Font>ark
<Font Size=+3>E</Font>lbert</H2><p>
<H3><Font Size=+3>B</Font>assist</H3><p>
```

**g.** **Add comment lines to your document (optional).**

Comment lines are ignored by the browser and will never show up on your Web page. They provide a means of documenting the details of how the document was constructed. Use <!....--> to create comments. For example:

```
<!--This text changes the first week of each month.-->
```
*(Note: Avoid using special characters such as <, >, & and !
in comment lines).*

**h.** **Add the body text and ending tags.**

```
<HTML>
<HEAD>
<TITLE>Wrapping Text</TITLE>
<BODY>
  </HEAD>
<IMG SRC = "MarkT.gif" ALIGN=LEFT>
<H2>Mark Elbert></H2><p>
<H3>Bassist</H3><p>
Mark, co-founder of Mother Mary, hails originally from
Bowie, Maryland…
</Body>
</HTML>
```

**i.** **Save the file.** Save the document in Notepad or your word processor. If you're using a word processor, save the text as ASCII or Text Only. Give the file a name and add an .html extension (.htm if the Web server you're using is a Windows 3.1 machine).

**3f.**

**j. Test the HTML document in Netscape.** Open your document in Netscape to test the appearance of your Web page.

## 3. Flip the image and try an ALIGN attribute.

Text can wrap differently if you use the ALIGN attribute in the <IMG> tag. In this example, to get text to wrap on the left side of the image, Mark used the ALIGN=RIGHT in the IMG tag:

**a. Open the image in Photoshop.** If the image needs to be reversed, flip it in Photoshop.

**b. Flip the image.** Select Flip|Horizontal from the Image pull-down menu.

**c. Resave as a GIF image.** Select Save As from the File pull-down menu and give the image another name.

**d. Make the background transparent.**

Use *LView Pro* or DeBabelizer to make the image transparent. *(Note: Since Photoshop cannot write the Transparent GIF information into the document header, this information is lost if you edit and save your document in Photoshop.)*

**e. Add the ALIGN attribute to the HTML file.**

```
<HTML>
<HEAD>
<TITLE>Wrapping Text</TITLE>
  </HEAD>
<BODY>
<IMG SRC = "MarkT.gif"ALIGN=RIGHT>
<H2>Mark Elbert></H2><p>
<H3>Bassist</H3><p>
Mark, co-founder of Mother Mary, hails originally from
Bowie, Maryland…
</Body>
</HTML>
```

**f. Resave the document and test it in Netscape.**

Although the other ALIGN attributes (RIGHT, TOP, BOTTOM and MIDDLE) are not appropriate for Mark's image, you may want to test others with smaller images.

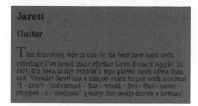

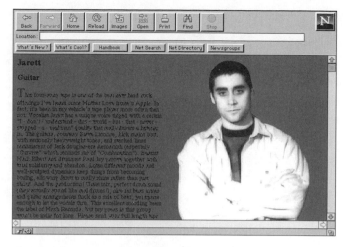

*Tip: Use the BBS Color Editor at:*

http://www.infocom.net/~bbs/cgi-
bin/colorEditor.cgi

*to find a hexadecimal red-green-
blue triplet for a body background
tag:*

<body bgcolor="#5c51d">

*(Note: For instructions, see
"Convert a Pantone RGB value to
a Web page color code with the
BBS Color Editor in the Online
Tools chapter.)*

## 4. Create an initial cap with the font size tag.

Large initial letters are called initial caps. The font size tag
<font size=value> can be used to create a raised initial cap
that rises above the text's baseline:

```
<HTML>
<HEAD>
<TITLE>Mesh</TITLE>
</HEAD>
<BODY BGCOLOR="#5c5c1d">>
<IMG SRC- "Jarett.gif"ALIGN-RIGHT>
<H2>Jarett</H2><p>
<H3>Guitar</H3><p>
<Fontsize=+3>T</font>his four-song tape is one of the best
new hard rock offerings I've heard since Mother Love
Bone's Apple. In fact, it's been in my vehicle's tape player
more often than not.
</Body>
</HTML>
```

# Controlling Text Wrap with HTML

*Summary:* Use HTML IMG tag attributes VSPACE and HSPACE as a way to control text wrap around an image.

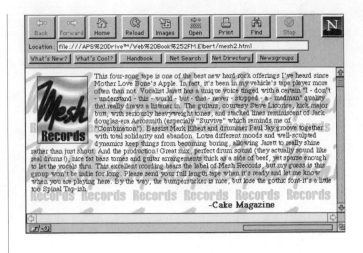

**1a.**

In this example, Mark used attributes HSPACE and VSPACE with an IMG tag. By assigning each a value in the HTML document, a "text offset" could be controlled.

## 1. An image with no extra background.

**a. Open the image in Photoshop.** Crop any extra background off the image that will have a text "runaround."

**b. Save as a GIF image.** Select Save As from the File pull-down menu and save the image as a CompuServe GIF file.

## 2. Create an HTML file.

**a. Open a text file editor.** Use Notepad or your word processor. If you use a word processor, be sure to save the document as Text Only.

**b. Create a new HTML document.** Start a new document with the following markup tags:

```
<HTML>
<HEAD>
<TITLE>Wrapping Text</TITLE>
</HEAD>
<BODY>
```

*Tip: With Netscape and your file editor both open, try varying the numbers assigned to VSPACE and HSPACE, re-save your text file, switch to Netscape and reload the file to see the results.*

**c.** **Add an Image tag.**

```
<HTML>
<HEAD>
<TITLE>Wrapping Text</TITLE>
</HEAD>
<BODY>
<IMG SRC = "Mesh Wave.gif">
```

**d.** **Add the alignment tags.**

```
<HTML>
<HEAD>
<TITLE>Wrapping Text</TITLE>
</HEAD>
<BODY>
<IMG SRC = "Mesh Wave.gif" ALIGN=LEFT VSPACE=5
HSPACE=10>
```

**e.** **Add the body text and ending tags.**

```
<HTML>
<HEAD>
<TITLE>Wrapping Text</TITLE>
</HEAD>
<BODY>
<IMG SRC = "Mesh Wave.gif" ALIGN=LEFT VSPACE=5
HSPACE=10>
This four-song tape is one of the best new hard rock
offerings I've heard since Mother Love Bone's Apple...
</Body>
</IITML>
```

**f.** **Test the HTML document in Netscape.** Open Netscape and then open your document by selecting Open File… from the File pull-down menu. Make sure your HTML document and your image are in the same directory.

*Tip: For information and instructions on how to upload files to your Internet provider's server, see the Image Map chapter.*

## 3. Summary of HTML tags used in this section.

The tags you see in this list (in alphabetical order) reflect the HTML3 specification:

**<BODY>…</BODY>**

A tag used to open and close the body of a document.

**<DL>…</DL>**

The "Definition List" tag is usually used for definitions or short paragraphs with no bullets or numbering. In this section, this tag is nested seven times to indent the word "Cake Magazine" For example:

```
<DL><DL><DL><DL><DL><DL><DL>Cake
Magazine</DL></DL></DL></DL></DL></DL></DL>
```

**<FONT SIZE=VALUE>…</FONT>**

A tag used to change the default font size. Values range from 1 to 7. The tag can also be written with a preceding + or - to indicate a size that is relative to the "Basefont."

**<H2>…</H2>**
**<H3>…</H3>**

Tags used to enlarge text, as to indicate a heading. Lower numbers indicate larger type; the options range from <H1> through <H6>.

**<HTML>…</HTML>**

A tag used to open and close a HTML document.

**<HEAD>…</HEAD>**

A tag used to open and close the header portion of a document.

**<IMG>**

Used to refer to an inline image, this tag uses the SRC="…" attribute that represents the the URL (location) of the image. For example:

```
<IMG SRC = "clear.gif">
```

This tag uses the ALIGN attribute (or parameter) to indicate the placement of an "inline" image. Options include TOP, BOTTOM, LEFT and RIGHT. For example:

```
<IMG SRC = "Mesh Wave.gif" ALIGN=LEFT>
```

The IMG tag also uses the HSPACE attribute, which adds space on either side of an image. For example:

```
<IMG SRC = "Mesh Wave.gif" ALIGN=LEFT HSPACE=20>
```

**<P>**

A tag used to indicate a new paragraph. This tag does not require an ending tag.

**<TITLE>...</TITLE>**

A tag used to describe the title of a document that shows up inside a document's title bar.

# Fading an image into the browser background

***Summary:*** *Photoshop's gradient tool and Quick Mask option can be used to "fade" an image to the gray that matches most browser backgrounds.*

**1a.**

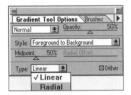

**1a, 1b, 1c, 1d.**

**2b.**

**2c.**

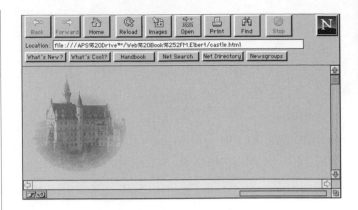

P hotoshop's strength is image editing. In this example, Mark Elbert discovered a method to fade an image into the browser background. A similar technique can also be used to create a "fuzzy" drop shadow.

## 1. Adjust Photoshop's gradient tool.
Open your image in Photoshop and adjust Photoshop's gradient tool setting:

**a.** Double click on the gradient tool (Figure 1a) and select Radial from the "Type" pop-up menu.

**b.** Drag the Opacity slider to 50%.

**c.** Drag the Radial Offset slider to 50%.

**d.** Drag the Midpoint slider to 50%.

## 2. Work in Quick Mask mode.

**a.** Double click on the Quick Mask icon at the base of the Toolbox.

**2a.**

**b.** Select "Color indicates Masked Areas" and type 50% in the Color, Opacity field.

**c.** With the Quick Mask icon still selected, use the crosshair pointer provided in this Mode and draw a radius line from the center of your image outward and release the mouse button.

**d.** Switch to Selection Mode by clicking the icon to the left of the QuickMask mode icon at the base of the Toolbox.

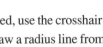

**2d.**

**3a.**

○ R: `201`
○ G: `201`
○ B: `201`

**3b.**

CASTLE.PSD [1:1]

**4.**

### 3. Set the background color.

**a.** Double click on the background color swatch at the base of the Toolbox.

**b.** Type 201 into the R, G and B fields. Click on OK.

### 4. Subtract the "unmasked" part of the image.

When you "mask" the middle of your image with a radial gradient mask, you protect the shaded area from further image manipulation in the "selection mode."

With a background shade equivalent to the gray you find in most browser backgrounds, press the Delete key.

The image will appear to fade into the gray color. By varying the Midpoint setting in the Gradient Tool Options palette, you can make the mask stronger, or weaker, in the middle.

### 5. Create an HTML file to test your image.

**a.** Create an HTML document with an IMG tag:

```
<HTML>
<HEAD>
<TITLE>Castle</TITLE>
</HEAD>
<BODY>
<IMG SRC ="Castle.gif">
</BODY>
</HTML>
```

**b.** **Save the file.** Save the document in Notepad or your word processor. If you're using a word processor, save the text as ASCII or Text Only. Give the file a name and add a .html extension.

**c.** **Test the HTML document in Netscape.** Open Netscape and then open your document by selecting Open File… from the File pull-down menu. Make sure your HTML document and your image are in the same directory.

# Create a tiled background

*Summary:* Using Netscape extensions to HTML, an image can be "tiled" in the browser window.

**1.**

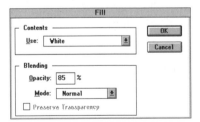

**2a.**

**2b.**

**2c, 2d, 2e.**

**2f.**

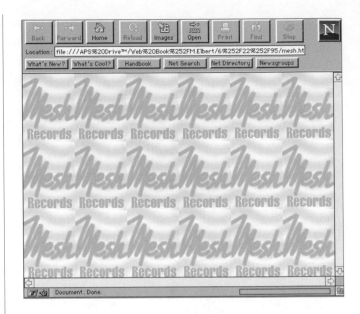

To create a wallpaper effect, Mark used a small photo and "ghosted" it with a white Fill at an opacity level of 85%. By keeping the background very light, type can be loaded on top and still be readable. Using the Netscape extensions to HTML, he created an HTML document that "tiled" the image across the browser's background.

## 1. Create a tile.

When you're planning a tile pattern, any size image may be used. Netscape will repeat the image to fill the background. Working in RGB Mode, reduce the size of your image to the desired size of your "tile."

## 2. Ghost the image.

**a.** Using Photoshop, choose All from the Select pull-down menu.

**b.** Select Fill from the Edit pull-down menu.

**c.** Select White from the Use pop-up menu.

**d.** Type 85% in the Opacity field.

**e.** Select "Normal" from the Mode pop-up menu. Click on OK.

**f.** The resulting image will have a "ghosted" appearance.

**4.**

**5c.**

### 3. Reduce the bit-depth.

Before you save, select Indexed Color from the Mode pull-down menu. Experiment to see how much you can reduce the bit depth without altering the image. Always select "Adaptive Palette, Diffusion Dither."

### 4. Save this Image as a GIF file.

Choose Save As from the File pull-down menu and select CompuServe GIF from among the choices on the Format pop-up box.

### 5. Create an HTML file to test your image.

**a.** Create an HTML document with an IMG tag:

```
<HTML>
<HEAD>
<TITLE>Mesh</TITLE>
</HEAD>
<BODY>
<IMG SRC ="Mesh.gif">
</BODY>
</HTML>
```

**b. Save the file.** Save the document in Notepad or your word processor. If you're using a word processor, save the text as ASCII or Text Only. Give the file a name and add an .html extension

**c. Test the HTML document in Netscape.** Open Netscape and then open your document by selecting Open File… from the File pull-down menu. Make sure your HTML document and your image are in the same directory.

# Create a "full bleed" photo background with larger tiles

*Summary: Netscape will "tile" any size image. Larger images will appear to be "full bleed" images.*

To create a "full-bleed" photo background, Mark filled in a black-and-white photo with white, in order to ghost the image. Using the Netscape extensions to HTML, he created an HTML document, which causes the full image to fill the browser's background.

## 1. Follow steps for "Create a tiled background."

When you're planning a tile pattern, any size image may be used. Netscape will repeat the image to fill the background. Follow the steps for "Create a tiled background," presented earlier in this chapter and shown here:

**a.** Create a tile.

**b.** Ghost the image.

**c.** Reduce the bit depth.

**d.** Save the image as a GIF file.

**e.** Create an HTML file to test your image.

## 2. The background "tiles" as you add content.

You will not be able to scroll and look at the "tiled" background until you've added content to your HTML file.

# Creating a silhouette on an image background

***Summary:*** *Silhouettes are created using a transparent GIF image. In this example, the background loads first when the Web page opens and the silhouette can be loaded on top as an "interlaced" or "non-interlaced" image.*

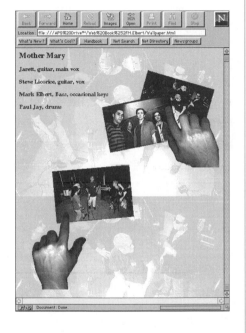

In this example, the positioning of the silhouette images was a greater challenge than the creation of the transparent GIF images. To position the transparent GIF images down the page, Mark Elbert experimented with the VSPACE attribute in the second image tag.

### 1. Make your image background transparent.
Follow these steps to use LView Pro:

**a.** Open a GIF image in LView Pro.

**b.** Select Background Color from the Options pull-down menu.

**c.** The Select Color Palette Entry will appear as a floating palette in the LView work area.

**d.** Click on the Dropper button at the base of the palette.

**e.** Position the eyedropper over the area you would like transparent and click your left mouse button.

**f.** With the image open, choose Save As from the File pull-down menu.

**g.** GIF89a will be displayed in the Format pop-up menu. This is the abbreviation for transparent GIF.

**h.** Enter a file name, use the GIF extension, and click OK.

*Tip:* *MacLink/Plus, a well-known trans-*
*lation utility from Dataviz now converts*
*Mac and Windows formats to and from*
*HTML.*

```
http://www.tile.net/tile/vendors/datavi
in.html
```

**2.** Follow these steps for *DeBabelizer (Macintosh):*

**a.** Use the File|Open command in DeBabelizer software to open the GIF file.

**b.** Select Options|Dithering & Background Color from the Palette pull-down menu.

**c.** Click the RGB radio dial or button at the bottom of the screen.

**d.** Use the Eyedropper tool to select the background shade you'd like to be transparent.

**e.** Choose Save As from the File pull-down menu.

**f.** Select GIF|Interlaced Transparent from the pop-up box.

**g.** DeBabelizer will give your file name a GIF extension. Save the file. Click on Save.

### 3. Create an HTML file.

**a.Open a text file editor.** Use Notepad or your word processor. If you use a word processor, be sure to save the document as Text Only.

**b. Create a new HTML document.** Start a new document with the following markup tags:

```
<HTML>
<HEAD>
<TITLE>Wrapping Text</TITLE>
</HEAD>
```

**c. Add a Body Background tag.**

```
<HTML>
<HEAD>
<TITLE>Wrapping Text</TITLE>
</HEAD>
<IMG SRC = "MarkT.gif">
<BODY Background="Toronto_Lg.gif">
```

**d. Add an image tag.**

```
<HTML>
<HEAD>
<TITLE>Wrapping text </TITLE>
<BODY Background="Toronto_Lg.gif">
<IMG SRC="MarkT.gif">
```

*Tip: FrameTechnology, makers of FrameMaker (for Unix, Windows and MacOS), has an export option that converts FrameMaker paragraph styles to HTML (Frame Technology is being acquired by Adobe Systems).*

```
http://www.frame.com/PRODUCTS/
fm5.html firstpage
```

**e.** **Add a Headline tag.**

```
<HTML>
<HEAD>
<TITLE>Wrapping Text</TITLE>
</HEAD>
<BODY Background="Toronto_Lg.gif">
<IMG SRC = "MarkT.gif">
<H2>Mother Mary</H2>
```

**f.** **Add a group of "nested" definition list tags.**

```
<HTML>
<HEAD>
<TITLE>Wrapping Text</TITLE>
</HEAD>
<BODY Background="Toronto_Lg.gif">
<IMG SRC = "MarkT.gif">
<H2>Mother Mary</H2>
<DL><DL><DL><DL><DL><IMG
SRC="Hand50_bbT.gif"></DL></DL></DL></DL></DL>
```

**g.** **Insert the ALIGN=RIGHT attribute in the image tag.**

```
<HTML>
<HEAD>
<TITLE>Wrapping Text</TITLE>
</HEAD>
<BODY Background="Toronto_Lg.gif">
<IMG SRC = "MarkT.gif">
<H2>Mother Mary</H2>
<DL><DL><DL><DL><DL><IMG
SRC="Hand50_bbT.gif"ALIGN=RIGHT></DL>
</DL></DL></DL></DL>
```

**h.** **Add four more headlines.**

```
<HTML>
<HEAD>
<TITLE>Wrapping Text</TITLE>
</HEAD>
<BODY Background="Toronto_Lg.gif">
<IMG SRC = "MarkT.gif">
<H2>Mother Mary</H2>
<DL><DL><DL><DL><DL><IMG
SRC="Hand50_bbT.gif"ALIGN=RIGHT></DL>
```

*Tip: Adobe Systems has an HTML export filter planned for Version 6.0 of PageMaker (for Windows and MacOS).*

http://www.adobe.com/Apps/PageMaker.html

```
</DL></DL></DL></DL>
<H3>Jarett, guitar, main vox</H3>
<H3>Steve Licorice, guitar, vox</H3>
<H3>Mark Elbert, bass, occasional keys</H3>
<H3>Paul Jay, drums</H3>
```

### i. Add a second image tag.

```
<HTML>
<HEAD>
<TITLE>Wrapping Text</TITLE>
</HEAD>
<BODY Background="Toronto_Lg.gif">
<IMG SRC = "MarkT.gif">
<H2>Mother Mary</H2>
<DL><DL><DL><DL><DL><IMG
SRC="Hand50_bbT.gif"ALIGN=RIGHT></DL>
</DL></DL></DL></DL>
<H3>Jarett, guitar, main vox</H3>
<H3>Steve Licorice, guitar, vox</H3>
<H3>Mark Elbert, bass, occasional keys</H3>
<H3>Paul Jay, drums</H3>
<IMG SRC="BackT2.gif">
```

### j. Add the VSPACE attribute to the second image tag.

```
<HTML>
<HEAD>
<TITLE>Wrapping Text</TITLE>
</HEAD>
<BODY Background="Toronto_Lg.gif">
<IMG SRC = "MarkT.gif">
<H2>Mother Mary</H2>
<DL><DL><DL><DL><DL><IMG
SRC="Hand50_bbT.gif"ALIGN=RIGHT></DL>
</DL></DL></DL></DL>
<H3>Jarett, guitar, main vox</H3>
<H3>Steve Licorice, guitar, vox</H3>
<H3>Mark Elbert, bass, occasional keys</H3>
<H3>Paul Jay, drums</H3>
<IMG SRC="BackT2.gif" VSPACE=120>
</Body>
</HTML>
```

*Note: Close your document with a </BODY> and </HTML> ending tag.*

*Tip:* *For information and instructions on how to upload files to your Internet provider's server, see the Image Map chapter.*

## 4. HTML tags used in this section.

The tags you see in this list (in alphabetical order) reflect the HTML3 specification:

### <BODY>...</BODY>

A tag used to open and close the body of a document. This tag can be used to refer to a background image in the form:

```
<Body background"Toronto_Lg.gif">
```

### <DL>...</DL>

The "Definition List" tag is usually used for definitions or short paragraphs with no bullets or numbering. In this section, this tag is nested seven times in order to indent the Mesh Records logo. For example:

```
<DL><DL><DL><DL><DL><DL><DL><IMG
SRC="Hand50_bbT.gif"></DL>
</DL></DL></DL></DL></DL></DL>
```

### <H2>...</H2>
### <H3>...</H3>

Tags used to enlarge text, as to indicate a heading. Lower numbers indicate larger type and the options range from <H1> through <H6>.

### <HEAD>...</HEAD>

A tag used to open and close the header portion of a document.

### <HTML>...</HTML>

A tag used to open and close a HTML document.

### <IMG>

Used to refer to an inline image, this tag uses the SRC="..." attribute that represents the the URL (location) of the image. For example:

```
<IMG SRC = "Mesh Wave.gif">
```

This tag uses the ALIGN attribute (or parameter) to indicate the placement of an "inline" image. Options include TOP, BOTTOM, LEFT and RIGHT. For example:

```
<IMG SRC="Hand50_bbT.gif" ALIGN-RIGHT>
```

*Tip:* BeyondPress, a QuarkXPress XTension from Astrobyte, converts QuarkXPress documents to HTML.

`http://www.astrobyte.com/Adtrobyte/Beyond`
`PressInfo.html`

This tag also uses the VSPACE attribute, which adds space on either side of an image. For example:

`<IMG SRC = "Mesh Wave.gif" VSPACE=120>`

### <TITLE>...</TITLE>

A tag used to describe the title of a document which shows up inside a document's title bar.

# Creating a drop shadow

*Summary:* Use Photoshop's selection tools and channels to record the outline of an image and create a drop shadow by blurring the edge of the shadow's channel image with the Gaussian Blur filter and filling the selection with 50% black.

1a.

○ R: 201
○ G: 201
○ B: 201

1b.

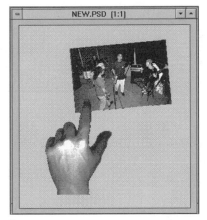

1c.

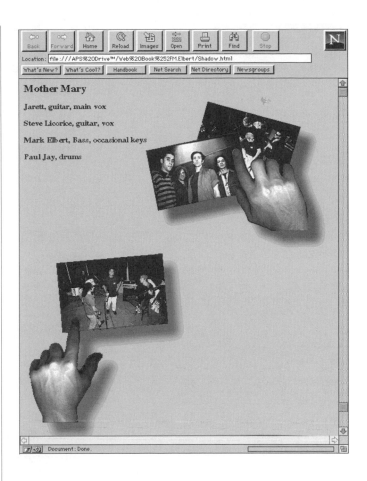

In this example, Mark created "fuzzy" drop shadows for photo silhouettes in Photoshop, by using channels. Since he planned to make the background of each silhouette transparent, Mark minimized the amount of "fringe" from the fuzzy drop shadow by starting with a gray background that was very similar to the gray in the browser background.

## 1. Set the image background color to gray.

**a.** With the Magic Wand tool, select the background of the object that will have a drop shadow.

**b.** Double click the background color sample in the ToolBox and type "201, 201, 201" as an RGB value. This gray is very close to the browser background.

**c.** With the background still selected, press the Select key to fill the background with the specified shade of gray.

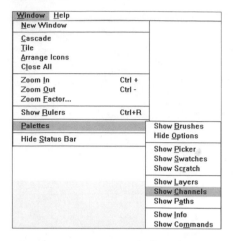

**2b.**

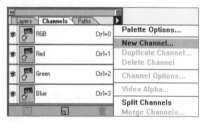

**2d.**

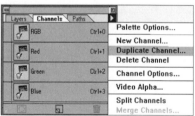

**2f.**

## 2. Create two channels.

**a.** If it is not still selected, select the background of the object that will be shadowed.

**b.** Choose Inverse from the Select pull-down menu.

**c.** With the object selected, select Palettes|Show Channels from the Window pull-down menu.

**d.** Press on the Channels pop-up menu and select New Channel

**e.** Give the channel the same name as your object.

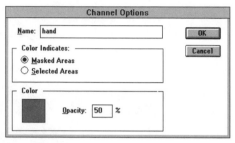

**2e.**

**f.** To create the second channel, which will be the shadow channel, select Duplicate Channel from the Channel pop-up menu.

**g.** Name this channel "shadow."

**2g.**

**3a.**

**3b.**

**4a.**

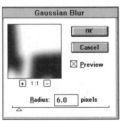

**4b.**

### 3. Use the Offset filter.

Since the shadow will need to be offset to the right and down at least 20 pixels in each direction, the offset filter will make this change.

**a.** Select the shadow channel in the Channels palette.

**b.** Select Other|Offset... from the Filter pull-down menu.

**c.** Select Repeat Edge Pixels, fill in 20 for Horizontal pixels right, and 20 for Vertical pixels down.

**d.** Click on OK.

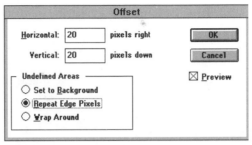

**3c, 3d.**

### 4. Gaussian Blur creates the "fuzziness."

**a.** With the shadow channel still selected, choose Blur|Gaussian Blur from the Filter pull-down menuu.

**b.** Type in 6 pixels and click on OK. The result is shown in Figure 4b.

**4c.**

**5a, 6a, 7a.**

**5b, 7b.**

**6b.**

**7c.**

## 5. Copy the hand to the Clipboard.

Use the Hand channel to select the hand and copy it to the Clipboard.

**a.** Choose Load Selection from the Select pull-down menu.

**b.** Select hand from the Channel pop-up menu in the dialog box.

**c.** Select Copy from the Edit pull-down menu.

## 6. Load the Shadow selection and do a Fill.

**a.** Choose Load Selection from the Select pull-down menu.

**b.** Select shadow from the pop-up menu that follows.

**c.** Choose Fill from the Edit pull-down menu.

**d.** Select Black from the Use pop-up box on the Fill dialog box.

**e.** Type 50% in the Opacity box, select Normal in the Mode pop-up, and click on OK.

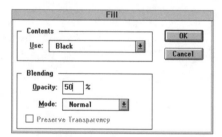

**6d, 6e.**

## 7. Paste an original of the hand on-top.

**a.** Reload the hand channel by choosing Load Selection from the Select pull-down menu.

**b.** Select hand from the Channel pop-up menu that follows.

**c.** Choose Paste from the Edit pull-down menu.

The result is shown in Figure 7c.

## 8. Reduce the pixel depth (in Photoshop).

When Mark finished editing the image in RGB Mode, he experimented with Photoshop's Indexed Color Mode to see how far he could reduce the pixel depth without altering the color. *(Note: See the next section for instructions on how to reduce the bit-depth in DeBabelizer.)*

**a.** Select Indexed Color from the Mode pull-down menu.

**b.** Experiment by selecting smaller bit depths with and without dithering to see how the color in your image holds up. If you don't like the color, select Edit|Undo.

Mark was able to reduce the image to a 6-bit color depth without a noticeable change in the color. This made a significant change in the file size:

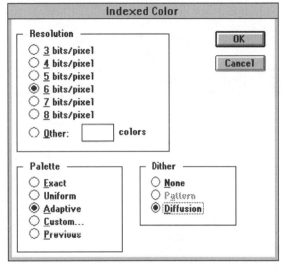

8b.

## 9. Reduce pixel depth (using DeBabelizer).

**a.** Open your RGB image in DeBabelizer.

**b.** Select Change Pixel Depth from the Palette pull-down menu. Equilibrium Technologies recommends that you always select dithering when you reduce the number of colors. Although you can change the amount of dithering by selecting Options|Dithering Options & Background Color from the Palette pull-down menu, DeBabelizer's default setting is the amount Equilibrium has determined is best.

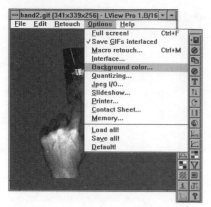

**9b.**

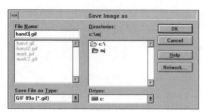

**10b.**

Start by reducing your image to 128 colors and look at the image. If you don't like the change, select Undo from the Edit pull-down menu. Keep stepping down to fewer colors to determine when the color change becomes visible. Mark was able to reduce the palette to 64 colors without a noticeable change in the image.

## 10. Save the Image.

**a.** Select Save As from the File pull-down menu *(in Photoshop or DeBabelizer).*

**b.** Select CompuServe GIF or JPEG from the pop-up menu.

*(Note: Photoshop 3.0 does not add interlacing to GIF images. Interlacing gives the Web visitor the impression of a faster download by quickly painting the image in low resolution and gradually filling it in.)*

To add interlacing to a Photoshop GIF image, you'll need LView Pro by *Leonardo Haddad Loreiro.* DeBabelizer also has an option to save a file as an Interlaced GIF. *(Note: LView Pro is available on the CD-ROM in the back of this book.)*

**c.** Give your image a name.

*Tip:* Visit the Submit It site and fill out a form that is part of a free service to list your site with 17 online directories—simultaneously.

http://submit-it.permalink.com/submit-it/

## 13. Create an HTML file.

**a. Open a text file editor.** Use Notepad or your word processor. If you use a word processor, be sure to save the document as Text Only.

**b. Create a new HTML document.** Every HTML document consists of a HEAD and a BODY. Start a new document with the following markup tags:

```
<HTML>
<HEAD>
<TITLE>Wrapping Text</TITLE>
</HEAD>
<BODY>
```

**c. Add an Image tag.**

```
<HTML>
<HEAD>
<TITLE>Wrapping Text</TITLE>
<BODY>
```

# Creating a blue duotone with Photoshop

**Summary:** *Use Photoshop's duotone presets to create a blue duotone.*

**1b.**

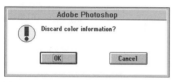

**1c.**

**2a.**

**2b, 2c.**

In print, a color duotone is a print made from a monochrome original with a second color added for greater detail. The technique is a way to add color to an image without using full color. For the Web, this means a smaller file size, and faster downloading.

## 1. Discard color from a color original.

**a.** Open your image in Photoshop.

**b.** Select Grayscale from the Mode pull-down menu.

**c.** Click on OK when a dialog appears that asks if you're sure you want to discard the color information.

## 2. Select a duotone.

**a.** Select Duotone from the Mode pull-down menu.

**b.** Select Duotone from the Type pop-up menu.

**c.** Click on Load to load the Photoshop duotone presets.

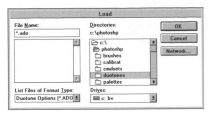

**2d.**

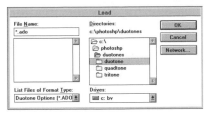

**2f.**

**2g.**

**d.** Find the Duotones folder inside the Photoshop software folder and click it open.

**e.** Click open the Duotone Presets folder.

**f.** Click open the Duotones folder.

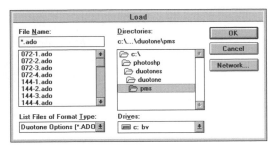

**2e.**

**g.** Click open the Pantone Duotone folder.

**h.** Mark selected Blue 286. When he applied this by clicking on the OK button on the Duotone Options dialog box, he decided he wanted the blue to look more saturated.

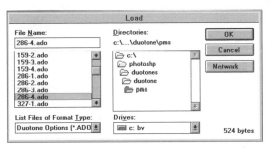

**2h.**

**i.** To adjust the amount of blue, Mark clicked opened the duotone curve. (Note: Click on the curve in the box to the right of "ink2.")

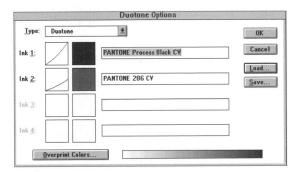

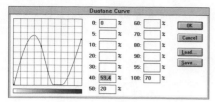

**2j.**

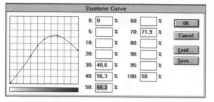

**2j.**

**3a.**

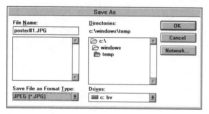

**3c.**

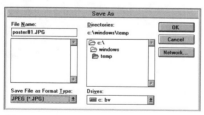

**3d.**

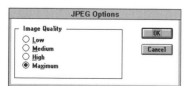

**3e.**

**j.** By pushing the curve up (shown at left) and to the left with the mouse, Mark altered the amount of blue in the duotone.

**k.** He reapplied the duotone information by clicking on OK in the Duotone Options dialog box.

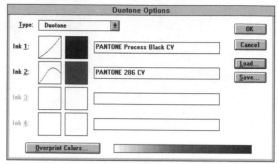

**2k.**

### 3. Save the image as a JPEG.

**a.** To save the image as a JPEG file, Mark chose RGB from the Mode pull-down menu.

**b.** Select Save As from the File pull-down menu.

**c.** Select JPEG from the Format pop-up menu in the Save dialog box.

**d.** Type in a file name and use a .jpeg or .jpg extension.

**e.** Select an image quality in the dialog box that follows.

## 4. Create an HTML file to test your image.

**a. Open a text file editor.** Use Notepad or your word processor. If you use a word processor, be sure to save the document as Text Only.

**b. Create a new HTML document.** Every HTML document consists of a HEAD and a BODY. Start a new document with the following markup tags:

```
<HTML>
<HEAD>
<TITLE>Duotone</TITLE>
</HEAD>
<BODY>
```

**c. Add the Image tag.** Reference your JPEG image with the addition of an <IMG> tag:

```
<HTML>
<HEAD>
<TITLE>Duotone</TITLE>
</HEAD>
<BODY>
<IMG SRC ="Poster1.jpcg">
</BODY>
</HTML>
```

**e. Test the HTML document in Netscape.** Open Netscape and then open your document by selecting Open File… from the File pull-down menu. Make sure your JPEG image and your HTML document are in the same directory.

# Digital cameras, Web photography and QuickTimeVR (virtual reality)

*Summary: Digital cameras that capture enough electronic data for print can capture more than enough data for an electronic medium. Visit the Ken Hansen Imaging showroom in New York City to see the latest digital cameras and imaging workstations. Bernard Furnival, an imaging specialist at Ken Hansen, gives a sales seminar on digital photography every Tuesday morning from 10:00 a.m. until 12 noon.*

*Tip: Ken Hansen Imaging (KHI) is at 920 Broadway, 3rd floor, New York, NY 10010 (212)777-5900.*

Digital photography has grown up—and it's ideal for capturing images for Web pages. Ken Hansen Imaging (KHI) in New York City is an electronic photography retailer that sells and rents a range of digital cameras. High-end print models can cost as much as $16,000. However, introductory models, which sell for under $1,000, can capture 24-bit images as large as 640×480 or 320×240 and offer photographers an efficient means to gather electronic data.

### Low-end digital cameras for Web work.

Ken Hansen sells the Apple QuickTake 150 for $725. The camera comes with a close-up attachment and a serial cable to transfer images to either a Macintosh or an IBM PC. Although Kodak made QuickTake for Apple, Kodak also introduced a slightly more versatile camera within the same price range.

| Camera | Price | Storage | Lenses |
|---|---|---|---|
| Apple QuickTake 150 | $725 | 20 images at 640×480 40 images at 320×240 | close-up attachment included |
| Kodak DC 40 | $995 | 48 images at 640×480 99 images 320×240 | telefoto, wide angle and close-up available from third parties |

Howard Goldstein (hrg@pipeline.com), who works for KHI, feels the QuickTake and Kodak DC40 are useful for Web work. Although neither camera has the functionality of a 35 mm, both cameras can capture more than enough information for Web images. Howard describes the QuickTake and the Kodak DC40 as "point-and-shoot" type cameras, or "fixed-focus." For example, unlike the lenses available for 35 mm cameras, the DC40's add-on lens attachments depend on the optics built into the camera.

### High-end digital cameras.

High-end digital cameras offer more features than the "point-and-shoot" variety. For example, Kodak's DCS 420 and 460 function like a true 35 mm camera with professional lens attachments and strobes. Both cameras are based on the Nikon N90 body and both can accommodate standard Nikon lenses. For photographers who already own Canon lenses, the Kodak DCS5 and the Canon EOS cameras offer similar flexibility. The Fujix (Fuji's division for electronic products) and the Nikon E2 camera are the same camera, because Fuji and Nikon collaborated on the development of a digital camera.

All of the digital cameras use PCMCIA hard disk cards to store images. Although the Fujix/Nikon camera PCMCIA card stores fewer images, images can be saved to the

*QTVR movie: Created for Ken Hansen Imaging by photographer Gabe Palacio, (gpalacio@aol.com), the QuickTime VR movie shown on this page is the interior of KHI showroom at 920 Broadway in New York City (available on the CD-ROM in the back of this book).*

removable PCMCIA card as standard JPEG or TIFF images. The credit-card-sized hard drive can be pulled out and handed to an assistant who's equipped with a PCMCIA slot in a workstation or notebook computer. Kodak's system stores more images, but each image is stored in a Kodak coded format. Each image must later be "acquired" or decoded through Photoshop, a single image at a time.

*QTVR movie: Created for the Macintosh New York Music Festival by photographer Gabe Palacio (gpalacio@aol.com), the QuickTimeVR movie shown on this page is the "dressing room" at CBGBs, a New York City club known for its thick graffiti. CBGBs is located at 315 Bowery, between Bleeker and Great Jones Streets, (212)982-4052.*

## Linear array scanning back systems.

In the $5,000 to $31,000 category are the powerful scanning back systems for studio work. Designed to sit on the film plane of popular large format cameras, these larger, more powerful cameras capture large, 20MB images, containing the highest resolution and the most color information.

Instead of capturing an image on film, these cameras make an Red, a Green and a Blue scanning pass, just like a flatbed scanner. Although there are constraints, such as no strobes and no movement, the scanning back system is tethered to a computer, so that a photographer can set color balance or calibrate the chip to accommodate special circumstances unique to each shoot. In contrast, the smaller digital cameras are considered "single capture." If color correction is needed in an image, it must be corrected later in Photoshop.

| Camera | Manufacturer | Price |
|--------|-------------|-------|
| Lumina | Leaf | $5,000 |
| DCB2 | Leaf | $27,900 |
| Dicomed | Dicomed | $20,588 |
| Catchlight | Leaf | $37,100 |
| Studio Kit | Phase 1 | $11,000-$13,000 |
| Photophase | Phase 1 | $19,000-$23,500 |

## Digital cameras and QuickTimeVR.

A QuickTimeVR "movie," which consists of still images stitched together to form a panorama, is an interesting new application for digital photography. Apple's new QuickTimeVR technology offers a "virtual reality" experience on a 320×240 movie (or full screen) that can be played via the QuickTimeVR player on a Macintosh or a Windows computer. The movie, which incorporates a new distortion-correction algorithm, corrects the distortion ordinarily associated with a panoramic image. Distortion correction occurs

*QTVR movie: The QuickTimeVR movie shown on this page is one of three movie nodes in Apple Computer's UK office movie demo.*

*Tip: APDA can be reached at: APDA, Apple Computer Inc., P.O. Box 319, Buffalo, NY 14207-0319, 1-800-282-2732.*

*Email:*

APDAorder@aol.com

*or*

apda@applelink.apple.com

on the fly while a viewer is panning a "scene." This makes the viewer feel as though he or she is actually in the scene, because movie movement can take a viewer forward, backward or shift perspective, left or right, up or down, or zoom in or out.

Although the point-and-shoot digital cameras (available for purchase at Ken Hansen for $995, or to rent for $35 per day) can be used for QuickTimeVR shots, Ken Hansen's larger cameras (also available for rent) are best suited for QuickTimeVR photography because of the wide-angle lens requirements. Apple recommends a 15 mm lens for indoor shots and a 24 mm lens for outdoor shots. This is due to the recommended amount of picture overlap, which should be from 30 to 50 percent.

Howard Goldstein at Ken Hansen explains that the smaller the number, the "wider" the angle. (Any number below 50 mm is considered to be wide angle and any number above 50 mm is considered telefoto). Ideally, the wide angle lens should be a rectilinear lens or a "corrected" wide angle lens that straightens out horizontal and vertical lines that are distorted in a wide angle.

### QuickTime VR movie "extras."

A movie can be much more than a panorama, and Apple Computer has a whole lot more planned for QuickTimeVR. In the future, QuickTimeVR will include music, interactivity and embedded URLs for World Wide Web applications.

At the present time, movies that have had additional "object movies" added can offer a viewer the ability to pick up an object, turn it up or down, or tip it on end. Still other movies can have "hot spots" that respond to mouse clicks. The mouse click can trigger a video, an audio clip, a still image or another QuickTimeVR "object movie."

*QTVR movie: The QuickTimeVR movie shown on this page is one of three movie nodes in Apple Computer's UK office movie demo.*

## Potential applications for QuickTImeVR

Apple Computer sees possibilities for QuickTimeVR applications in the computer game industry, real estate, the travel business, museums, education, architecture, kiosks and engineering. In contrast to a digital video, which would require tens of megabytes to capture a similar 360 degree scene, a 360 degree view of a scene captured as a "panorama" requires from 500 to 700K per "node." A "node" refers to the position in a scene from which a viewer sees a 360 degree panoramic image. QuickTimeVR movies can have one or more "nodes" that can link to other "nodes" to form a scene.

## Apple's UK office, a "multi-node" movie.

The complexity of a "multi-node" QuickTimeVR movie can best be understood by viewing Apple's UK office movie demo. The movie consists of three 360-degree panoramic movies stitched together. The viewer travels to different movie nodes by using an arrow icon. When the arrow icon appears, a click in the direction that's implied launches the viewer to another movie node.

## QTVR Authoring Tools Suite and the Players.

Although Apple's QuickTimeVR Authoring tools are only available for the Macintosh, the QuickTimeVR Player is available for both Macintosh and Windows machines.

As a standalone product, the QTVR Authoring Tools Suite is available from the Apple Developer's Association (APDA) for $495. MPW Pro software (Macintosh Programmer's Workbench, which, combined with HyperCard, is required for authoring the more complex QTVR movies) sells for $695. Apple also bundles the QTVR Tools Suite, MPW Pro and one seat in a three-day training class at Apple's Developer University for $1,995.

*QTVR movie: The QuickTime VR movie shown on this page is one of three movie nodes in Apple Computer's UK office movie demo. Also shown is the arrow icon used to navigate from movie node to movie node.*

## Royalties.

Apple waives royalties for non-commercial use of QuickTimeVR. Apple's royalty fees for distributing the run-time player software with QuickTimeVR titles:

| Item | No Royalty | Royalty |
| --- | --- | --- |
| CD-ROM Title | < 25,000 units | $400/5,000 units |
| Enhanced Audio C | < 50,000 units | $750/25,000 units |

## Hardware requirements.

Although the hardware requirements to run a QuickTimeVR movie are minimal, the QuickTime Authoring Tools need a very substantial system:

Requirements for running QTVR Authoring Tools:

| Item | Macintosh | IBM |
| --- | --- | --- |
| Computer | 68040, 33 MHz with a floating point unit (FPU) or any Power Macintosh | not available |
| Display | 16-bit color | not available |
| RAM | 40 MB | not available |
| Disk Space | 10 MB per panorama | |
| QuickTime | 2.0 or later | not available |
| System | 7.0.1 or later (68040) 7.1.2 or later (PowerPC) | not available |
| HyperCard | version 2.2 | not available |
| ResEdit | version 2.1.1 | not available |
| MPW | version 3.2 (68040) version 3.4b2 (PowerPC) | not available |

# Running the QuickTime VR Player

**Summary:** *Apple's QuickTimeVR (virtual reality) Player for Windows can be used to run QTVR movies at 320×240 pixels in the default-sized view or full-screen (640×480 pixels). To try out a QuickTimeVR movie, look for Ken Hansen's movie of their showroom on the CD-ROM in the back of this book.*

Apple's QuickTime VR (virtual reality) Player has three principle functions: viewing, zooming, or navigating objects.

## 1. To view a scene:

**a.** Place your mouse pointer over a scene.

**b.** Hold the mouse button down and move your pointer in the direction you'd like to view.

## 2. To zoom in a scene:

Zooming refers to magnifying a scene or pulling back to see a larger area.

**a.** Place your mouse pointer on an area in the scene.

**b.** Press and hold down the Shift key to Zoom in.

**c.** Press and hold down the Control key to Zoom out.

## 3. To navigate an object:

Navigating an object refers to turning it around or upside down.

**a.** Place your mouse pointer on an object. You'll see the pointer turn into a hand.

**b.** Press and hold down the mouse button and the hand will appear to grab the object.

**c.** Move the hand to turn or tilt the object.

**Artist featured in this chapter:**

*Kleber Santos is a senior graphic designer with Straightline International, a New York-based firm specializing in strategic marketing communications. In addition to print, Kleber specializes in the development of electronic programs and multimedia.*

*ksantos@echonyc.com*

*http://www.echonyc.com/ ~art/santos/santos.html*

# Chapter 6

# Image Maps

Map files? CGI scripts? cgi-bin? default URLs? In this chapter, Kleber Santos sorts out the details related to image maps including finding marker definitions for a map file, creating a map file and referencing an image map in an HTML file.

If you're a Web traveler, you've probably used an image map to navigate. Image maps are inline images that have special regions "mapped" to URLs. Anyone who clicks on one of the pre-defined regions (or "hot spots") will be taken to the page referenced in the URL. Well known sites with image maps include Disney's MoviePlex (http://www.disney.com), The Spot, a Web site of "episodes" (http://www.thespot.com), Condé Nast Traveler (http://www.cntraveler.com), SONY (http://www.sony.com), IUMA or the Internet Underground Music Archive (http://www.iuma.com) and Hot Wired (http://www.hotwired.com).

If you're renting space on an Internet provider's server, this chapter will help you understand the components you'll need to create image maps. It will also lead you through the steps of how to "upload" your files from your studio or office to your provider's computer.

# A virtual walking tour of NY's World Financial Center

***Summary:*** *In this chapter, Kleber Santos provides thorough details on the steps required to create image maps. The first image map (in its present form) was invented by Kevin Hughes (kev-inh@eit.com) while he was Webmaster at Honolulu Community College. Although image maps are slightly complicated to assemble, they're popular because they are an interesting addition to a Web page.*

In the World Financial Center, sixteen palm trees, each forty five feet high, line the glass-enclosed "Winter Garden."

K leber Santos, a graphic designer with Straightline International in New York City, likes to challenge himself with computer projects to satisfy a curiosity about "how things work."

To learn how image maps work, Kleber created a "virtual walking tour" of New York's World Financial Center (http://www.echo-nyc.com/~art/santos/santos.html). Image maps are inline images with "hot spots." Clicking on a hot spot links the user to another document with more hotspots.

*Ann Taylor is one of several retail tenants in the World Financial Center (WFC). Created on a landfill adjacent to New York's financial district, the WFC contains more than eight million square feet of office, retail and recreational space.*

## Building image maps.

Planning a strategy for setting up image maps requires an investigation of the type of server your firm owns or your provider owns. It also requires that you investigate what Web server software is being used. For his virtual walking tour, Kleber Santos worked with ECHO, an Internet provider in New York that uses the CERN software written for the Unix platform. Unix computers dominate the Web because the operating system is powerful and capable of multitasking. The two most popular Web server programs for the Unix platform are the CERN server and the NCSA server, which both exist in the public domain:

| Server | Notes |
|---|---|
| CERN httpd | ftp://info.cern.ch/pub/www/bin |
| | From Conseil Européen pour la Recherche Nucléaire (European Laboratory for Particle Physics), the birthplace of the Web, CERN httpd was written by Ari Luotonen, Henrik Frystyk and Tim Berners-Lee. |
| | The CERN Web server software comes with *htimage*, a script that is required to run image maps on the CERN server. |
| NCSA | http://boohoo.ncsa.uiuc.edu |
| | From the National Center for Supercomputer Applications, located at the University of Illinois, Urbana-Champaign, where the Mosaic browser was developed by Marc Andreessen. |
| | The NCSA software comes with *imagemap*, a script originally called *mapper* (by K. Hughes). *imagemap* is required to run image maps on the NCSA server. |

The image map scripts that come with the CERN and NCSA server are similar but have different formatting requirements for assembling the map configuration file and the HTML link inside your HTML document. *(Note: See "Finding marker definitions for a map file with Mapedit" and "Referencing an image map in an HTML file" in this chapter.)*

*Outside view of the World Financial Center designed by Cesar Palli & Associates and built in 1981.*

## The components of Kleber's map project.

Although Kleber Santos' studio is relatively close to ECHO in New York City, he never had to physically go to the ECHO site because he uploaded his project components through a dial-up PPP connection. (Although you don't have to be in the same city as your provider, it is recommended that you and your provider be located on the same coast because Internet traffic across country can be challenging.) To complete his project, Kleber needed:

| Item | Notes |
| --- | --- |
| An image | Kleber used Photoshop to create his photo montage of the shops and restaurants surrounding the World Financial Center's "Winter Garden." This step will be the most familiar to designers since Photoshop is a popular image editor. For one of his image maps, Kleber needed transparent GIF images for silhouetted buttons (Sfuzzi). He used Leonardo Haddad Loureiro's LView Pro, an image file editor for Microsoft Windows 3.1, Win32s and Windows NT. *(Note: LView Pro is available on the CD-ROM in the back of this book.)* |
| Space on an http server. | Kleber's image map project resides on ECHO's Web server in New York City The services a designer can obtain from an Internet provider vary a great deal. Minimally, Kleber needed a dial-up PPP account, which provides access to the Internet; server space; a provider willing to allow Web pages with image maps and a technical support specialist at the provider's site accessible by phone or email. Considerable research is required to investigate these services and a Web designer may need to try out two to three providers before finding the right one. |

*The North Cove Harbor Marina is tucked behind the World Financial Center along the Hudson Riverfront.*

*When a clickable image map exists on a web page, the mouse arrow will turn into a hand pointer.*

| | |
|---|---|
| A text processor | A text processor is required to build Web pages. On the IBM platform, Notepad is a good choice because it automatically saves files in the required ASCII format. An HTML link with a reference to the image, the imagemap script and a map configuration file is an important step in the process involving the text processor. *(Note: See "Referencing an image map in an HTML file" later in this chapter.)* |
| A browser | Browser software is used to view the Web and it's also a tool that can be used locally (without a modem connection) to view Web pages throughout the design process. Web documents are ASCII text files that can be opened by selecting Open File from the File pull-down menu. |
| A software program to create a "map" file | A "map" file or map configuration file describes the special regions or the clickable "hot spots" on an image map with x, y coordinates. *Mapedit* by Thomas Boutell is an application that makes this part of the process easy to follow. |
| Software to transfer files over a modem | *Windows Sockets FTP Client Application (WS FTP)* is a popular Windows FTP software program used to transfer files over a modem. Although files can also be transferred to your provider's server with popular communications programs, *WS FTP* is useful because it has functions that allow you to create directories and delete files. |

*The World Financial Center is located on three and a half acres of landscaped parkland along the Hudson River.*

IMAGE MAP.CONF file

If your provider uses the NCSA server, the IMAGEMAP.CONF file is a special file that your provider will need to edit. It will need one line added for each image map you create. Each line starts with a symbolic map name (which you will invent) followed by a colon and a pathname describing the map configuration file that can be found. For example:

```
symbolicname.map:/dirname/
filename.map
```

# Finding marker definitions for a map file with Photoshop

***Summary:*** *Photoshop's Info palette can be used to find marker definitions for your map file.*

Adobe
Photoshop

## 1. Plan the "hot spot" areas.

The "hot spots" on Kleber's image map are restaurant and retail store logos (Figure 1). Although image maps can have clickable regions shaped as circles, polygons, rectangles or points, Kleber decided to use rectangular areas to cover the various store and restaurant names. *(Note: Photoshop is a convenient tool to find coordinates if you already work in Photoshop. However, if your plan includes image map shapes other than rectangles, see "Finding marker definitions for a map file with Mapedit.")*

Photoshop's Info palette shows the coordinate position of the mouse pointer (measured from the upper-left corner of the image). Kleber recorded the palette's readings for a map text file. To obtain upper-left and lower-right coordinate readings for all the restaurant and store logos, he positioned the mouse pointer on the upper-left corners and the lower-right corners of each of the images.

**1.**

## 2. Open your image map in Photoshop.

**a.** Open Photoshop and select Open from the File pull-down menu.

| File | Edit | Mode | Image | Filter | Select | |
|---|---|---|---|---|---|---|
| New... | | | | | | Ctrl+N |
| Open... | | | | | | Ctrl+O |
| Open As... | | | | | | |
| Place... | | | | | | |
| Close | | | | | | Ctrl+W |
| Save | | | | | | Ctrl+S |
| Save As... | | | | | | |
| Save a Copy... | | | | | | |
| Revert... | | | | | | |
| Acquire | | | | | | ▶ |
| Export | | | | | | ▶ |
| File Info... | | | | | | |
| Page Setup... | | | | | | |
| Print... | | | | | | Ctrl+P |
| Preferences | | | | | | ▶ |
| Exit | | | | | | Ctrl+Q |

**2a.**

**b.** Select a graphic in the dialog box that follows and click on OK.

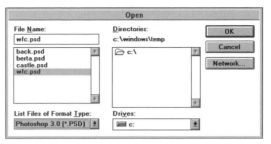

2b.

## 3. Open the Info palette.

**a.** Select Show Info from the Window|Palettes pull-down menu.

**b.** The Info palette will appear as a floating palette in the Photoshop work area. Click on Info palette's pop-up menu and select Palette Options.

**c.** Click on the Mouse Coordinates Ruler Units pop-up menu and select Pixels. Click on OK.

3a.

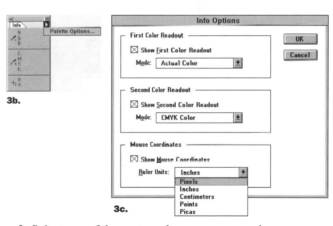

3b.

3c.

**d.** Select one of the rectangular areas on your image map and place the mouse pointer (*in the shape of a crosshair*) in the upper-left corner.

3d.

**3e.**

**e.** Look at the Info palette and record the x and y readings (*in a notebook*) as follows:

```
x: 210
y: 257
```

**f.** Place the mouse pointer (*in the shape of a crosshair*) in the lower-right corner.

**3f.**

**3g.**

**g.** Look at the Info palette and record the x and y readings as follows:

```
x: 295
y: 305
```

**h.** You will need to repeat these steps for all of your planned "hot spots."

## 4. Save the image as a GIF.

**a.** Select Save a Copy from the File pull-down menu.

**b.** Press on the Format pop-up menu and select CompuServe GIF.

**4a.**

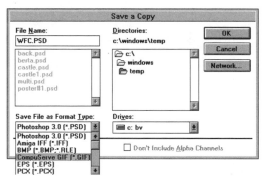

**4b.**

*Tip: GIF and JPEG images can both be used in image maps. Although JPEG images cannot be seen by as many browsers, the file size is very small compared to GIF. In this example, Kleber's montage was 70K as a GIF and only 30K as a JPEG.*

**c.** Enter a file name for your image and Photoshop will add a GIF extension.

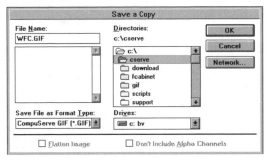

**4c.**

# Use Programmer's File Editor to create a map file

*Summary: Although the Mapedit application can be used to generate a map configuration file, designers who have gathered coordinate information from Photoshop can also create a map configuration file with Programmer's File Editor or a word processor.*

**2.**

**3a.**

**3b.**

## 1. Plan your map document.

Map configuration files are text files saved with the .map extension added to the filename. Use Notepad or a word processor. If you use a word processor, be sure to save the document as Text Only.

## 2. Start a new document.

Open the Programmer's File Editor (or any text editor) and select New from the File pull-down menu.

## 3. Save the text file.

**a.** Select Save As from the File pull-down menu.

**b.** Create a map configuration file name and add .map as an extension.

## 4. Add text descriptions of "hot spot" areas.

**a.** In the CERN map format (used with the CERN web server software), text descriptions of hot spot areas are written in the form

```
method coord1 coord2 url
```

where *method* refers to one of the following:

| Method | Meaning |
|--------|---------|
| default | default |
| circle | circle |
| poly | polygon |
| rect | rectangle |

where *coord1* or *coord2* refer to:

| Method | Coordinates |
|--------|-------------|
| default | no coordinates |
| circle | center and edgepoint |
| poly | each coordinate is a vertex |
| rect | upper left, lower right |

**Tip:** *The NCSA map format is written in the form:*

`method url coord1 coord2`

*There are no parentheses around the coordinates as there are in the CERN map format.*

*The shapes for the CERN and the NSCA map format are identical except the NCSA gives you one extra shape—the point.*

*(Note: In the CERN format, coord1 and coord2 are written in parentheses)*

and *url* refers to the location of the Web document to be "returned" if the viewer clicks inside the set of described coordinates.

**b.** Using the coordinates gathered from the previous Photoshop example, add to your text file as as shown in Figure 4b. *(Note: You will need to consult your provider about a path name for your file.)*

**c.** Continue to add similar lines of text reflecting each additional hot spot on your image map.

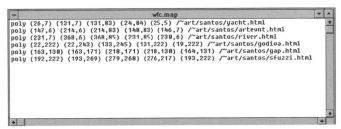

```
wfc.map
poly (26,7) (131,7) (131,83) (24,84) (25,5) /~art/santos/yacht.html
poly (147,6) (214,6) (214,83) (148,83) (146,7) /~art/santos/artevnt.html
poly (231,7) (368,6) (368,85) (231,85) (230,6) /~art/santos/river.html
poly (22,222) (22,243) (133,245) (131,222) (19,222) /~art/santos/godiva.html
poly (163,130) (163,171) (218,171) (218,130) (164,131) /~art/santos/gap.html
poly (192,222) (193,269) (279,268) (276,217) (193,222) /~art/santos/sfuzzi.html
```

**4b.**

## 5. Add a text description of a "default" area.

A default line item will be needed to specify the file to be returned if the user clicks outside of the specified areas. This can be written in the form (as shown in Figure 5).

`default/directoryname/filename.html`

```
wfc.map
poly (26,7) (131,7) (131,83) (24,84) (25,5) /~art/santos/yacht.html
poly (147,6) (214,6) (214,83) (148,83) (146,7) /~art/santos/artevnt.html
poly (231,7) (368,6) (368,85) (231,85) (230,6) /~art/santos/river.html
poly (22,222) (22,243) (133,245) (131,222) (19,222) /~art/santos/godiva.html
poly (163,130) (163,171) (218,171) (218,130) (164,131) /~art/santos/gap.html
poly (192,222) (193,269) (279,268) (276,217) (193,222) /~art/santos/sfuzzi.html
default /~art/santos/santos.html
```

**5.**

# Referencing an image map in an HTML file

**Summary:** *The HTML document that supports an image map needs a link to refer to the map configuration file, the image map script and the image.*

## 1. Open a text editor.

Use *Notepad* or a word processor. If you use a word processor, be sure to save the document as Text Only.

## 2. Create a new HTML document.

Start a new document with the following markup tags:

```
<HTML>
<HEAD>
<TITLE>The World Financial Center</TITLE>
</HEAD>
```

## 3. Add a BODY tag.

Kleber wanted the browser background color to be white, which can be accomplished with a BGCOLOR attribute added to the BODY tag:

```
<HTML>
<HEAD>
<TITLE>The World Financial Center</TITLE>
</HEAD>
<BODY BGCOLOR=#FFFFFF>
</HTML>
```

## 4. Add a CENTER tag.

To center the remaining elements, Kleber added a <CENTER> tag:

```
<HTML>
<HEAD>
<TITLE>The World Financial Center</TITLE>
</HEAD>
<BODY BGCOLOR=#FFFFFF>
<CENTER>
</HTML>
```

*Tip: Although Kleber used GIF images for his image maps, JPEG images can also be used. JPEG images are smaller than GIFs but they can only be seen with the Netscape browser.*

## 5. Add an Image tag.

The IMG tag contains a "source" or SRC parameter that contains the name of an image file. In this case the image is a banner graphic at the top of the page:

```
<HTML>
<HEAD>
<TITLE>The World Financial Center</TITLE>
</HEAD>
<BODY BGCOLOR=#FFFFFF>
<CENTER>
<IMG SRC="virtual.gif">
</CENTER>
</BODY>
</HTML>
```

## 6. Add an image map link.

The HTML document that supports an image map needs a link to refer to the map configuration file, the image map script and the image. (*Note: You will need to consult your provider about a path name for your image map link.*)

```
<HTML>
<HEAD>
<TITLE>The World Financial Center</TITLE>
</HEAD>
<BODY BGCOLOR=#FFFFFF>
<CENTER>
<IMG SRC="virtual.gif">
<A HREF="/cgi-bin/htimage/~art/santos/wfc.map">
    <IMG SRC="/~art/santos/WFC.gif" ISMAP></A>
</CENTER>
</BODY>
</HTML>
```

### 7. Add BORDER, WIDTH and HEIGHT attributes.

Kleber turned off the image border with a Border=0 attribute and added image sizing to the IMG tag. By adding Width=399 and Height=402, Netscape speeds downloading because it can anticipate the size requirements without a delay:

```
<HTML>
<HEAD>
<TITLE>The World Financial Center</TITLE>
</HEAD>
<BODY BGCOLOR=#FFFFFF>
<CENTER>
<IMG SRC="virtual.gif">
<A HREF="/cgi-bin/htimage/~art/santos/wfc.map">
   <IMG SRC="/~art/santos/WFC.gif" border=0 width=399
   height=402 ISMAP></A>
</CENTER>
</BODY>
</HTML>
```

### 8. Add line breaks.

Line breaks add space below the image map graphic:

```
<HTML>
<HEAD>
<TITLE>The World Financial Center</TITLE>
</HEAD>
<BODY BGCOLOR=#FFFFFF>
<CENTER>
<IMG SRC="virtual.gif">
<A HREF="/cgi-bin/htimage/~art/santos/wfc.map">
   <IMG SRC="/~art/santos/WFC.gif" border=0 width=399
   height=402 ISMAP></A>
<BR>
<BR>
```

## 9. Add text.

Kleber added a line of text below the graphic to give Web visitors directions:

```
<HTML>
<HEAD>
<TITLE>The World Financial Center</TITLE>
</HEAD>
<BODY BGCOLOR=#FFFFFF>
<CENTER>
<IMG SRC="virtual.gif">
<A HREF="/cgi-bin/htimage/~art/santos/wfc.map">
    <IMG SRC="/~art/santos/WFC.gif" border=0 width=399
    height=402 ISMAP></A>
<BR>
<BR>
Select individual elements of the above image to go on a
    virtual tour.
</CENTER>
</BODY>
</HTML>
```

## 10. Add the signature area.

Although signature areas generally contain the <ADDRESS> tag, Kleber limited the signature area to an email address. He added a Mailto URL to the HREF attribute so viewers get an empty email form when they click on the email address (Figure 10).

```
<HTML>
<HEAD>
<TITLE>The World Financial Center</TITLE>
</HEAD>
<BODY BGCOLOR=#FFFFFF>
<CENTER>
<IMG SRC="virtual.gif">
<A HREF="/cgi-bin/htimage/~art/santos/wfc.map">
    <IMG SRC="/~art/santos/WFC.gif" border=0 width=399
```

*Kleber's email address has a Mailto URL added to the HREF attribute, which is part of an anchor link.*

E-MAIL address: ksantos@echonyc.com

*When a Web visitor clicks on the email link with a Mailto URL, an empty email form appears with the address already filled out (Figure 10).*

**10.**

```
height=402 ISMAP></A>
<BR>
<BR>
Kleber Santos can be contacted at E-MAIL address:
<A HREF="mailto:ksantos@echonyc.com">
ksantos@echonyc.com</A>
</CENTER>
</BODY>
</HTML>
```

## 11. Summary of HTML tags used in this section.

The tags you see in this list (in alphabetical order) reflect the HTML3 specification:

### <A>...</A>

Referred to as an "anchor," this tag uses the HREF attribute to link to an graphic file or "anchor." In the following example, the HREF and ISMAP attributes refer to an image map:

```
A HREF="/cgi-bin/htimage/~art/santos/wfc.map">
<IMG SRC="/~art/santos/WFC5.gif" border=0 width=399
height=402 ISMAP></A>
```

BORDER, WIDTH and HEIGHT attributes have been added to the IMG tag in this example to turn off the border and add image sizing. Image sizing speeds downloading.

### <B>...</B>

A tag used to apply boldfacing to text.

### <BR>

A tag used to add a line break. This tag does not require an ending tag.

### &lt;BODY&gt;...&lt;/BODY&gt;

A tag used to open and close the body of a document. This tag uses the BGCOLOR=#RRGGBB or hexadecimal red-green-blue triplet attribute, which adds color to a browser page. For example:

```
<BODY BGCOLOR=#FFFFFF>
```

### &lt;CENTER&gt;...&lt;/CENTER&gt;

A tag used to center elements on a page.

### &lt;HEAD&gt;...&lt;/HEAD&gt;

A tag used to open and close the header portion of a document.

### &lt;HTML&gt;...&lt;/HTML&gt;

A tag used to open and close an HTML document.

### &lt;IMG&gt;

Used to refer to an inline image, this tag uses the SRC="..." attribute, which represents the the URL (location) of the image. For example:

```
<img src="virtual.gif">
```

### Mailto URL

The Mailto URL is used in an email link inside the signature area of a document. Viewers who click on a link containing a Mailto URL will get an empty email form with the address filled out.

### &lt;TITLE&gt;...&lt;/TITLE&gt;

A tag used to describes the title of a document, which shows up inside a document's title bar.

# Use LView Pro to create a transparent GIF

*Summary: Use an image editor to save transparent GIFs and interlaced GIFs.*

LView Pro
1.B/16

When a Web visitor clicks on the Sfuzzi logo (top left), they branch to another HTML document with its own image map. On this page the button choices are transparent GIF images, which Kleber created in Photoshop. To make the color around the buttons transparent, he used Leonardo Haddad Loreiro's LView Pro. (*Note: LView Pro is a shareware software program available on the CD-ROM in the back of this book.*)

1a.

# 1. Open a GIF image in LView Pro.

**a.** Open LView and select Open from the File pull-down menu.

**b.** Select an image from the dialog box and click on OK.

**c.** The image will open in a LView window.

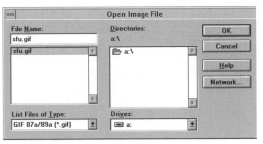

1b.

1c.

2a.

# 2. Select a background color.

The background color you select will be saved as a transparent shade.

**a.** Select Background color from the Options pull-down menu.

**b.** The Select Color Palette Entry will appear as a floating palette in the LView work area.

**c.** Click on the Dropper button at the base of the palette.

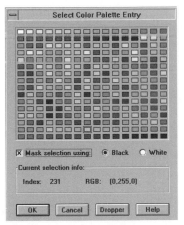

2b.

Dropper

2c.

**2d.**

**3a.**

**d.** Position the eyedropper over the area you would like to make transparent and click your left mouse button.

## 3. Save the image as a transparent GIF.

**a.** With the image open, choose Save as from the File pull-down menu.

**b.** GIF89a will be displayed in the Format pop-up menu. This is the abbreviation for transparent GIF.

**c.** Enter a file name and use the GIF extension.

**d.** Click on OK.

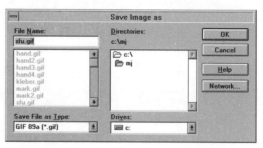

**3c, 3d.**

# Finding marker definitions for a map file with Mapedit

*Summary:* Use Mapedit to draw object primitives over your hot spots, set URLs and save the marker definitions into a map file. Unless you're running your own server, you'll need to find out if your Internet provider is using the CERN or NCSA server. You will need this information to export your map file from Mapedit.

Mapedit

## 1. Open Mapedit and a GIF image.

**a.** Open Mapedit and select Open/ Create from the File pull-down menu.

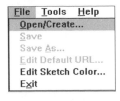

1a.

**b.** Type a map file name and a GIF file name in the dialog box that follows. If you're not sure of the file name or the directory, use the browse button to locate the file(s).

**c.** Select NCSA or CERN as the map file format (you will need to obtain this information from your provider).

**d.** If you're creating a new map file, Mapedit will recognize the map file does not exist and a dialog box will be displayed. Click OK.

**e.** Your GIF image will be displayed in a window.

1b, 1c.

1d.

1e.

**2a.**

**2b.**

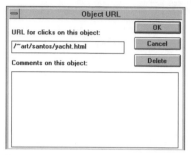

**3.**

File  Tools  Help
Open/Create...
Save
Save As...
Edit Default URL...
Edit Sketch Color...
Exit

**4.**

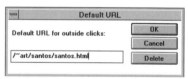

**4b.**

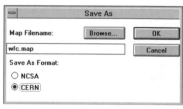

**5b.**

Confirmation

Map saved.

OK

**5c.**

## 2. Draw an object primitive on your image.

**a.** Select an object primitive tool from the Tools pull-down menu. (*Note: Kleber found the polygon tool worked better than the rectangle tool.*)

**b.** Click in each corner of the area you would like to define. When you have completed the shape, click the right mouse button. A dialog box will be displayed.

## 3. Enter an object URL.

Type in a URL, which includes the name of the page to be displayed when a viewer clicks on the region you've defined. Click OK.

## 4. Add a default URL.

The default URL refers to the page that will be displayed if a Web visitor clicks outside of the regions you've defined.

**a.** Select Edit Default URL from the File pull-down menu. A dialog box will be displayed.

**b.** Enter a URL. Click OK.

## 5. Open your map file in Notepad or another text editor.

**a.** Select Save As from the File pull-down menu.

File  Tools  Help
Open/Create...
Save
Save As...
Edit Default URL...
Edit Sketch Color...
Exit

**5a.**

**b.** Enter a map file name and select a format. Click OK.

**c.** A confirmation message will be displayed.

## 6. Check your map file in a text editor.

Open your map file in Programmer's File Editor, your HTML editor, or another text editor.

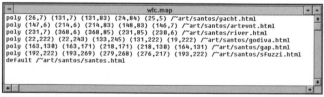

**6.**

# Use WS FTP to upload files to a provider's server

*Summary: John A. Junod's Windows Sockets FTP Client Application is a Windows shareware FTP utility which can be used to transfer files to and from file servers on the Internet. Look for WS FTP on the CD-ROM in the back of this book.*

To use WS FTP to transfer files to your provider's server, you'll need to obtain a Host name (the name of the server), a User ID and a Password.

### 1. Open WS FTP.

Open the Windows Sockets FTP Client Application. A dialog window will open that displays your local system on the left and the remote system (your provider's server) on the right.

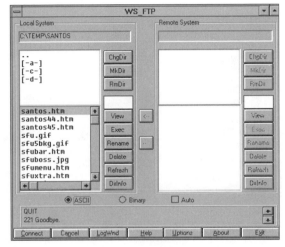

**1.**

### 2. Log in to your provider's server.

**a.** Click on the Connect button at the base of the dialog window.

**b.** A Session Profile window will be displayed.

**c.** Type in a Host Name, User ID, Password, and Remote host directory. (*Note: you will need to obtain these from your provider.*) Click on OK.

**d.** Within seconds, you will be connected to your provider's server.

**2a.**

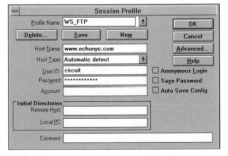

**2b, 2c.**

**3b.**

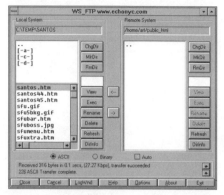

**4a, 4b, 4c.**

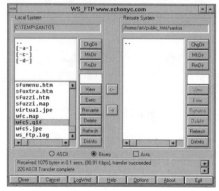

**5a, 5b, 5c.**

### 3. Create a directory (optional).

**a.** Click on the MkDir button along the right edge of the WS FTP dialog window.

**3a.**

**b.** Enter a new directory name in the dialog box that follows.

### 4. Upload a text file.

**a.** Use the file list window on the left to locate a  text file (*Example: an HTML file*).

**b.** Click to select the ASCII radio button at the base of the file list window.

**4b.**

**c.** Click the right arrow located in the middle of the WS FTP dialog window.

**4c.**

### 5. Upload a graphic file.

**a.** Use the file list window on the left to locate a graphic file (*Example: a GIF File*).

**b.** Click to select the Binary radio dial at the base of the file list window.

**5b.**

**c.** Click the right arrow located in the middle of the WS FTP dialog window.

**5c.**

### 6. Delete a file (optional).

**a.** Select a file in the file list window.

**b.** Click the Delete button to the right of the window where you selected the file.

**6b.**

### 7. Exit WS FTP.

**a.** Click on the Close button.

**7a.**

**a.** Click on the Exit button.

**7b.**

**Artist featured in this chapter:**

*Steven McGrew is a Senior Production Associate at the New Media Center/University of Oregon Computing Center. Throughout the past ten years, Steve has worked in both digital and analog video and audio production. He has a B.S. from the University of Oregon in visual design/ computer graphics.*

*(smcgrew@oregon. uoregon.edu)*

http://darkwing.
uoregon.edu/
~smcgrew/

# Chapter 7

# Video

Although Web page developers will need to create movies that are tiny in size and relatively slow, they will still entertain Web visitors because moving images *always* captivate viewers.

In this chapter, you'll see several examples of Web sites with video. You'll see how Premiere's Movie Analysis Tool can be used to examine movies you download, plus Steven McGrew offers tips on capturing and compressing.

If you're new to the Web and to Netscape, take a look at how to configure the MoviePlayer and the VMPEG player as Netscape helper applications.

# Web sites with video

*Summary:* Learn about the conventions used to format video-linked Web pages by visiting sites with video. For example, Web visitors can determine the amount of time required for downloading from the clues you offer in your "link."

*Tip:* Download time depends on the type of connection to the Internet. Most people are connected to the Web via a dial-up SLIP or PPP connection accessed with a 14.4 Kbps or a 28.8 Kbps modem. Although it's not available everywhere, 20-year-old ISDN technology has suddenly become popular as a means to "step-up" connection speed to the Internet. ISDN service is available through local Internet providers and the regional Baby Bell telephone companies (both are involved in providing the service). ISDN options include dial-up, direct (no modem) and 64K or 128K (refers to the data transfer rate).

Madonna's home page, created by IUMA for Warner Brothers Records, is actually part of the IUMA Web "system" (Internet Underground Music Archive). It can be accessed directly (http://www.iuma.com/Warner/html/Madonna.html) or indirectly through the IUMA home page (http://www.iuma.com).

Madonna's page is unique because it offers Web visitors a clip from her "Secret" video in both QuickTime and a video-only MPEG file format. QuickTime is Apple Computer's file format for time-based data such as anima-

[MPEG (3MB), QuickTime (3.3MB)]

tion, sound and video. With an appropriate player program, QuickTime files can be played on platforms other than the Macintosh. MPEG (Motion Picture Experts Group) is an evolving standard defined by an international committee that sets goals for the digital compression of movie (and audio) data.

QuickTime and MPEG file formats both have benefits and drawbacks. QuickTime is a more versatile format because it can contain embedded text and MIDI tracks, but movie playback without hardware acceleration looks good only at a very small frame size (160×120 pixels).

MPEG movies have superior compression and can look good at a larger frame size (320×240).

| Movie | File Size | Duration | Frame Size | Sound |
|---|---|---|---|---|
| Secret.qt (QuickTime) | 3.33 MB | 40 sec. | 160×120 | 11 kHz 8-bit mono |
| Secret.mpeg 320×240 (MPEG) | | 3.01 MB | 40 sec. | 11 kHz 8-bit sound |

**2.**

**3.**

**1.**

Disney's home page (http://www.disney.com) is popular with visitors who love movies. The Buena Vista MoviePlex is a beautifully illustrated series of Web pages that simulate a tour through a Hollywood Pictures or a Touchstone Pictures theater. Mouse clicks on each of the illustrations takes you through a lobby and then into separate theaters, where QuickTime movie trailers can be downloaded and saved to your hard drive with the following steps:

### 1. Click on the MoviePlex front doors.

After clicking on the MoviePlex link on the Disney home page, click on the front doors to the movie theater.

### 2. Select a theater.

Click on the Hollywood Pictures sign or the Touchstone Pictures sign at the top of the stairs.

### 3. Select a movie.

Click on a movie poster to enter the movie theater of your choice.

## 4. Select a movie trailer or a still image.

To download a movie file or a still image, click on an icon. The progress of the file download will be displayed.

4.

## 5. Save the movie or image to your hard drive.

**a.** Select Save As from the File pull-down menu.

**b.** Select a folder for saving.

**c.** Enter a file name.

**d.** Select "Make movie self-contained."

**e.** Click on Save.

*(Look for the MoviePlayer application on the CD-ROM in the back of this book and see "Configuring MoviePlayer as Netscape a helper application" in this chapter.)*

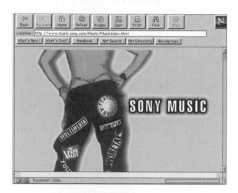

- View some of our new video clips.

Spin Doctors - *You Let Your Heart Go Fast*
From *Turn It Upside Down* - **EKS2907**
( 7M, 22 Secs, 6fps, Quicktime)

S ony's Web site (http://www.sony.com) is dense with music videos, which are small QuickTime clips. This entertainment industry giant hosts an enormous Web site, offering sound clips as well as video.

Videos are easy to find on the Sony site. First, click on the "on music" button on the home page. Although Sony changes the graphics frequently, just follow screen "hot spots" that read "Multimedia."

Maynard Handley, the New Zealander who wrote Sparkle, introduced me to Phade's site during our email correspondence about his software (http://www.cs.tu-berlin.de/~phade/).

The site belongs to Frank Gadegast, a Berlin resident who studies computer science at Technische Universitat. Frank's collection of information about MPEG technology is very valuable if you're interested in advanced technical details.

Born in Frankfurt, Germany in 1966, Frank started working with computers when he was fourteen. He nicknames himself and his software company Phade, in honor of a "very early graffiti sprayer, DJ, and computer freak from New York." He can be reached at phade@contrib.de.

*Tip: Click on Heini's name at the bottom of the page to visit the "Heini Withagen... everything you wanted to know but were afraid to ask" page. His list of interests includes Anne-Marie, a Ph.D. student who works as a helicopter pilot. Heini has created a link to his girlfriend Anne-Marie's page, which displays a picture of her in her helicopter.*

The MPEG Movie Archive (http://w3.eeb.ele.tue.nl/mpeg) is run by Heini Withagen at Eindhoven University in The Netherlands. The site contains a very large, well-organized collection of MPEG movies to download.

*Tip:* *The film clip image on this page was provided by Fabulous Footage at:*

http://www.FOOTAGE.net:2900/

FOOTAGE.net (http://www.footage.net:2900/) is a stock footage "catalog of catalogs" on the Web. It's run by publisher John Tariot (publisher@footage.net) as a service of Full Circle Productions, Inc., a broadcast television production company. While visiting the FOOTAGE.net system of pages, Web visitors can:

- Do a keyword search of the holdings of more than 100 major sources of stock footage around the world

- Order catalogs and demo reels online

- Do on-demand footage screening

- Send "zap" messages for hard-to-find footage directly to stock footage companies via email

- Order transcripts from *Journal Graphics*, a collection of over 75,000 records of broadcasts on CNN, ABC, CBS, PBS and National Public Radio

- Read government publications concerning footage copyright issues

**1a.**

**1b.**

**2a.**

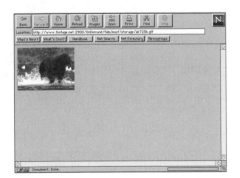

**2b.**

- Access information on the public domain audiovisual holdings of the National Archives

- Connect to the Motion Picture, Broadcast and Recorded Sound Division of the Library of Congress

- Browse the holdings of the Vanderbilt Television News Archives, which lists more than 23,000 network evening news broadcasts

The on-demand footage screening has a well-organized format, which allows Web visitors to take a look at a thumbnail image before deciding to download a QuickTime clip.

## 1. Select ON DEMAND STOCK FOOTAGE SERVER.

**a.** On the Footage.net home page, click on the button labeled "ON DEMAND STOCK FOOTAGE SERVER."

**b.** On the ON DEMAND STOCK FOOTAGE Server page, click on the Fabulous Footage Inc: button.

## 2. Screen stock thumbnails or footage.

**a.** On the Fabulous Inc: page, select a subject and click on the word "Thumbnail" next to the name of the subject.

**b.** If you would like to see the clip, click on Clip.

# Use Premiere's Movie Analysis Tool to learn about data rate and compression settings

**Summary:** *Familiarize yourself with the performance specs of movies you download from the Web.*

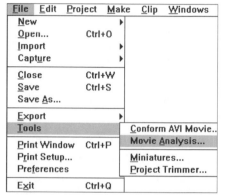

**1.**

**2.**

*Tip: The film clip image on this page was provided by The Image Bank, Inc., a source for still photographs, film footage and illustrations. 800-TIB-images.*

Premiere 4.0

Adobe Premiere's Movie Analysis Tool provides a valuable means to learn about movie specs, including average frame rate, data rate, compression settings and audio quality.

## 1. Select the Movie Analysis Tool.
Select Tools|Movie Analysis from the File pull-down menu.

## 2. Select a movie to analyze.
Use the file-list window in the dialog box to locate the movie you would like to analyze. Click on OK.

## 3. Print the specs.
Select Print from the File pull-down menu to print the specs.

### The WWW is considered "low bandwidth"
The World Wide Web is considered a "low bandwidth" application for digital movies, considering that the average Web visitor uses a 14.4 Kbps modem to download movie files. Compare this to an average hard drive, which can transfer data at only 300 Kbps. If you want Web visitors to download movie files, special attention should be given to file size.

### Capture settings
Nearly every item in this movie analysis report (except for the file name) can be traced back to the capture settings.

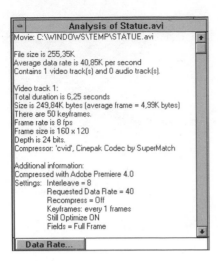

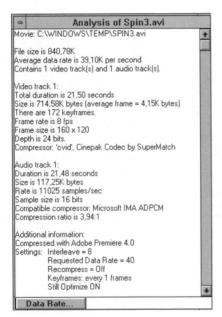

The choices you make when you digitize movie data will determine a movie's characteristics. Consider the following movie characteristics with respect to the World Wide Web:

| Movie "spec" | If the movie is for the Web... |
|---|---|
| file size | File size will affect the amount of time a Web visitor will have to wait for a download to be complete. |
| | To calculate the amount of time it will take to download a movie at different modem speeds, divide the modem speed (14,400 or 28,800) by 8 because there are 8 bits to one byte of data in this situation. Divide the number that represents the size of your movie file by this number, then divide by 60 (60 seconds per minute). This will give the (theoretical) number of minutes required to download a movie file. |
| | *(Note: When movie data is transferred over telephone wire, even if a Web visitor has a 28.8 Kbps modem, this bandwidth may not be available everywhere. Certain areas have a maximum bandwidth of 2.4 Kbps).* |
| average data rate | Data transfer inside a computer is measured in kilobytes per second. Since a Web visitor downloads movies and then plays them on a hard drive, your movie's data rate should not exceed 100-200 Kbps, because the data rate of an "average" hard drive is only 300 Kbps. If the movie data rate is too fast, the movie will drop frames. |

# Gail Garcia, New York, NY

**Above:** *Gail's Web catalog page created for Elaine Arsenault, a handbag designer in New York City.*

*http://www.echonyc.com/~art/arsenault/arsenault.html*

Graphic Designer Gail Garcia (gjgarcia@interport.net) specializes in product promotion and has a background in print. When Gail's clients approached her about designing Web pages, she experimented with software programs already familiar to her from her print work.

## Gail's design tips:

1. **Use Quark XPress as a layout tool.** Use Quark XPress to build a layout, saving each page as a separate EPS file.

2. **Open the image in Photoshop.** A Quark XPress EPS image will open as an EPS Pict Preview image in Photoshop 3.0 and as a Pict Resource in version 2.5.

3. **Reduce the bit-depth.** If you're designing splash screens, be careful of file size. Reduce the bit-depth by selecting Indexed Color from the Mode pull-down menu. (*Note: If you already have Indexed Color selected, select RGB and reselect Indexed Color. Experiment with smaller bit-depths for a smaller file size.*)

# Diana DeLucia
# Design,
# New York, NY

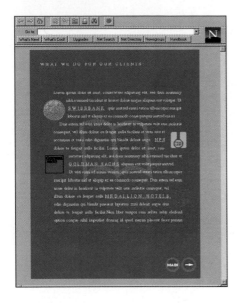

*Above:* A sample Web page from the
Diana DeLucia Design Web site designed
by Frauke Ebinger and art directed by
Diana DeLucia.

*http://www.echonyc.com/~art/DeLucia/*
*DeLucia.html*

Diana DeLucia (dddnyc@interport.net) sees the role of
the graphic designer changing and the changes are
being driven by technology. As Diana explains, "today, a
graphic designer is as much a marketing consultant as an
artist. A graphic designer who is familiar with the Web is in
a better position to help a client solve big-picture issues
than a designer who limits himself/herself to print."

## Diana's design tips:

1. **Don't forget your role as a marketer.** Create an incen-
   tive on a Web page for Web visitors to return. Examples
   include a flow of updated information and possibly art
   or multimedia files to download.

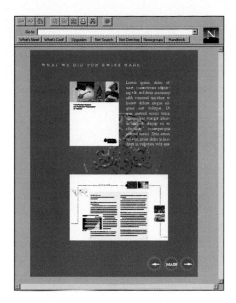

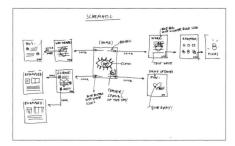

**1.**

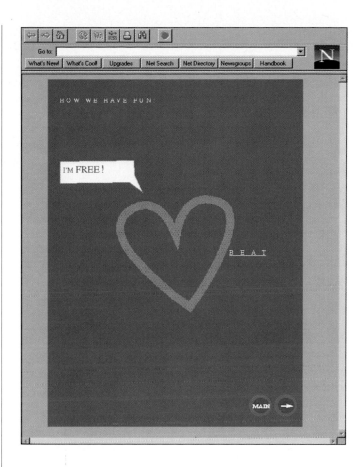

2. **Web pages should be easy to read.** Web visitors spend very little time reading pages. Make pages easy to read for quick scanning.

### Frauke's design tips:

1. **Work out a schematic before creating pages.** Even if it's rough, a schematic helps to focus your ideas before you start designing Web pages (Figure 1).

2. **Watch for improvements in HTML.** HTML has already improved in just a few short months. Watch for new developments that will make Web page construction easier.

# Shankweiler Nestor Design, New York, NY

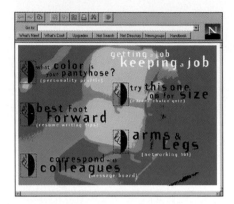

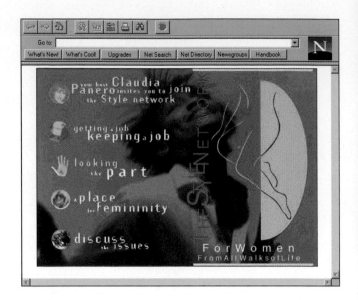

**Above:** *A sample Web page from a Shankweiler Nestor Web site, art directed by Okey Nestor (okey@interport.net) and designed by Lindsey Payne.*

*http://www.echonyc.com/~art/Nestor/Okey.html*

Okey Nestor, who taught Corporate Identity at Kent State University and owns Shankweiler Nestor Design in New York City, feels Web graphics offer a graphic designer broad new potentials in communication, with characteristics such as sound, video and animation.

## Okey's design tips:

1. **Integrate your Web site into your Corporate Identity program.** Instead of treating your Web site as a totally different entity, integrate it into your Identity program and make it work with the goals and strategies of your company's marketing plans.

2. **Offer compelling content within your design.** Design is not the only part of the story. Since the Web is an interactive medium, exploit the potential by offering your customers the ability to place orders, pose questions or look up information in a database. Be creative with both design and content.

# David Reinfurt, San Francisco, CA

*Above: Sample pages from three Reuters sites: News Machine, the Reuters Corporate Web site and Reuters Business Information.*

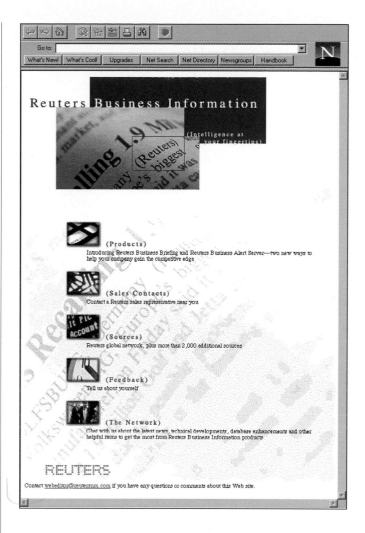

Graphic Designer David Reinfurt (reinfurt@ideo.com) recommends that Web designers put energy into planning before starting graphic design.

## David's design tips:

1. **Don't jump into design and skip the planning phase.**
   By skipping the planning phase of a Web project, content, design and interaction issues will become confused and the process will take twice as long.

2. **Create a schematic prototype (no graphics).**
   A prototype with text and no graphics focuses the design team's attention on content before graphics are created.

# Brandee Amber Selck, Santa Cruz, CA

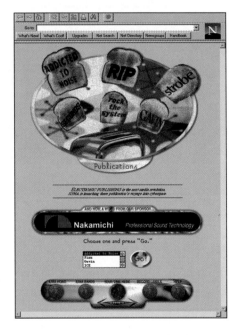

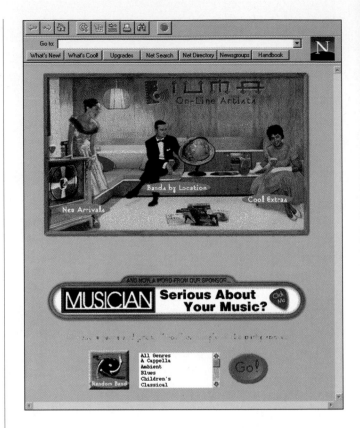

*Above: Brandee's sample Web pages from the IUMA site. Many of the IUMA pages provide Web visitors with a scrolling database window they can use to access artists or labels.*

B randee Amber Selck's artwork is one of the most popular Web sites on the Internet. The IUMA (Internet Underground Music Archive) site at http://www.iuma.com is a home for over 500 independent, unsigned artists who want to reach people directly on the Internet.

## Brandee's design tip:

Brandee (brandee@iuma.com) encourages Web artists to go "hog wild" with their scanners. When Brandee and artist David Beach began designing for the IUMA Web pages, they scavenged for everyday items around the office, at home and at thrift stores. Brandee explains, "a lot of the best stuff came

*Above:* All of the Web graphics on the IUMA site have a fifties theme.

from Beach's parents' kitchen and junk drawer: a cooking pot with a copper bottom, tin foil, a gas stove dial, a radio knob from a reproduction radio that David bought his Dad at K-Mart when he was a kid and various knobs from an old Zenith television."

# Christina Sun, New York, NY

http://www.echonyc.com/~art/
sun_studio/sun_studio.html

Christina Sun (csun@echonyc.com) is an illustrator who specializes in watercolor and collage for books, magazines, newsletters, posters and fabric design.

## Christina's design tips:

While working with Photoshop, Christina discovered changes she made in a feature known as Target Gamma had a dramatic effect on the detail in her images. She noticed that a high (2.2) Target Gamma made her images look washed out. A Target Gamma of 2.2 is optimum for preparing images for transparencies, but too high for preparing images for the Web or print. Photoshop artists have the option of using Curves to compensate for the decreased saturation (see step 3.)

Gamma is a measure of the amount of neutral midtone values displayed in an image. Although Target Gamma won't be written into the file, the value is significant since it will affect the adjustments an artist makes to a file when it's displayed.

1. Try to match the Target Gamma of the output device you intend to use. For example, the Target Gamma of IBM PC monitors that display Web graphics is 1.8, and the Target Gamma of Macintosh monitors that display Web graphics is 2.0.

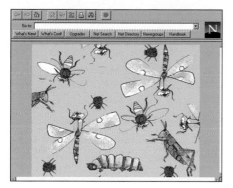

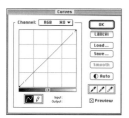

**3a.**

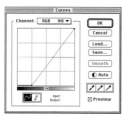

**3b.**

**2.** To control the Target Gamma settings on the Macintosh, use the Knoll Control Panel that comes with Photoshop; for the PC, use the Monitor Setup dialog box under Preferences in Photoshop.

| Gamma | Meaning |
|---|---|
| Low number | A narrow midtone range provides high contrast. Although a low Target Gamma will result in dramatic blacks and brilliant whites, it could mean a loss of detail in images that need a variation of tones (e.g. skin tones). |
| High number | A Target Gamma that is too high may result in images that look washed out. |

**3.** To increase the saturation in an image, use Curves in Photoshop. Open the Curves dialog box by selecting Adjust|Curves from the Image pull-down menu. Instead of making the entire image darker by dragging the curve in the center, try dragging the handle on the curve from its starting point (Figure 3a) to the first gridline (Figure 3b). This technique causes darker areas to become more saturated but doesn't affect the light areas.

# Merry Esparza, New York, NY

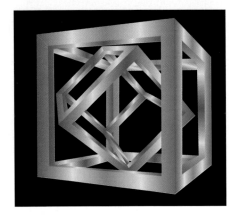

*Above: Sample images from the "Mobius Gallery" Web site.*

*http://www.echonyc.com/~art/merry/merry.html*

**2.**

For her work on Web pages, Merry Esparza (mesparza @echonyc.com) uses Photoshop and Illustrator. Because these two programs have different properties, she likes to transfer graphics from one program to the other.

## Merry's design tips:

1. Begin an illustration with a black and white line art drawing in Illustrator and import it into Photoshop.

2. Once the drawing is in Photoshop, create channels for all the distinct areas in your drawing. Do this before applying any color or textures. Channels provide a means to record selection areas and with the various areas recorded, an artist can easily reselect an area and experiment with color (and textures) over and over.

For example, Merry created the tiled floor in the Mobius Gallery splash screen (Figure 2) with straight lines in Illustrator. When she imported her black and white line art drawing into Photoshop, she used the magic wand tool with the Shift Key held down to select the tiles she wanted to fill with color. She made a channel to record the selection and then experimented with color fills.

# Curtis Eberhardt, New York, NY

*Above: A Macromedia Director self promotion animation movie that Curtis offers as a downloadable file on his Web site.*

*http://www.echonyc.com/~art/curtis/curtis.html*

As an animator, Curtis Eberhardt (CurtisAE@aol.com) is very conscious of bit-depth and related file sizes. He recommends that Web artists reduce bit-depth as much as possible to maintain a reasonable bandwidth.

## Curtis' design tips:

1. **Use Photoshop or DeBabelizer to reduce bit-depth.** Photoshop and DeBabelizer can both be used as tools to optimize color depth for Web graphics. Always use dithering because it fools the eye into believing there is more color present.

2. **Use one-bit (black and white) cast members in Director movies.** Instead of importing color cast members into a Director movie, colorize one-bit cast members on Stage to make very small movies for downloading.

# Frank
# De Crescenzo,
# New York, NY

*Above: Frank created silhouettes of instruments for the background of the "Slappers" pages he designed for the Web.*

*http://www.echonyc.com/~art/slappers/ slappers.html*

Graphic designer Frank De Crescenzo (deac@echo nyc.com) feels designing Web pages is challenging, but he likes challenges. Slappers are flat drumsticks, for drummers and percussionists who are willing to try something radically different.

## Frank's design tips:

Create a light background with silhouettes for your Web page. A wallpaper effect can be created for your Web pages using scanned images and Photoshop.

1. **Scan your images.** Scan the images for your wallpaper at 72 dots per inch RGB. Make sure the images are the

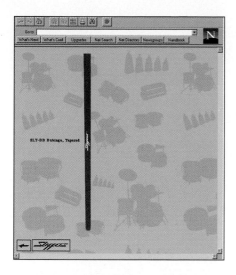

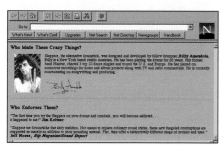

same size as the size you intend to use on your final image because resizing or resampling up will degrade your image.

2. **Silhouette the images.** Create silhouettes by first selecting the images with the pen, lasso or magic wand tool and then filling the background with a solid color.

3. **Create a new document.** Fill a new RGB document with 200 Red, 200 Blue and 200 Green to approximate the gray color of the browser background. Any color can be used but this one is very neutral and won't interfere with foreground images you decide to add to your page.

4. **Paste your silhouettes into the new document.** Select the background of each of the silhouetted images, inverse the selection, copy the image and paste it into the new document.

5. **Fill the pasted images with dark gray.** A slightly darker gray tone such as 190 Red, 190 Blue and 190 Green can be used to fill the silhouettes.

6. **Position the images while they're still selected.** While the images are still selected, they can be repositioned, rotated and scaled.

7. **Convert the document to Indexed Color and reduce the bit-depth.** By selecting a smaller bit-depth of 3 bits per pixel, Frank was able to make the file size very small without a loss in image quality.

8. **Save the image as a GIF file.** By saving the image as a GIF file, the image size was reduced even further since the GIF format contains a lossless compression algorithm.

# Kleber Santos, New York, NY

*Above: Kleber's Sfuzzi Web page was created for his virtual tour of the World Financial Center.*

*http://www.echonyc.com/~art/santos/ santos.html*

Graphic designer Kleber Santos (ksantos@echonyc.com) recommends that Web designers watch the HTML 3.0 draft at http://www.w3.org/hypertext/WWW/MarkUp/html3 /CoverPage.html to keep up with changes in the Hypertext Markup Language.

## Kleber's design tips:

1. **To conserve on bandwidth, consider black and white images.** For his virtual tour of the World Financial Center, Kleber used black and white images instead of color. Since some of his images are large, black and white means smaller file sizes.

2. **Use Adobe Illustrator to create type, rasterize it in Photoshop and save it as GIF or JPEG.** Since HTML does not provide a variation in type faces, Illustrator is the best tool to create original type. Save the file as EPS, open it in Photoshop and save the type as a GIF or JPEG.

# Mark Elbert
# New York, NY

**Above:** *Mark experimented with Photoshop's Composite Controls to combine two images for a button image.*

*http://www.echonyc.com/~art/mesh/ mesh.html*

Mark Elbert (mother@interport.net) is a graphic artist, songwriter and musician who specializes in promoting music on the Web.

## Mark's design tips:

1. **Experiment with Photoshop's tools.** Whether you're working with brushes, the opacity slider or the rubber stamp, challenge yourself to try something different each time you work on a new project.

2. **Work at 72 pixels per inch.** Netscape will resize graphics that are higher than 72 ppi. To avoid resizing your images, work at 72 ppi.

3. **Gather ideas for Web graphics from Web publications.** The new online publications are a good source of ideas for Web site design. Study these (or visit the Web site) and try to think ways you can improve the graphics.

4. **Web visitors will expect fresh material.** Web designers will be expected to update their Web graphics at least once a month. As a result, try to think of ways to update your images without starting from scratch. For example, updating can be accomplished by rearranging the art or floating new objects on the same background.

# Steven McGrew
# Eugene, OR

**Above:** *Steven McGrew invites Web visitors to copy images from his "Gizmo" collection.*

*http://darkwing.uoregon.edu/~smcgrew/*

# Arch Garland
# New York, NY

**Right:** *Arch Garland's splash screen graphic created for his Web site.*

*http://www.echonyc.com/~art/arch/arch.html*

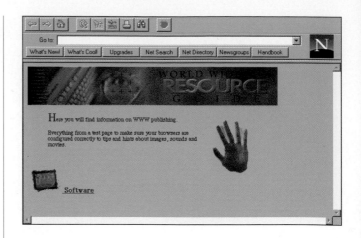

S teven McGrew (smcgrew@oregon.uoregon.edu) is Senior Production Associate at the New Media Center/ University of Oregon Computing Center. Look for Steven's tips on video compression in the Video chapter.

G raphic designer Arch Garland is a graduate of the Cranbrook Academy of Art and owner of Flyleaf in New York City. He recommends keeping dimensions and colors to a minimum when designing a splash screen graphic.

| | |
|---|---|
| average frame rate | When you capture a movie, frame rate is a function of the computer's processing power or the speed of the hard drive, depending on whether the movie is captured to RAM or to the hard drive. Ideally, the frame rate should be a function of the playback requirement. However, download time is an important factor when you create movie files for the Web and a higher frame rate implies larger files. *(Note: See Steven McGrew's tips on capturing and compressing.)* |
| frame size | Since frame size effects file size, Web movie frame size should be limited to 160×120. |
| compressor | QuickTime has seven software compressors built in: Animation, Cinepak, Component Video, Graphics, Photo-JPEG, None and Video. |
| audio format | Three sound components effect sound data rate: |
| *sample rate* | the number of sound samples per second |
| *sample size* | 8-bit or 16-bit |
| *number of channels* | *mono or stereo; choose mono since* stereo sound can only be heard on stereo-capable hardware |

# Steven McGrew's tips on capturing and compressing

**Summary:** *When you're creating movies for the World Wide Web, the choices you make during capturing and compression set the file characteristics. Learn about the variables that will affect the size and quality of your movies.*

**Tip:** *The film clip image on this page was provided by The Image Bank, Inc., a source for still photographs, film footage and illustrations. 800-TIB-images.*

Steven McGrew, who is a digital media designer/animator at the University of Oregon, offers the following advice on capturing and compressing:

### Evaluate your material.

Before you capture a single frame, look at your material and think about issues such as frame size. Can the movie be captured at 320×240 or is 160×120 large enough? Is color necessary, or will black and white be good enough?

### Uncompressed raw data.

If disk space is not a problem and your capturing hardware supports uncompressed capturing, this is the best choice. When you start with uncompressed footage, you'll always get superior results—especially if you post-produce your footage in a movie editor program such as Adobe Premiere. Compression adds artifacts such as jaggies and blurring, which are always compounded by effects, transitions and filters in the editing software.

### Post-production blues.

Limit the post-production process and remove as much material from the clip as possible. If the subject doesn't move, cut the frame!

### Compression is about compromise.

For World Wide Web movies, use the lowest possible frame rate. You'll be able to get away with a very low frame rate if your subject is static or doesn't move very much. Fast action requires a much higher frame rate. Since compression involves a tradeoff between frame rate and image quality, use a "give-a-little, take-a-little" philosophy when determining the final compression/frames per second settings.

### Selecting a type of compression.

QuickTime and MPEG are currently the most widely used compression standards. QuickTime is easy to use and gives good performance. It can include sound and can be played on both Macintosh and IBM PCs. Of the software compressors built into QuickTime, the Cinepak CODEC (compressor decompressor) is the best.

MPEG is difficult to use and is not well supported on Macs. However, MPEG can produce movies that are several times smaller than QuickTime movies. Use MPEG for longer movies that do not require audio, since this format gives the maximum amount of compression and the best final product.

### An emerging standard: MPEG system files.

MPEG system files combine an MPEG video and an MPEG audio file. These files are considerably smaller than anything that could be obtained from the QuickTime CODECs. Although players for this type of data will be available in the future, this type of video requires a very fast computer for playback, or a special hardware card that supports MPEG.

### Conclusion.

When you're creating a movie for the World Wide Web, make it as small as possible. Try to design your material around the Web's bandwidth limitation and be aware of the time required to download your movie.

Each clip should be evaluated separately to determine the best compression method. When in doubt, use QuickTime Cinepak.

# Configuring MoviePlayer as a Netscape helper application

*Summary:* Configure MoviePlayer as a Netscape helper application to automatically play any QuickTime movie files you encounter on the Web.

*Tip:* Try out the latest version of MoviePlayer helper application at the following sites:

http://www.iuma.com
(Internet Underground Music Archive)

http://www.sony.com
(Sony)

http://www.disney.com
(Disney)

http://www.mtv.com
(MTV)

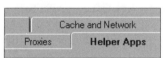

2.

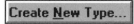

3.

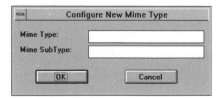

1.

MoviePlayer is the most popular PC movie player add-on (in addition to the AVI player). Use it for playing QuickTime movies on the PC. Apple distributes it with QuickTime. The most current version is stored at apple.info.com and can be downloaded for free.

Movie Player

## 1. Open Preferences.
Choose Preferences from Netscape's Options pull-down menu.

## 2. Select the Helper Apps tab.
Select the Helper Apps tab from among the choices at the top of the Preferences dialog window.

## 3. Click on the Create New Type button.
To add a new helper application, click on the Create New Type button.

## 4. Identify the Mime type and subtype.
Fill in "video" for the Mime type and "quicktime" for the Mime subtype. (Mime, or Multiple Independent Mail Extensions, is a method of describing audio, video and graphics data on the Internet.) Click on OK to exit.

**Configure New Mime Type**

Mime Type:
Mime SubType:

[OK]     [Cancel]

4.

File Extensions: 

**5.**

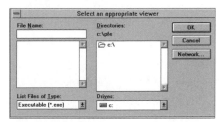

**6.**

**7a.**

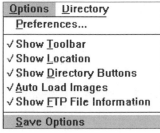

**7b.**

| Options | Directory |
|---------|-----------|
| Preferences... | |
| √ Show Toolbar | |
| √ Show Location | |
| √ Show Directory Buttons | |
| √ Auto Load Images | |
| √ Show FTP File Information | |
| Save Options | |

**8.**

## 5. Identify the file extension.

Enter .qt, .mov in the Extensions box.

## 6. Identify an action.

In the Action set of buttons, click on Launch the Application.

## 7. Locate the application by browsing.

**a.** Click on Browse.

**a.** Select your MoviePlayer application.

## 8. Save.

Select Save Options from the Options pull-down menu (Figure 8).

# Configuring the VMPEG player as a Netscape helper application

*Summary: Configure the VMPEG player as a Netscape helper application to automatically play any MPEG movie files you encounter on the Web. Look for the VMPEG player on the CD-ROM in the back of this book*

*Tip: Try out the latest version of the VMPEG player helper application at the following sites:*

http://www.iuma.com
(Internet Underground Music Archive)

http://www.cs .tu-berlin.de/~phade/
(Frank Gadegast or "Phade")

(http://w3.eeb.ele.tue.nl/mpeg
(MPEG Movie Archive, Netherlands)

http://www.ccsf.caltech.edu/~johns/s19.html
(CalTech)

http://seds.lpl.arizona.edu/s19/s19.html
(University of Arizona)

**1.**

### 1. Open Preferences.
Choose Preferences from Netscape's Options pull-down menu.

### 2. Select the Helper Apps tab.
Select the Helper Apps tab from among the choices at the top of the Preferences dialog window.

### 3. Click on the Create New Type button.
To add a new helper application, click on the Create New Type button.

### 4. Identify the Mime type and subtype.
Fill in "video" for the Mime type and "mpeg" for the Mime subtype. (Mime, or Multiple Independent Mail Extensions is a method of describing audio, video, and graphics data on the Internet.)

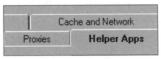

**2.**

Create New Type...

**3.**

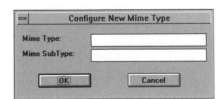

**4.**

**5.**

**6.**

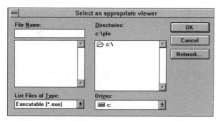

**7a.**

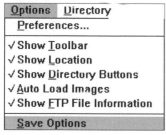

**7b.**

**8.**

## 5. Identify the file extension.

Enter .mpg, .mpeg, .mpe in the File Extensions box.

## 6. Identify an action.

In the Action set of buttons, click on Launch the Application.

## 7. Locate the application by browsing.

a. Click on Browse.

a. Select your MoviePlayer application.

## 8. Save.

Select Save Options from the Options pull-down menu (Figure 8).

# Creating a link to a movie on your Web page

*Summary:* *Create HTML links to QuickTime movie files. Include the file type and file size to help Web visitors make a decision whether to download.*

*Tip:* *The film clip image on this page was provided by The Image Bank, Inc., a source for still photographs, film footage and illustrations. 800-TIB-images.*

Nested Definition List tags can be used to create a "paragraph indent" against a background GIF image that has been downloaded with the <Body Background> tag. To start the type down the page, begin with an IMG tag that references a small, clear GIF image.

Try this example, which contains four links to movie files:

### 1. Open a text editor.
Use NOTEPAD or a word processor. If you use a word processor, be sure to save the document as a Text Only file.

### 2. Create a new HTML document.
Every HTML document consists of a HEAD and a BODY. Start a new document with the following markup tags:

```
<HTML>
<HEAD>
<TITLE>Kids</TITLE>
</HEAD>
```

### 3. Try the <Body Background> tag.
In this example, the "multicolored" background was downloaded as a small tile from the Netscape's Background Samples page (http://home.netscape.com/assist/net_sites/bg/backgrounds.html):

  **a.** Open the tile called multicolordots.gif in Photoshop as a CompuServe GIF image.

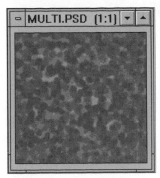

**3a.**

**3d.**

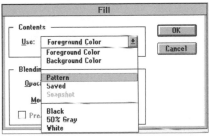

**3f.**

**3j.**

**b.** Select RGB from the Mode pull-down menu.

**c.** Choose All from the Select pull-down menu.

**3c.**

**d.** Choose Define Pattern from the Edit pull-down menu.

**e.** Open a New document, name it multi.gif and make it 603×317 pixels and 72 ppi.

**f.** Choose Fill from the Edit pull-down menu. Select Pattern from the Use pop-up menu, 100% Opacity and Normal Mode.

**g.** To create the "vellum" (to make the type readable against a busy background), drag to select an area of thebackground art, and choose Fill from the Edit pull-down menu.

**h.** Choose White from the Use pop-up menu, 50% Opacity, and Normal Mode.

**i.** Choose Indexed Color from the Mode pull-down menu, and click on OK.

**3i.**

**j.** Choose Save As from the File pull-down menu and select Compuserve GIF from the choices on the Format pop-up menu. The result is shown in Figure 3j.

**k.** Refer to this image in the <Body Background> tag:

```
<HTML>
<HEAD>
<TITLE>Kids</TITLE>
</HEAD>
<Body Background="multi.gif">
```

*Tip: For information and instructions on how to upload files to your Internet provider's server, see the Image Map chapter.*

## 4. Start the type down the page.

To start the type down the page, use the <BR> tag to add line breaks:

```
<HTML>
<HEAD>
<TITLE>Kids</TITLE>
</HEAD>
<Body Background="multi.gif">
<BR>
<BR>
```

## 5. Add a group of nested Definition List tags.

To create the equivalent of a paragraph indent, use the <DL> or Definition List tag. In this example, eight opening tags are used and eight ending tags are used. Adding more than one is called "nesting" the tags:

```
<HTML>
<HEAD>
<TITLE>Kids</TITLE>
</HEAD>
<Body Background="multi.gif">
<BR>
<BR>
<DL><DL><DL><DL><DL><DL><DL>
</DL></DL></DL></DL></DL></DL></DL></DL>
```

## 6. Add a headline between the <DL> tags.

Once the required number of <DL> tags are in place, add the text in between the opening and ending tags. *(Note: The <H2>...</H2> tag is for headline type.)*

```
<HTML>
<HEAD>
<TITLE>Kids</TITLE>
</HEAD>
<Body Background="multi.gif">
<BR>
<BR>
<DL><DL><DL><DL><DL><DL><DL><H2>Videos:</H2></DL></DL>
</DL></DL></DL></DL></DL></DL>
</Body>
</HTML>
```

*Tip: Artists who are inertested in displaying a portfolio on a Web site should visit the Beverly Hills Internet site at:*

http://www.bhi90210.com/

*See "Homesteading on the Web-Free Personal Home Pges."*

## 7. Add a paragraph tag.

The <p> tag will create a new paragraph:

```
<HTML>
<HEAD>
<TITLE>Kids</TITLE>
</HEAD>
<Body Background="multi.gif">
<BR>
<BR>
<DL><DL><DL><DL><DL><DL><DL><H2>Videos:</H2><p></DL>
</DL></DL></DL></DL></DL></DL></DL>
</Body>
</HTML>
```

## 8. Add the links to movie files.

Create links to movie files by opening with the link tag <A> in conjunction with the HREF attribute, and placing text between the opening and closing tags. This text will serve as a clickable "hot spot" on the Web page, and can be identified with an underline. (*Note: End each line with a paragraph tag <p>.*)

```
<HTML>
<HEAD>
<TITLE>Kids</TITLE>
</HEAD>
<Body Background="multi.gif">
<BR>
<BR>
<DL><DL><DL><DL><DL><DL><DL><H2>Videos:</H2><p>
<A HREF="Child1.mov">Boy with Ice Cream 1.4 MB,
Macintosh QT </A><p>
<A HREF="Child2.mov">Little Girl 1.4 MB, Macintosh QT
</A><p>
<A HREF="Child3.mov">Kids with Giraffe 1.4 MB,
Macintosh QT </A><p>
<A HREF="Child4.mov">Boy and Elephant 1.4 MB, Macintosh
QT </A><p>
</DL></DL></DL></DL></DL></DL></DL></DL>
</Body>
</HTML>
```

## 9. Add bolding to the underlined (link) text.

In this example, the <B> and </B> tags will bold the text that visitors will click on. The text will appear underlined and bold faced.

```
<HTML>
<HEAD>
<TITLE>Kids</TITLE>
</HEAD>
<Body Background="multi.gif">
<BR>
<BR>
<DL><DL><DL><DL><DL><DL><DL><H2>Videos:</H2><p>
<A HREF="Child1.mov"><B>Boy with Ice Cream 1.4 MB,
Macintosh QT </B></A><p>
<A HREF="Child2.mov"><B>Little Girl 1.4 MB, Macintosh
QT </B></A><p>
<A HREF="Child3.mov"><B>Kids with Giraffe 1.4 MB,
Macintosh QT </B></A><p>
<A HREF="Child4.mov"><B>Boy and Elephant 1.4 MB,
Macintosh QT </B></A><p>
</DL></DL></DL></DL></DL></DL></DL>
</Body>
</HTML>
```

*Tip:* One of the best ways to learn how to use HTML tags is to view the tags used in your favorite pages on the Web. To see the HTML tags that make up a page, select Source from Netscape's View pull-down menu.

## Summary of HTML tags used in this section.

The tags you see in this list (in alphabetical order) reflect the HTML3 specification:

**<A>…</A>**

Referred to as an "anchor," this tag uses the HREF attribute to link to an external sound file or anchor." For example:

```
<A HREF="Child4.mov"><B>Boy and Elephant 1.4 MB,
Macintosh QT </B></A>
```

*Note: the movie file name must include the path name if the file is located in another directory.*

**<B>…</B>**

A tag used to apply bold facing to text.

**<BODY>…</BODY>**

A tag used to open and close the body of a document.

**<BR>**

A tag used to insert a line break.

**<DL>…</DL>**

The Definition List tag is usually used for definitions or short paragraphs with no bullets or numbering. In this chapter, this tag is nested seven times to indent the word "Video" at the bottom of each page. For example:

```
<DL><DL><DL><DL><DL><DL><DL>Videos</DL>
</DL></DL></DL></DL></DL></DL>
```

**<HTML>…</HTML>**

A tag used to open and close a HTML document.

**<HEAD>…</HEAD>**

A tag used to open and close the header portion of a document.

**<IMG>**

Used to refer to an inline image, this tag uses the SRC="…" attribute, which represents the the URL (location) of the image. For example:

```
<IMG SRC = "clear.gif">
```

**<TITLE>…</TITLE>**

A tag used to describe the title of a document, which shows up inside a document's title bar.

**Artist featured in this chapter:**

*Tom Cipolla is a writer and producer of audio visual educational materials. In this chapter, he teaches how to "hear with your mind."*

*cipolla@echonyc.com*

*http://www.echonyc.com/ ~art/cipolla/cipolla.html*

# Chapter 8

# Sound

If you're considering putting sound on your Web pages, you'll be working with one of the most innovative and rapidly changing technologies on the Web. At the time of this writing, Modem Media, which developed the Zima site, is just beginning to add real-time audio to its sites, a development that allows you to download and play audio at the same time.

This chapter begins with a tour of some well-known Web sites that offer sound. You'll learn technical tips from the developers who created the sites, including Modem Media (Zima), Fry Multimedia (Ragu) and Robert Lord (IUMA). Tom Cipolla offers tips on selecting sound effects for your images. In this chapter, he works with clip sounds to create sound effects for photos from Pacific Coast Software (http://www.pacific-coast.com). Using Andrew Bulhak's Waveform Hold and Modify (*WHAM*, available on the CD ROM in the back of this book) and Adobe Premiere, Tom alters sounds and reformats sound files for use on other platforms.

If you're new to the Web and Netscape, you'll want to take a look at the section on getting Netscape to identify your helper applications. There's also a how-to section on using Cambium Development's Sound Choice CD, a unique database of music clips you can use on your Web pages.

# Web sites with sound

**Summary:** *Visit pages with sound to gather ideas for your own pages. The artists who have created the Web pages you see in this chapter are among the first to take advantage of the Web's multimedia characteristics.*

**Tip:** *Charles Marelli, the writer who created the Duncan character and Duncan's sound effects, uses clip sound effects from a variety of public domain sound archives, as well as a sound effects CD-ROM. (See "Creating sound effects with clip media for addresses of public sound archives.") Charles also creates sound effects from scratch using a 16-bit sound card and a microphone.*

The Zima site, developed by Modem Media in Westport, Connecticut, uses sound effects the same way sound was once used on radio. Visit http://www.zima.com and follow soap-opera-like installments about Duncan, the site's fictional Generation X character.

Weekly episodes contain inline audio links to sound effects. For example, in this segment, Duncan is dropping his date off at her door. He swings open an iron gate in front of her apartment and the word "swung" has an audio link attached. A mouse click on the word swung will automatically play the sound of a gate swinging open:

```
"Duncan, I had a wonderful time."
Duncan's bountiful pool of clichés immediately evaporated.
"Um, ,,.. me too," he stammered.
Duncan swung open the small iron gate in front of her
apartment.
```

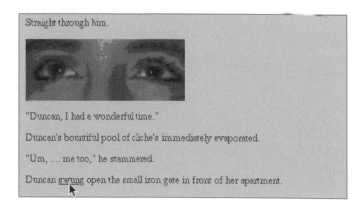

**Tip:** *Watch for further sound developments on the Zima site; Modem Media developers are planning to add real-time audio to give visitors the ability to download and listen at the same time. RealAudio information can be obtained at:*

`http://www.realaudio.com`

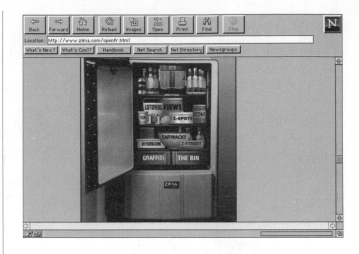

At the Zima site, you'll also find sound files in the "fridge." Click on the Earwacks bowl inside the refrigerator and you'll visit a page of sound icons with links to WAV files for Windows or AU files for Macintosh and Unix:

 Smooch date.au (18 K) | date.wav(36 K)

 Batter up! ball.au (21 K) | ball.wav(42 K)

 Ding. elevator.au (14 K) | elevator.wav(37 K)

 A slight drizzle...rain.au (23 K) | rain.wav(62 K)

John Nardone (JNardone@ModemMedia .com) of Modem Media recommends that Web site developers follow "ubique," a Web technology that "facilitates communication on a Web site." It provides real-time chat and can set up automated tours with a list of predefined sites. For more information, visit:

`http://www.ubique.com`

**"I made a lasagna so good the other day, I swear it would have made Michelangelo cry from joy."**

*Tip: Fry Multimedia estimates it takes about one second to download one kilobyte of data over a 14.4 Kbps modem. They prefer to hold file sizes under 40 K so that visitors never have to wait more than 40 seconds for sound to download.*

R agu's Web site (http://www .eat.com/index.html), produced by Fry Multimedia in Ann Arbor, Michigan, has a clever theme called Mama's Cucina (or Mama's kitchen).  Included are Mama's Cookbook, Contests, Mama's Secrets, Italian lessons, Cooking/Pasta Glossaries, Stories Around the Family Table, and Mama's Favorite Places.

Professor "Antonio" teaches Italian. A mouse click on the appropriate file type (WAV, AU or AIFF) will play a phrase in Italian. The idea for the site came from David Fry (dfry@fry-multi.com) and Michael Clemens. Writer Tom Cunniff creates much of the content for the site and "Professor Antonio" is Antonio Antiochia, a software engineer with Fry Multimedia.

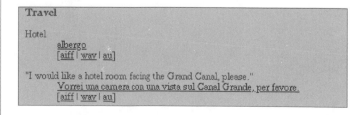

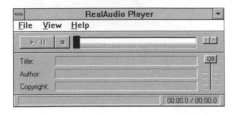

*Tip: The RealAudio Web site contains listings of radio servers being formed around the globe. To access the Web sites, use the following addresses:*

http://www.batmanforever.com

http://www.hkweb.com/radio/
(Radio HK, Los Angeles)

http://bam.nuri.net/Entertainment/Gayo/
(KBS, Seoul, South Korea)

http://nt.access.com.net/wwoz/
(WWOZ FM Radio, Metairie, LA)

O ne of the most exciting developments on Web pages is RealAudio, by Progressive Networks, Inc. (http://www.realaudio.com). This interesting new technology allows you to simultaneously download and play sound. The Progressive Network Web site hosts pages that contain ABC, National Public Radio, and Radio Yesteryear radio programs.

Progressive Networks, Inc. sells RealAudio server software to sites that wish to offer "streaming" audio files or real-time playback. Web site visitors who have a RealAudio player installed will have only a two-second delay compared to the longer delays required for WAV files.

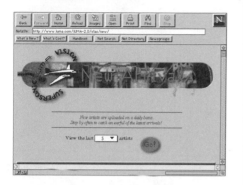

*Tip:* *Netscape can guess at a Web site's protocol, which means you don't need to type http://. For example, try:*

www.iuma.com

The IUMA site at http://iuma.com (Internet Underground Music Archive) is the epitome of organization, advanced sound technology, and beautiful graphics. Founders Robert Lord and Jeff Patterson are recent computer science graduates from the University of California at Santa Cruz. Created in 1993, the site is intended for independent, unsigned artists who want to reach the estimated 30 million people on the Internet. In 1994, IUMA was awarded "Best of the Web" by Internet book publisher O'Reilly & Associates for "contributions that have significantly improved the Internet."

For musicians, "base service" on IUMA is $120 per year and includes one song, one logo, two band or other images, up to two pages of text, cross-indexing by artist, song title, location, and genre.

Songs submitted on DAT tape or CD are digitized and compressed to disk using MPEG2 audio compression techniques. MPEG (Motion Picture Experts Group) is a high fidelity sound format (cassette quality) that offers better compression than WAV files.

IUMA artists Brandee Amber Selck and David Beach create graphics with Macintosh computers, but create sound on Silicon Graphics Indys. Upon entering the site, the database of over 500 musicians can be viewed in five different ways:

**1.**

**2.**

**3.**

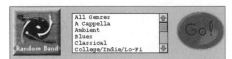

**4.**

**5.**

### 1. New Arrivals.

A list of the newest bands on IUMA.

### 2. By Artist.

An alphabetical listing of all IUMA bands.

### 3. By Genre.

A listing of musical genres or styles. Note that bands may be under multiple categories.

### 4. By Location.

Bands can be sorted by country, state, and city.

### 5. By Label (from the IUMA home page).

Several record labels have their own home page on IUMA. To access this section, click on the washing machine pictured on the IUMA home page.

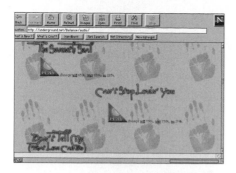

**Tip:** *When you discover a site you like, select Add Bookmark from the Bookmarks pull-down menu in Netscape. This will record the site address so you don't have to enter it the next time you want to visit. To view the list, select View Bookmarks from the Bookmarks pull-down menu.*
*Click on the Export button if you want a copy of the list. Netscape will create a file, which you might email to a friend.*

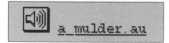

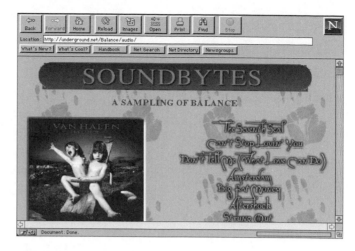

The Van Halen sound samples (http://vanhalen.warner rcrds.com/Balance/ ) are arranged on a beautiful page of "wallpaper" graphics and half buttons, which is the artist's clever scheme to use sound excerpts rather than full songs. Visitors have their choice of WAV (Windows), AIFF (Macintosh), or AU (Unix) files.

Enter X-Files on the Yahoo search page (http://www .yahoo.com/search.html) and you'll get a list of several Web sites and several newsgroups. Charles McGrew's Web site has the best sound: http://www.rutgers.edu/x-files.html.

# Configuring the Media Player as a Netscape helper application

*Summary:* Configure the Media Player as a Netscape helper application to automatically play WAV sound files you encounter on the Web.

*Tip:* Try out the Media Helper Application player helper application at the following sites (without the name in parentheses):

http://www.iuma.com
(Internet Underground Music Archive)

http://www.classicalmus.com/audio cen-
ter.html
(BMG audio)

http://web.msu.edu/vincent/presi-
dents.html
(Michigan State University
Archive of Presidents)

http://www.aaj.com/aaj/motherm/index.html
(Worldwide Alternative Jukebox, Mother
Mary, New York City)

*Tip:* Visit the IUMA Help page to download a sound player for Windows:

http://www.iuma.com/IUMA-
2.0/help/help-windows.html

| Options | Directory |
|---|---|
| **Preferences...** | |
| ✓ Show Toolbar | |
| ✓ Show Location | |
| ✓ Show Directory Buttons | |
| ✓ Auto Load Images | |
| ✓ Show FTP File Information | |
| Save Options | |

**1.**

## 1. Open Preferences.
Choose Preferences from Netscape's Options pull-down menu.

## 2. Select the Helper Apps tab.
Select the Helper Apps tab from among the choices at the top of the Preferences dialog window.

## 3. Click on the Create New Type button.
To add a new helper application, click on the Create New Type button.

## 4. Identify the Mime type and subtype.
Fill in "audio" for the Mime type and "x-wav" for the Mime subtype. (Mime, or Multiple Independent Mail Extensions, is a method of describing audio, video, and graphics data on the Internet.) Click on OK to exit.

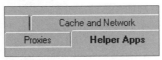

**2.**

**Create New Type...**

**3.**

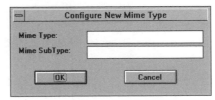

**4.**

File Extensions: [                    ]

**5.**

**6.**

Browse...

**7a.**

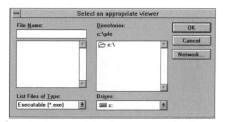

**7b.**

| Options | Directory |
|---------|-----------|
| Preferences... | |

√ Show Toolhar
√ Show Location
√ Show Directory Buttons
√ Auto Load Images
√ Show FTP File Information

Save Options

**8.**

## 5. Identify the file extension.

Enter wav in the File Extensions box.

## 6. Identify an action.

In the Action set of buttons, click on Launch the Application.

## 7. Locate the application by browsing.

Click on Browse and select the MPEG helper application application.

## 8. Save.

Select Save Options from the Options pull-down menu (Figure 8).

# Configuring an MPEG player as a Netscape helper application

*Summary:* *Configure an MPEG player as a Netscape helper application to automatically play MP2 sound files you encounter on the Web.*

*Tip:* *Try out the Media Player at the following sites:*

```
http://www.zima.com
```
(Zima)

```
http://www.eat.com
```
(Ragu)

```
http://vanhalen.warnerrcrds.com/
Balance/
```
(Van Halen)

```
http://www.sony.com
```
(Sony)

```
http://www.mca.com
```
(MCA Records)

*Tip:* *Visit the IUMA Help page to download a sound player for Windows:*

```
http://www.iuma.com/IUMA-
2.0/help/help-windows.html
```

| Options | Directory |
|---------|-----------|
| Preferences... | |
| √ Show Toolbar | |
| √ Show Location | |
| √ Show Directory Buttons | |
| √ Auto Load Images | |
| √ Show FTP File Information | |
| Save Options | |

1.

### 1. Open Preferences.
Choose Preferences from Netscape's Options pull-down menu.

### 2. Select the Helper Apps tab.
Select the Helper Apps tab from among the choices at the top of the Preferences dialog window.

### 3. Click on the Create New Type button.
To add a new helper application, click on the Create New Type button.

### 4. Identify the Mime type and subtype.
Fill in "audio" for the Mime type and "x-mpeg" for the Mime subtype. (Mime, or Multiple Independent Mail Extensions, is a method of describing audio, video and graphics data on the Internet.) Click on OK to exit.

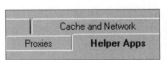

2.

Create New Type...

3.

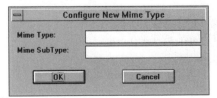

4.

**5.**

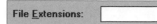

**6.**

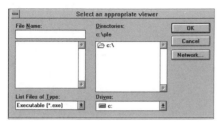

**7a.**

**7b.**

| Options | Directory |
| --- | --- |
| Preferences... | |
| √ Show Toolbar | |
| √ Show Location | |
| √ Show Directory Buttons | |
| √ Auto Load Images | |
| √ Show FTP File Information | |
| Save Options | |

**8.**

## 5. Identify the file extension.

Enter MP2 in the File Extensions box.

## 6. Identify an action.

In the Action set of buttons, click on Launch the Application.

## 7. Locate the application by browsing.

Click on Browse and select an MPEG player application.

## 8. Save.

Select Save Options from the Options pull-down menu (Figure 8).

# Creating a link to sound files on your Web page

*Summary:* Create HTML links to WAV (Windows), AIFF, AU (Mac and Unix μ-law, pronounced mu law), MP2 (MPEG audio), or RA (RealAudio) sound files.

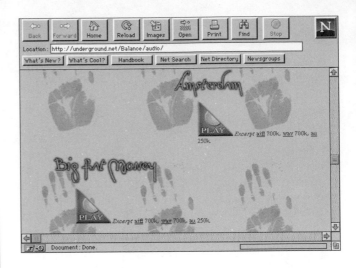

The Van Halen Soundbytes page offers WAV, AIFF, or AU files for downloading. To see the HTML tags that make up a page in Netscape, select Source from the View pull-down menu. This is a practical way to learn how to use HTML tags. For example, the HTML tags for the links to the Van Halen "Amsterdam" sound bytes include:

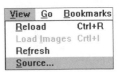

```
<DL><DL><DL><DL><DL>
<DD><IMG ALT="Amsterdam"
WIDTH=118 HEIGHT=50
SRC="/Balance/audio/balance-amsterdam.gif">
<BR>
<DL>
<DD><FONT SIZE=2>
<IMG ALT="" WIDTH=58 HEIGHT=58 ALIGN= BOTTOM
SRC="butt_play.gif"> <I>Excerpt</I>
<A HREF="/Balance/sounds/amstrdm.aiff">aiff</A> 700k,
<A HREF="/Balance/sounds/amstrdm.wav">wav</A> 700k,
<A HREF="/Balance/sounds/amstrdm.au">au</A> 250k.
</DL></FONT>
</DL></DL></DL></DL></DL>
<P>
```

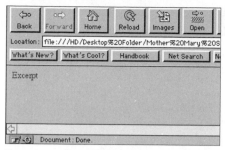

**3.**

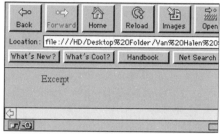

**4.**

Follow these steps to get an understanding of the effect these same type of tags have on the Web page:

### 1. Open a text file editor.

Use Notepad or your word processor. If you use a word processor, be sure to save the document as Text Only.

### 2. Create a new HTML document.

Start a new document with the following markup tags:

```
<HTML>
<HEAD>
<TITLE>Mother Mary:Soundbytes</TITLE>
</HEAD>
<BODY>
```

### 3. Try the Definition List tag <DL>.

Add <DL> at the end of your HTML document, followed by the word "Excerpt". Add an ending </DL> tag.

```
<HTML>
<HEAD>
<TITLE>Mother Mary:Soundbytes</TITLE>
</HEAD>
<BODY>
<DL>Excerpt</DL>
```

Save this document as "Definition List Sample" and open it in Netscape. Select Open File from the File pull-down menu to view your HTML document.

### 4. Try nesting two <DL> tags.

Add another <DL> and another </DL> tag around the word "Excerpt."

```
<HTML>
<HEAD>
<TITLE>Mother Mary:Soundbytes</TITLE>
</HEAD>
<BODY>
<DL><DL>Excerpt</DL></DL>
```

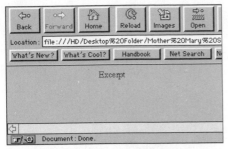

**5.**

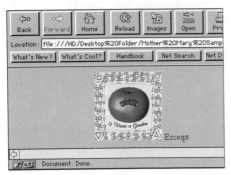

**6.**

### 5. Try nesting four <DL> tags.

Add two more <DL> and two more </DL> tags around the word "Excerpt."

```
<HTML>
<HEAD>
<TITLE>Mother Mary:Soundbytes</TITLE>
</HEAD>
<BODY>
<DL><DL><DL><DL>Excerpt</DL></DL></DL></DL>
```

### 6. Add an inline image.

Insert an <IMG> tag below the Definition List tags in the form <IMG SRC="mesh.gif">. The SRC attribute indicates the file name of the image. *Note: The file name alone without a path name, indicates the image file is in the same directory as the HTML document.*

```
<HTML>
<HEAD>
<TITLE>Mother Mary:Soundbytes</TITLE>
</HEAD>
<BODY>
<DL><DL><DL><DL>
<IMG SRC = "mesh.gif">
Excerpt
</DL></DL></DL></DL>
```

### 7. Add an ALT attribute to the image tag.

The ALT attribute in an <IMG> tag is an accommodation for people with text browsers. They see the word "Apple" instead of the GIF image.

```
<HTML>
<HEAD>
<TITLE>Mother Mary:Soundbytes</TITLE>
</HEAD>
<BODY>
<DL><DL><DL><DL>
<IMG ALT="Apple"
SRC = "mesh.gif">
<i>Excerpt</i>
</DL></DL></DL></DL>
```

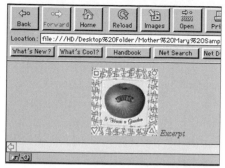

**8.**

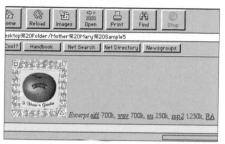

**9.**

## 8. Add an italic tag around "Excerpt."

Add a set of italic tags around the word "Excerpt" with the pair <i> and </i>.

```
<HTML>
<HEAD>
<TITLE>Mother Mary:Soundbytes</TITLE>
</HEAD>
<BODY>
<DL><DL><DL><DL>
<IMG ALT="Apple" WIDTH =100 HEIGHT = 102
SRC = "mesh.gif">
<i>Excerpt</i>
</DL></DL></DL></DL>
```

## 9. Specify the Height and Width.

Insert WIDTH =100 and HEIGHT =102 in the <IMG> tag. This information may be obtained from the Image Size dialog box in Photoshop. Specifying the HEIGHT and WIDTH as attributes of the <IMG> tag speeds the loading of the image on the Web page.

```
<HTML>
<HEAD>
<TITLE>Mother Mary:Soundbytes</TITLE>
</HFAD>
<BODY>
<DL><DL><DL><DL>
<IMG ALT="Apple" WIDTH =100 HEIGHT = 102
SRC = "mesh.gif">
<i>Excerpt</i>
</DL></DL></DL></DL>
```

*Tip: The HOMR site at http://jeeves.media. mit.edu:80/homr/ is a "music recommendation" system written by Max Metral at the MIT Media Lab. The system helps you determine your music taste, based on how you rate various artists and groups.*

## 10. Add links to sound files.

Create links to sound files by opening with the link tag <A> and the HREF attribute and entering text and then the closing tag. This text serves as the clickable "hot spot" on the Web page, and can be identified with an underline.

```
<HTML>
<HEAD>
<TITLE>Mother Mary:Soundbytes</TITLE>
</HEAD>
<BODY>
<DL><DL><DL><DL>
<IMG SRC = "mesh.gif">
<i>Excerpt</i>
<A HREF="/sounds/"garden.aiff">aiff</A> 700k,
<A HREF="/sounds/"garden.wav">wav</A> 700k,
<A HREF="/sounds/"garden.au">au</A> 250k,
<A HREF="/sounds/"garden.mp2">mp2</A> 250k,
<A HREF="/sounds/"garden.RA">RA</A> 250k.
</DL></DL></DL></DL>
```

| File Format | Notes |
| --- | --- |
| WAV | An audio file format used on the Windows platform. |
| AIFF | An audio file format used on the Macintosh platform. |
| AU | An audio file format read by Sun Sparc, NeXT workstations and Macintosh computers. |
| MP2 | A hi-fidelity file format used on the Windows, Macintosh and Unix platforms. |
| RA | An audio file format developed by Progressive Technology, Inc. for instant playback or "audio streaming." Instant playback is only available from servers equipped with RealAudio server software, although the RA file will do a normal download to Windows, Macintosh and Unix machines. |

*Tip: The ultimate band list at*

`http://american recordings.com///wwwof-music/ubl/ubl.shtml`

*is the Web's largest list of music links where a Web visitor can add the la music links for new bands. Browse the site alphabetically, by genre, by resource (newsgroups, mailing lists, FAQ files, lyrics, guitar tablatures, digitized songs or Web pages) or view the complete list.*

## 11. Summary of HTML tags used in this section.

The tags you see in this list (in alphabetical order) reflect the HTML3 specification:

### <A>...</A>

Referred to as an "anchor," this tag uses the HREF attribute to link to an external sound file or "anchor." For example:

`<A HREF="/sounds/"garden.aiff">aiff</A> 700k,`

*Note: The sound file name must include the path name if the file is located in another directory.*

### <BODY>...</BODY>

A tag used to open and close the body of a document.

### <DL>...</DL>

The Definition List tag is usually used for definitions or short paragraphs with no bullets or numbering. In this section, this tag is nested four times to indent the word "Excerpt." For example:

`<DL><DL><DL><DL>Excerpt</DL></DL></DL></DL>`

### <HTML>...</HTML>

A tag used to open and close an HTML document.

### <HEAD>...</HEAD>

A tag used to open and close the header portion of a document.

### <i>...</i>

A tag used to format with italics.

### <IMG>

Used to refer to an inline image, this tag uses the SRC= "..." attribute, which represents the URL (location) of the image. In this section, the <IMG> tag also uses the WIDTH and HEIGHT attributes, which speed up the downloading of the image and the ALT attribute, which accommodates users limited to text browsers. For example:

`<IMG ALT="Apple" WIDTH —100 HEIGHT = 102`
`SRC = "mesh.gif">`

### <TITLE>...</TITLE>

Used under the <HEAD> tag, the <TITLE> tag describes the title of a document, which shows up inside a document's title bar.

# Creating sound effects with clip media

*Summary: By using free-of-rights clip media from public sound archives on the Web, you can add sound effects to photographic images.*

*Tip: Look for sound effects at the following locations:*

http://www.eecs.nwu.edu/~jmyers/other-sounds.html

http://sunsite.unc.edu/pub/multimedia/sunsounds/sound_effects/

http://sunsite.sut.ac.jp/multimed/sounds/

http://info.fuw.edu.pl/multimedia/sounds/animals/

*Tip: The images on this page are from Pacific Coast Software's collection of stock photography at:*

http://www.pacific-coast.com

Applying what he learned when working with an analog sound medium, Tom Cipolla selected electronic images from Pacific Coast Software's collection of stock photography, and used Andrew Bulhak's *Waveform Hold and Modify* (*WHAM*, available on the CD-ROM in the back of this book), to shape the sound and converted files to formats for playback on Unix and Windows machines.

## 1. Select your photographs.

When selecting photographs to combine with sound effects, look for shots with elements that evoke sounds. Pictures with human content offer the greatest range of potential sounds.

## 2. How many sounds?

When sound waves are mixed in an 8-bit environment, there seems to be too little information for individual sounds to maintain their integrity. Clip sounds from the Web or sound effect CD-ROMs are usually 8-bit. Try to limit your selection to two sounds unless you start with 16-bit sound.

Country .WAV

Rio2 .WAV

**4b.**

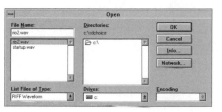

**4c.**

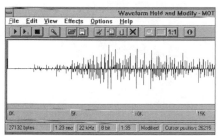

**4d.**

| 27132 bytes | 1.23 sec | 22 kHz | 8 bit |

**4e.**

### 3. "Listening" with your mind.

Put yourself in the picture and try to imagine what you would hear. Look for sounds that are strong enough to convey what's happening in the photo. Since you cannot expect to hold a viewer's attention for long, fifteen or twenty seconds should be the maximum duration.

### 4. Compare clip sound format, sample rate and other characteristics.

WHAM can be used to compare sound file characteristics such as file formats, sample rate, sample size, compression, and total time.

Tom Cipolla noted the following information about the files country.wav and horse.wav:

**a.** Open the WHAM software.

**b.** Select Open from the File pull-down menu.

**c.** Select a sound file to open.

**d.** The sound file will open into a wave form.

**e.** Note the sound file characteristics at the base of the waveform panel.

**country.wav**
Format: WAV
Sample Size: 8 bits
Total Time: 7 seconds
Sample Rate: 22.3 kHz

**horse.wav**
Format: WAV
Sample Size: 8 bits
Total Time: 1 second
Sample Rate: 22.3 kHz

# File conversion: WAV to AU or AIFF

***Summary:*** *Use WHAM to convert WAV files to AU or AIFF.*

**1.**

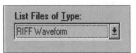

**2a.**

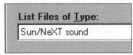

**2b.**

**2c.**

The "clip" sound files found on numerous sites across the Web may need to be converted to a file format that your sound edit software can read. For example, Windows WAV files can be converted to AIFF or AU with Andrew Bulhak's *Waveform Hold and Modify* (*look for WHAM on the CD-ROM in the back of this book*).

### 1. Select the file you'd like to convert.
Open a sound file into the *WHAM* software and select Save As from the File pull-down menu.

### 2. Identify the file and format you need.
Use the file type pop-up box to locate the file format you need.

### 3. Select a directory for the new file.
Either create a new destination folder for the converted file or select the default directory by clicking on OK.

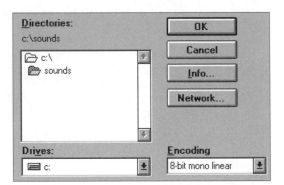

**3.**

# Edit a waveform with WHAM

***Summary:*** *Use Andrew Bulhak's WHAM software to alter and mix sounds.*

Tom Cipolla located the sound of a horse whinneying on a public domain archive on the Web. (*Note: the locations of the public archives are listed in the "Creating sound effects with clip media" section in this chapter.*) The sounds you collect from the archives or from sound effects CD-ROMs vary in file format, length, and sampling rate. Tom was able to shorten the length of a sound clip with the *WHAM* sound editor.

## 1. Clip a portion of a sound file.

Open a music file in *WHAM*, play the file, and determine the duration of the clip you'd like to use. Sections of the wave pattern may also be altered with the Cut, Copy, and Paste commands. Start by drag-selecting a section of the wave pat tern and then use the Cut, Copy, or Paste commands.

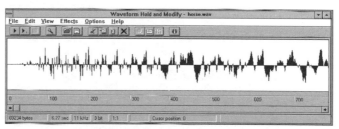

1a.

1b.

## 2. Save the sound clip.

Select Save from the File pull-down menu and save this music clip to your hard drive.

# Use Cambium Development's Sound Choice Lite database to locate clip music

*Summary:* Cambium Development has created a unique database of music clips you can use on your Web pages.

*Tip: Cambium Development's Sound Choice CD-ROM won the 1995 Multimedia World Reader's Choice Award and was named by PC Magazine as one of the top 100 CD-ROMs for 1995.*

*The Sound Choice Lite CD-ROM described in this chapter can be found bundled with Astound 2.0, Turtle Tools, Q-Media, Adobe Premiere 4.0, Sound Forge 3.0 and Microsoft Office '95 as part of the PowerPoint Multimedia CD-ROM.*

*For more information about Cambium's Sound Choice Volumes 1 & 2, contact:*

*Cambium Development, Inc.*
*P.O. Box 296-H*
*Scarsdale, NY 10583*
*1-800-231-1779*
*1-914-472-6246*

## 1. Open the Sound Choice Lite software.

Open Cambium's Sound Choice software. An "Audition Music" panel will be displayed.

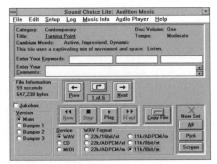

1.

## 2. Review categories and titles.

Click on the Next or Previous buttons to cycle through the categories and titles on the Sound Choice CD. The categories, titles, and database keywords will be displayed at the top of the Audition Music Panel (Figure 1).

2.

## 3. Play a title.

Click on the Play button to audition a title.

3.

**4a.**

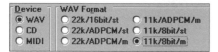

**4b.**

**4c.**

## 4. Copy a title to your hard drive.

Cambium Development provides a copy function to copy the sound files from the CD-ROM to your hard drive. Each of the sounds has a "main" version (full-length sound) and several "bumpers" of varying lengths.

Bumpers are short versions which can be used for a transition or punctuation in CD-ROM productions. In this example, Tom Cipolla chose "Main" since he wanted to edit the sound in Adobe Premiere (*see "Fade a sound with Adobe Premiere's editing tools" in the next section*). He also chose 11kH, 8-bit, mono (Figure 4b) since it would be a smaller file.

**a.** Select a sound version.

**b.** Select a sound format.

**c.** Click on Copy File.

**d.** The "Copy music from the CD-ROM" panel will be displayed.

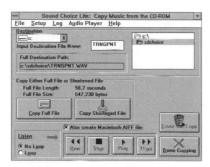

**4d, 4f, 4g.**

**e.** Select a destination drive and directory.

**f.** (Option) Click on the "Also create a Macintosh aiff file" if you need a Macintosh version for your Web page.

**g.** Click on the Copy Full File button.

**h.** A dialog box will notify you that the file has been copied. Click on OK.

**4h.**

# Fade a sound with Adobe Premiere's editing tools

**Summary:** *Although Adobe Premiere is usually associated with video editing, it can also be used to edit sound files.*

**1.**

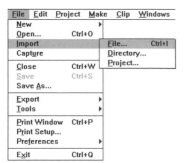

**2a.**

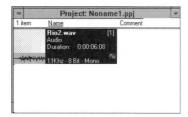

**2c, 3a.**

## 1. Open Premiere.

Open Adobe Premiere. A dialog box labeled "New Project Presets" will be displayed. Click on OK to accept the default settings.

## 2. Import a sound clip to edit.

**a.** Select Import|File from the File pull-down menu.

**b.** Select a sound to import in the dialog box that follows.

**c.** The sound clip will be displayed in a Project Window.

## 3. Move the sound to the Construction window.

**a.** Position your mouse pointer over the waveform minia-ture in the Project Window. Your pointer will turn into a grabber hand.

**b.** Drag the clip into the track labeled "Audio" in the Construction window.

**3b.**

**4a.**

**4b.**

**4c.**

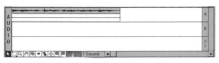

**4d.**

**5a.**

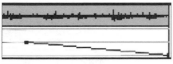

**5b, 5c.**

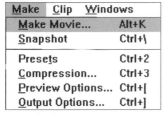

**6a.**

**6b.**

# 4. Clip off the trailing silence.

**a.** Select the razor tool at the base of the Construction window.

**b.** Click on the trailing silence part of the wave in the Audio track.

**c.** Select the trailing silence form and delete it with the Delete key.

**d.** Without the trailing silence, the waveform file will be significantly smaller.

# 5. Fade the sound.

**a.** Position the mouse pointer (hand) over the fade line in the Audio track where you want the fade to start.

**b.** Click on the line to form a handle (a black dot).

**c.** Create an additional handle at the end of the line and drag it downward so the fade line has a slope. Since a downward slope in the line decreases the volume, the sound will fade.

# 6. Make a movie.

**a.** Select Make Movie from the Make pull-down menu.

**b.** A Make Movie save dialog box will appear. Click on Output Options.

**c.** A Project Output Options dialog box will appear.

**6c.**

☐ Video

**6d.**

**6e.**

**d.** Click to remove the "X" in the box labeled "Video."

**e.** Select AVI Movie from the "Output As" pop-up menu.

**f.** Select 11kHz from the Rate pop-up menu.

**g.** Select 8-bit mono from the Format pop-up menu.

**h.** Select MS-ADPCM from the Type pop-up menu.

**i.** Select 1 Second from the Interleave pop-up menu.

**j.** Click on OK. Premiere will display a status bar as the movie is assembled.

**k.** When the movie is assembled, it will be displayed in a Clip window..

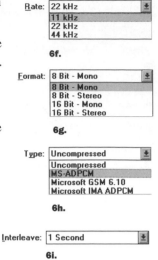

Rate: 22 kHz
11 kHz
22 kHz
44 kHz

**6f.**

Format: 8 Bit - Mono
8 Bit - Mono
8 Bit - Stereo
16 Bit - Mono
16 Bit - Stereo

**6g.**

Type: Uncompressed
Uncompressed
MS-ADPCM
Microsoft GSM 6.10
Microsoft IMA ADPCM

**6h.**

Interleave: 1 Second

**6i.**

**6j.**

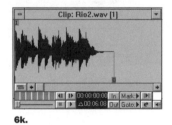
**6k.**

## 7. Export the AVI movie as a Waveform file.

**a.** With the Clip Window selected, select Export|Waveform from the File pull-down menu.

**b.** Create a file name in the dialog window that follows and click on OK.

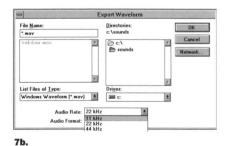
**7a.**

**7b.**

# File optimization: Resample and downsample sound files for playback on the Web

**Summary:** *Take an inventory of file sizes and use downsampling techniques to reduce them.*

**7b.**

Tom Cipolla found that Premiere's layered audio tracks (Figure 1) could be used to mix sound. After mixing sound for each of the photographs, Tom Cipolla took an accounting of the file components and total file sizes to see whether the files would be appropriate for the Web. File size is related to duration and sampling rate. Larger files can be scaled down by resampling, although there is a loss of quality.

| | File Size | Characteristics |
|---|---|---|
| **Picture: Horse** | | |
| music (country) | 330 K | Stereo, 8-bit, 22.254 kHz |
| horse | 110 K | Mono, 8-bit, 22.050 kHz |
| Mix | 605 K | Stereo, 8-bit, 22.3 kHz |
| **Picture: Crowd** | | |
| crowd | 286 K | Stereo, 8-bit, 22.3 kHz |
| National Anthem | 100 K | Mono, 8-bit, 22.3 kHz |
| Mix | 561 K | Stereo, 8-bit, 22.3 kHz |
| **Picture: Cruise Ship** | | |
| steamship whistle | 330 K | Mono, 8-bit, 22.3 kHz |
| **Picture: Waterfall** | | |
| music (orchestral) | 1276 K | Sterco, 8-bit, 22.3 kHz |
| waterfall | 33 K | Stereo, 8-bit, 22.3 kHz |
| Mix | 649 K | Stereo, 8-bit, 22.3 kHz |

Use the following steps to reduce a sound's file size:

## 1. Remove trailing silence.

Remove any following silence parts. This often reduces the file as much as 100 K.

## 2. Resample sound and mix to mono sound.

Downsample 16-bit sounds to 8 bit. If stereo sound is not essential, this step will reduce the file size. (*Note: If you're using Adobe Premiere to edit a sound file, select these options in the Project Output Options dialog box.*)

## 4. Resample to 11 kHz or 8 kHz.

If the sound still sounds good, resampling to 11 kHz or 8 kHz will reduce the file size. (*Note: If you're using WHAM to edit a sound file, select Playback Rate from the Effects pull-down menu to resample sound.*)

After trailing silence was removed, stereo sounds were mixed as mono, and the sounds were resampled to 11 kHz, the resulting sounds were substantially smaller. To reduce the sounds even further would require shortening the sound duration.

| Picture | File Size (Mix) | New File Size |
|---|---|---|
| Horse | 605 K | 99 K |
| Crowd | 561 K | 154 K |
| Cruise ship | 660 K | 176 K |
| Waterfall | 649 K | 143 K |

# Chapter 9

**Artist featured in this chapter:**

*Curtis Eberhardt has a B.A. from the Art Institute of Chicago and an M.A. from New York University. Curtis specializes in Macromedia Director, Strata Studio Pro and Photoshop. He also teaches computer graphics at New York University and The New School for Social Research.*

*CurtisAE@aol.com*

http://www.cchonyc.com/
~art/curtis/curtis.html

# Animation & 3D

Animation and 3D graphics are well-represented on the Web with several new developments. In the months ahead, artists will use VRML and 3DMF files to describe 3D worlds on the Web, and animation software will be able to "write" VRML and 3DMF files for display on Web pages.

In this chapter, Curtis Eberhardt shows us how to build an interactive Director animation and offers tips on how to create Director movies for Macromedia's new "streaming" multimedia technology designed for the Web.

# Web sites with animation

**Summary:** *Web designers will want to tour the Web to examine the growing number of animation formats, including AVI, QuickTime and MPEG movies; Macromedia's new shockwave Director Internet Player technology, which allows viewers to run Director animations, CGI scripts that animate Web graphics; QuickTime VR movies assembled from pre-rendered 3D scenes and virtual interactive "worlds" accessed with 3D graphics viewers for the World Wide Web.*

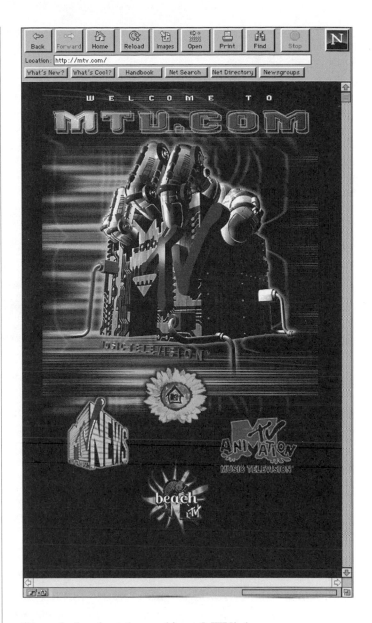

Look closely at the graphic on MTV's home page (http://mtv.com/) and you'll see robot fingers crunching an MTV logo. Look further into the site and you'll find Beavis and Butthead in MTV's collection of animations and still images.

Although Netscape has a JPEG viewer built in (for still images), you'll need the MoviePlayer or some other QuickTime movie player to see the animations.

**1a.**

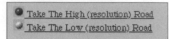

**1b.**

**1c.**

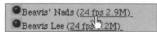

**1e.**

*Tip: Visit the IUMA Help page to download a movie player for Windows:*

```
http://www.iuma.com/IUMA-
2.0/help/help-windows.html
```

## 1. Find an animation to download.

**a.** Click on the MTV animation logo on the MTV home page.

**b.** Click on Take The High (resolution) Road or the Take The Low (resolution) Road.

**c.** Click on MTV Animation on the MTV Oddities site.

**d.** Scroll down the MTV Animation page to view the list of animations.

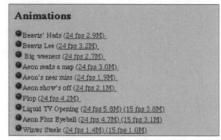

**1d.**

**e.** Click on an animation you would like to download. Several of the MTV animations are available as 24 fps (frames per second) or 15 fps. Note the difference in file size.

**f.** Netscape will begin the download immediately.

**g.** If you have a QuickTime movie player installed as a Netscape helper application, the player will launch when the movie is done downloading.

**h.** Click on the Play button on the movie controller bar to start the animation. **1g.**

**1h.**

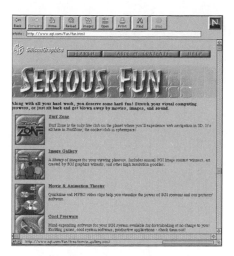

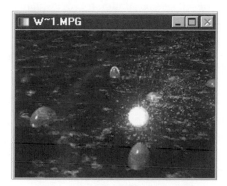

**1e.**

The Silicon Graphics Web site (http://www.sgi.com/Fun/fun.html) is where you'll see sophisticated, high-end 3D graphics and animation. According to Mark Rand (mark@oceana.com), a graphic systems integrator at Oceana in Orchard Park, NY, "the learning curve is tougher but the horsepower is much greater. In 3D graphics, horsepower represents fewer rendering hours."

The available movie downloads at the Silicon Graphics' site are both QuickTime and MPEG files. MPEG (Motion Picture Experts Group) movies' high quality is due to superior compression.

## 1. Download an animation.

**a.** The Movies and Animation Theater link will take you to a page of available movie files to download.

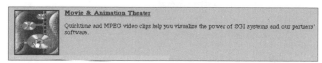

**1a.**

**b.** Click on any one of the animation movie links to start a movie download.

**1b.**

**c.** Netscape will begin the download immediately.

**d.** With an MPEG player configured as a Netscape helper application, an MPEG movie will launch when the movie is done downloading.

**e.** Click on the Play button on the movie controller bar to start the animation.

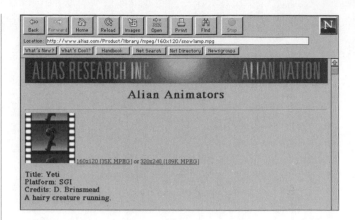

Alias and Wavefront, companies that were once separate business entities, have merged with Silicon Graphics. Both companies have a reputation for high-quality animation software that runs on high-end computer workstations. Visit the Alias Animators page (http://www.alias.com/Product/library/mpeg/160X120/snowlamp.mpg) or the Wavefront Animations page (http://www.alias.com/Day1/AliasWavefront-welcome.html) to view workstation-class MPEG animations.

### The WebForce Indy.

Although Microsoft and Apple intend to claim a portion of the 3D graphics and animation market, Silicon Graphics (SGI) is still king. Even the smallest of SGI's servers, the WebForce Indy, can multitask and handle an artist using authoring tools, serve Web documents in the background and withstand 600,000 hits per day. (The CPU will withstand more hits if the machine is dedicated to one task.) The company's larger servers, such as the Indigo2 and the Challenge, are popular for Web sites with very large bandwidth requirements, such as multimedia and new database applications.

Of the twelve largest sites on the Web, seven are set up on Silicon Graphics' machines. SGI has positioned their WebForce Indy as an integrated hardware and software solution for companies who want to publish and get online. The teal blue "screamer" has a price tag that may surprise many business people in the 3D market. The WebForce Indy bundle, which sells for $10,995, includes an 8-bit, 133 MHz

*Tip:* To stay current on developments in VRML *(Virtual Reality Modeling Language), visit* Wired's *VRML Forum at:*

http://vrml.wired.com/

*Tip: Mark Pesce, one of the key people who initiated the development of VRML (Virtual Reality Modeling Language), has written* VRML Browsing and Building Cyberspace. *Chapter 2, entitled "The VRML Equinox" (published by New Riders), can be found at:*

http://www.mcp.com/general/news7/chap
2.html

*Tip: A growing number of 3D application software programs support VRML.*

*Examples include* Strata's Studio Pro Blitz for Windows *(available in December '95) and Autodesk's next release of* 3DStudio *(available in the Spring of '96).*

*For information about software manufacturers which support VRML watch the following Web site:*

http://rosebud.sdsc.edu/SDSC/Partn
ers/vrml/about.html

*Tip: AdHoc Software has created a utility to convert Autodesk 3DStudio files to VRML (the utility is available on the CD-ROM in the back of this book).*

R4600 WebForce Indy with a 1 GB system disk, 32 MB of RAM memory and a 16-inch color monitor, Netscape's Netsite server software (a $1,495 value), Photoshop, Illustrator and WebMagic Pro (an HTML editor). Users can also opt to upgrade to the Netsite Commerce Server for conducting electronic commerce.

## Microsoft's pursuit of the 3D market.

Microsoft's move to acquire SoftImage has started to reshape the 3D graphics software market. Prior to the purchase, SoftImage, a highly revered 3D graphics program, only ran on high-end workstations. It now runs under Windows NT and has a much smaller price tag.

## Where is the 3D market?

3D graphics have been popular in the computer game, movie, and television industries—and the Web represents an untapped new market segment. Among the companies building Web strategies into their business plan, Silicon Graphics is one of the most aggressive. SGI has formed a "WebForce" division to market products for the Web. As a result of this marketing focus, the company has teamed up with Template Graphics to provide a publicly available file format for describing 3D graphics on the Web. VRML, or Virtual Reality Modeling Language, is an adaptation of Silicon Graphics' Open Inventor ASCII file format. Although SGI and Template Graphics adopted the idea, the driving force behind the VRML effort belongs to a group of far-sighted individuals who contributed to the idea long before computer firms were involved. The names include Mark Pesce, Tony Parisi, Brian Behlendorf, Gavin Bell, Paul Strauss and Robert Weideman.

## 3D applications that support VRML.

Software application programs that support VRML have a selection on the File menu for exporting a 3D image as a VRML file. The same applications also have built-in features that enable artists to specify the location of a "network anchor" or "hot spot." Network anchors are clickable spots in a 3D world that hold URL information. When clicked, the Web visitor hyperlinks or travels to a related Web site.

**1a.**

*Tip:* *Visit the IUMA Help page to download a movie player for Windows:*

```
http://www.iuma.com/IUMA-
2.0/help/help-windows.html
```

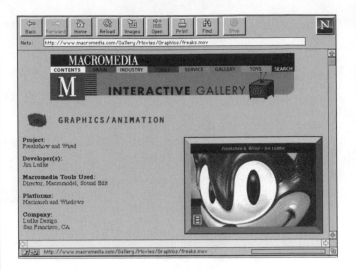

Although Macromedia is about to provide a unique new tool to deliver multimedia directly over the Internet, their Interactive Gallery contains interesting movie samples in a format that you'll need to download with a movie player application. Visit http://www.macromedia.com/Gallery/ Movies/Graphics/freaks.mov to see a clip of The Residents Freak Show. The movie you'll download will also contain artist Jim Ludtke's model for a *Wired* magazine cover.

## 1. Download an animation.

**a.** When you visit Macromedia's Interactive Gallery, click on the movie window to start the movie download.

**b.** Netscape will begin the download immediately.

**c.** With a movie player configured as a Netscape helper application, a QuickTime movie will launch when the movie is done downloading.

**d.** Click on the Play button on the movie controller bar to start the animation.

 **1d.**

*Tip: The Residents new CD-ROM, called Bad Day on the Midway, features more work from artist Jim Ludtke. Published by Warner Brothers/Home Box Office-backed Inscape, the new CD-ROM will be released on Halloween. Like the Freak Show, the CD-ROM will have a carnival theme and will feature Jim Ludtke's innovative new animation techniques. The Residents hot line:1-800-795-3933.*

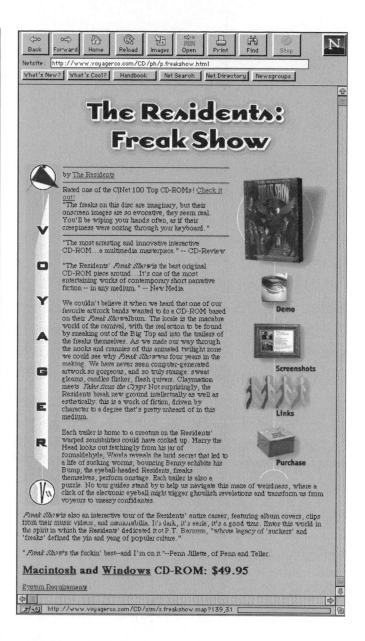

The Voyager site (http://www.voyagerco.com/CD /ph/p.freakshow.html) has animation clips available for downloading. However, the site is significant for several other reasons. For example, Web designers can familiarize themselves with Voyager's CD-Link technology, a technology that links Web pages to music CDs. (Voyager will give

**1a.**

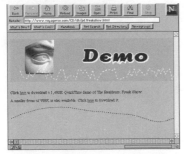

**1b.**

**1d.**

*Tip: Visit the IUMA Help page to download a movie player for Windows:*

`http://www.iuma.com/IUMA-2.0/help/help-windows.html`

a free license to companies that do not sell CDs.) If the subject of a Web site has anything to do with an audio CD and a Web visitor happens to have the CD, CD-Link will play a song or part of a song off the audio CD. For example, if the Web page contains a discussion about Sergeant Pepper and the Web visitor has Sergeant Pepper's Lonely Hearts Club Band on a CD, he or she can put in their audio CD and a song or any amount of music will play in response to a time code message sent from the Web page to the CD-ROM.

Voyager is also leading the way with Web commerce because they sell CDs on the Web via a secure server. NetGuide Magazine has praised their site, saying, "Voyager does commerce correctly." Trevor Kaufman, who runs Voyager's online department explains that the Web order form is encrypted and it's actually more secure than placing a similar order by telephone.

With online sales, Voyager has been able to drop the price of their expanded books from $20 to $5, since no packaging is required. Trevor feels customers are becoming less skittish about online transactions and the Web site now represents $5,000 a week in revenue.

### 1. Download an animation.

**a.** Click on the Demo icon.

**b.** Click on a movie link.

**c.** Netscape will begin the download immediately.

**d.** With a movie player configured as a Netscape helper application, a QuickTime movie will launch when the movie is done downloading.

**e.** Click on the Play button on the movie controller bar to start the animation.

 **1e.**

**2a.**

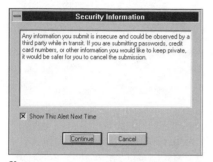

**2b.**

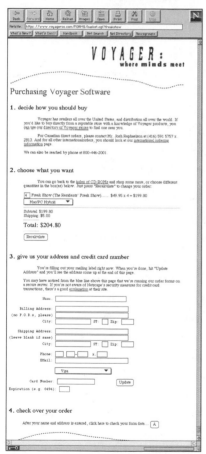

**2c.**

## 2. Order a CD-ROM online.

If you're interested in seeing how transactions are handled online, Voyager's site is certainly a model.

**a.** Click on the brown-paper package icon.

**b.** A secure document warning will be displayed explaining that the information you provide in the Voyager order form will be encrypted for privacy. Click on OK.

**c.** Fill out the Voyager order form.

**d.** Click on the Update button to register the item in your "virtual shopping cart."

**2d.**

**e.** Note the Netscape "secure server" icon. The small key in the lower-left portion of the Netscape browser window is now unbroken.

**2e.**

**f.** Click on the A button to review your order.

**g.** Click on the f button to register your form.

**2f.**

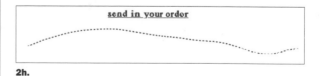

**2g.**

**h.** Scroll down to the bottom of the page and click on send in your order.

**2h.**

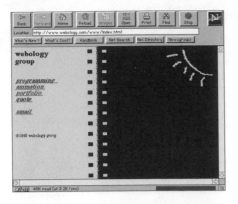

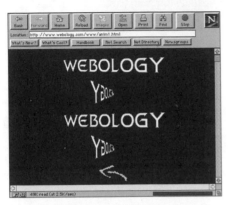

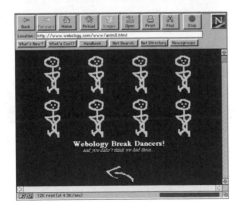

Inline animations, which are based on CGI scripts (Common Gateway Interface), are instantaneous because they're part of the Web page. Most of the programming is done using PERL, a powerful scripting language. Nicknamed "server-push" and "client-pull," the scripts consist of small executable programs that can make simple graphics wiggle, dance or move across a page.

Bill Murphy, a computer programmer and partner in the Webology Group (http://www.webology.com/www/index .html), explains that CGI animation scripts require that graphics be kept to a minimum. Artists can work out their ideas in Photoshop for speed, but the total combination of frames should not exceed 50 K.

Bill's firm is a Web design company that specializes in scripting. At this time, only 20 percent of the nation's Internet provider's allow CGI scripts on their servers, since CGI scripts are tricky and CGI scripting skills are hard to find. Many providers are also reluctant to put their customers' scripts on a server because bulky inefficient scripts can be detrimental to a server's performance. Other forms of CGI scripts provide Web pages with image map clickable hot spots for navigation and fill-in forms to collect data from Web visitors.

When Netscape Communications Corporation added the Webology Group (http://www.webology.com/www/animation.html) to their What's New What's Cool list, the number of hits to their server skyrocketed from 50,000 hits per day to 350,000. The group was not aware that they had been added to the list and had to optimize their server for the increased traffic.

### 1. To see an example of CGI animation.

**a.** Click on animation on the Webology home page.

**b.** Click on an animation link.

1a.

### 2. To see another example.

**a.** Click on the return arrow.

**b.** Click on another animation link.

2a.

1b, 2b.

### 3. Note the "open connection" light.

"Inline" animation is accomplished with a "server-push" technique, which maintains an open connection between the browser and the server. The Netscape's status bar at the bottom of the screen is filled in with red while the animation is running.

3.

# Web sites with 3D graphics

**Summary:** *Visit Time Warner's pathfinder site to see S.P.Q.R., an online adventure game containing scenes created in SoftImage. Also look for the S.P.Q.R. QuickTime VR movie of the Roman Forum on the CD-ROM in the back of this book.*

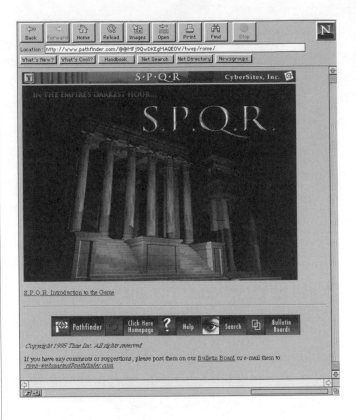

S.P.Q.R. (http://www.pathfinder.com/twep/rome/), an online adventure game with over 300 beautifully rendered scenes of ancient Rome, has a unique history of its own. Authors Eden Muir and Rory O'Neill are part-time professors at Columbia University's School of Architecture, founders of the school's Digital Design Lab and partners in Cybersites, a game development company specializing in the creation of 3D worlds.

## A story embedded in a real space.

Although very little of ancient Rome is standing today, Eden and Rory have worked hard to create a game that is historically accurate, combing through a library of over sixty books on ancient Rome to find historical facts. For example, the name S.P.Q.R. meaning the Senate and the People of Rome is an inscription that can still be seen throughout Rome. Recently, a professor of Archaeology at the University of Michigan wrote that he found the site so

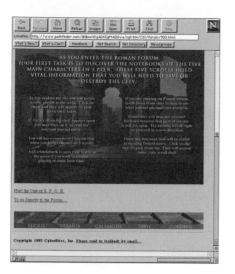

impressive that he intends to introduce S.P.Q.R. to his students and ask them to wander through the site and take in the Roman Forum.

### The "play."

There are two types of computer games. There are action games, which might be called arcade-style, and adventure games, which are mysteries to solve. An adventure game like S.P.Q.R. or Myst is divided into separate sections with separate puzzles. In Myst, the sections are called "ages," and in S.P.Q.R. they are called "chapters." During the game, a player looks for clues and objects that might help solve the mystery. Players navigate to one of the few exit portals, and if successful, they'll move on. Inside a chapter, events occur randomly and each player can have a unique, one-of-a-kind experience.

### Characters communicate with players.

Throughout the S.P.Q.R. game, players learn about events, clues and the history of Rome through scrolls belonging to each of the game's characters. In chapter one, players wander through Rome, collecting scrolls and getting acquainted with the characters. Characters Lucius, Verania, Calamitus, Sibyl and Gordian all have bookshelf areas along the bottom of the screen. As the game proceeds, an open scroll on the character's shelf indicates a character has something to communicate and a mouse click on the scroll displays a text message that will serve as a clue.

### Outcomes.

Adventure game players are not mere witnesses to events; their actions can determine an outcome. For example, S.P.Q.R. takes place during the late Empire when the city of Rome is threatened by vandal invasions. The character Calamitus is a vandal spy who wants to learn how to cripple Rome to help the vandals invade. At the end of Chapter 1,

*Tip: For instruction on how to run the QuickTime VR Player, see "Running the QuickTime VR Player" in the Photography chapter. Look for the S.P.Q.R. QuickTime VR movie of the Roman forum on the CD-ROM in the back of this book.*

while Calamitus is waiting to be tried by the State, the player's character is holding his journal. The trial will be jeopardized unless the player chooses to turn his journal over to the State.

### Web site beta testing for a future CD-ROM.

Eden and Rory will be developing new chapters for their free Web site game over the next eight months. Their objective is to build a multimedia-rich CD-ROM version, which will include QuickTime VR movies, sound effects and music. Although the Web version can only offer static images, Eden and Rory collect valuable feedback (via email) from Web visitors who play the game. As Rory explains, "game development is an iterative process. If several players complain that they cannot get into the Temple of Saturn, we know a change is necessary."

### Reality Action Graphics Environment (RAGE).

People who understand HTML know that a Web server does not know who you are or where you've been. Since it may take weeks to play an adventure game, a history of where each player has been is critical information that must be stored. Although players are encouraged to use Netscape's bookmark feature in the browser software, the uniqueness of each game requires that the server keep track of variables for each player's game. To compensate for an http server's inability to track history, Glen and Rory have developed *Reality Action Graphics Environment* or RAGE, which is designed to run on a Web server. They have plans to license the software to other game developers and will develop the software for a variety of server platforms.

### QuickTime VR.

Eden and Rory will be using Apple's new QuickTime VR technology in the S.P.Q.R. game. This cross-platform movie format offers a "virtual reality" experience in the form of a 320×240 (or full-screen size) 360 degree panoramic image. Depending on the complexity of the movie, viewers can rotate the scene around a stationary "node," zoom in or out and "navigate" objects by turning them upside down.

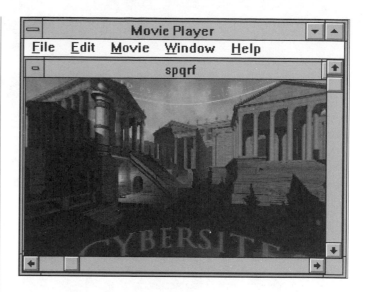

Complex "multi-node" movies allow viewers to travel to different nodes for a similar experience. In S.P.Q.R., viewers will see QuickTime movies as they navigate from node to node. As the QuickTime VR technology evolves, Apple plans to add music, interactivity and embedded URLs.

### QuickTime VR and game development.

QuickTime VR movies may be formed from either still photographs or computer-generated images. Although the development process is similar, rendered 3D images are a little easier to stitch together, since they're very precise and line up perfectly. *(Note: For more information, see "Digital cameras, Web photography and QuickTime VR" in the Photography chapter.)*

# VRML

*Summary: 3D graphics are hot and so is VRML, the language that describes 3D space on the World Wide Web.*

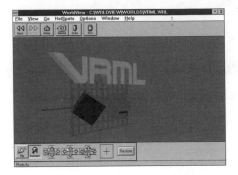

*Tip: To stay current on developments in VRML (Virtual Reality Modeling Language), visit* Wired's *VRML Forum at:*

http://vrml.wired.com/

*Tip: Mark Pesce, one of the key people who initiated the development of VRML (Virtual Reality Modeling Language), has written* VRML Browsing and Building Cyberspace. *Chapter 2, entitled "The VRML Equinox" (published by New Riders), can be found at:*

http://www.mcp.com/general/news7/chap2.html

*Tip: AdHoc Software has created a utility to convert Autodesk 3DStudio files to VRML. (The utility is available on the CD-ROM in the back of this book.)*

VRML (Virtual Reality Modeling Language) has an interesting history which began late in 1993 when Mark Pesce and Tony Parisi developed a three dimensional interface to the World Wide Web. When they described their interface to Tim Berners Lee, the software engineer who developed the World Wide Web, he invited Mark Pesce to present a paper at the First International Conference on the World Wide Web in Geneva Switzerland.

During that conference, the term VRML was coined and a mailing list was formed. Later, with support from the mailing list which quickly grew to one thousand members, the group (headed by Mark Pesce and Brian Behlendorf of *Wired* Magazine) decided to adapt Silicon Graphic's Open Inventor File Format to form the basis of VRML.

To make VRML an "open" file format, SGI contributed a file format parser to the public domain and has stated the Inventor File Format for VRML, a subset of the original Inventor File Format, should be available to the open market.

## How does an artist create a VRML file?

Software application programs that support VRML have a selection on the File menu for exporting a 3D image as a VRML file. The same applications also have built-in features that enable artists to specify the location of a "network anchor" or "hot spot." Network anchors are clickable spots in a 3D world that hold URL information. When clicked, the Web visitor hyperlinks or travels to a related Web site.

*Strata's Studio Pro Blitz for Windows* (available in December '95) and Autodesk's next release of *3DStudio* (available in the Spring of '96) are two examples of 3D applications that will support VRML.

## Following WWW anchors in VRML with the WorldView browser

**Summary:** *Use the WorldView browser, the first VRML browser to be released for the PC, to view VRML worlds and to jump to other VRML sites.*

**Tip:** *For information about 3D software manufacturers which support VRML, watch the following Web site:*

http://rosebud.sdsc.edu/SDSC/Partn

### 1. Open a URL for a site with VRML.
(Note: For instruction on locating the WorldView browser for your PC, see "Finding a VRML browser for your PC.")

**a.** Open the Netscape browser and click on the Open button in the Toolbar.

**1a.**

**b.** Type:

http://www.vrml.com/models/

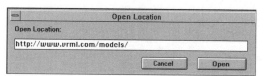

**1b.**

**c.** Scroll down the Web page and click on the startrek link.

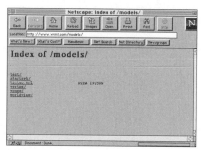

**1c1.**

**1c2.**

**d.** On the next Web page you'll see the "reliant" link. Click on the link.

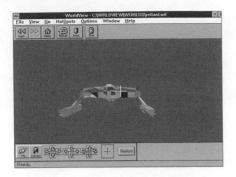

*Above:* *A view of the Reliant through the WorldView browser window.*
*Below:* *A view of the Reliant after navigating forward with the WorldView browser.*

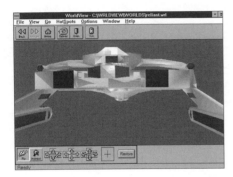

**3a.**        **3b.**

**4a.**

**4b.**

**e.** Netscape will begin the download immediately.

**f.** With the WorldView browser installed as a Netscape helper application, the browser window will open automatically when the file is done downloading.

## 2. Use the WorldView navigation crosshair.

The crosshair tool on the WorldView navigation panel will provide a means to navigate in 3D space. The mode buttons, which provide alternative navigation controls, are described in the next section.

**2a, 2b, 2c, 2d, 2e.**

**a.** Press and hold the mouse button above the crosshair to move forward.

**b.** Press and hold the mouse button below the crosshair to move back.

**c.** Press and hold the mouse button with the Shift key to pan.

**d.** Press and hold the mouse button with the Control key to pitch and roll.

**e.** Click on the Restore button to return to the first view you encountered.

## 3. Use the navigation modes (optional).

**a.** **Fly** mode moves you around a 3D world.

**b.** **Inspect** mode moves and tilts a 3D model.

## 4. Use the navigation arrows (optional).

**a. Move Forward**

• Fly mode moves the model closer to you.

• Inspect mode moves the model away from you.

**b. Move Backward**

• Fly mode moves the model away from you.

• Inspect mode moves the model closer to you.

**4c.**

**c. Look Left**

- Fly mode moves the model to the right.

- Inspect mode tilts the top of the model to the right (*Note: The Alt or Control keys act as accelerators to simulate spinning.*)

**4d.**

**d. Look Right**

- Fly mode moves the model to the left.

- Inspect mode tilts the top of the model to the left (*Note: The Alt or Control keys act as accelerators to simulate spinning.*)

**4e.**

**e. Tilt Left**

- Fly mode tilts your viewpoint to the right.

- Inspect mode tilts the top of the model to the left (*Note: The Alt or Control keys act as accelerators to simulate spinning.*)

**4f.**

**f. Tilt Right**

- Fly mode tilts your viewpoint to the left.

- Inspect mode tilts the top of the model to the right (*Note: The Alt or Control keys act as accelerators to simulate spinning.*)

**4g.**

**g. Look Up**

- Fly mode tilts your viewpoint up.

- Inspect mode tilts the top of the model toward you.

**4h.**

**h. Look Down**

- Fly mode tilts your viewpoint down.

- Inspect mode tilts the top of the model away from you.

**4i.**

**i. Move Up**

- Fly mode moves you up or moves the world down.

- Inspect mode moves the model up.

**4j.**

**j. Move Down**

- Fly mode moves you down or moves the world up.

- Inspect mode moves the model down.

### k. Move Left
- Fly mode moves the camera view to the left..
- Inspect mode moves the model to the left..

### l. Move Right
- Fly mode moves the camera view to the right..
- Inspect mode moves the model to the right..

## 5. Jump to another WWW location.

**a.** Click on an embedded URL or Web link *(Note: You'll know you've encountered a Web link when the pointer turns into a hand as you move it over the 3D model.)*

**b.** A click on the Web anchor on the side of the spaceship will *hyperlink* you to a page on Paramount's Voyager site, which Netscape will display in the background behind the WorldView window.

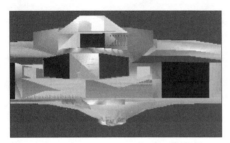

5a.

5b.

# Finding a VRML browser for your PC

***Summary:*** *Several VRML browsers are now available for the PC. Use this section as a guide for finding the right one for your computer.*

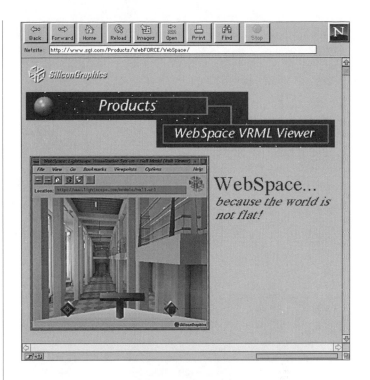

### InterVista's WorldView browser.

Look for the InterVista's WorldView browser at (http://www.webmaster.com:80/vrml/).

### WebSpace.

Look for the WebSpace browser at Silicon Graphics' site (http://www.sgi.com/Products/WebFORCE /WebSpace/) or the Template Graphics site (http://www.cts.com/~template/).

### WebFX.

WebFX, from Paper Software, (http://www. paperinc.com) is a browser designed to embed itself into Web browsers. WebFX supports 3D space in Internet Relay Chat (IRC) rooms.

### The Virtus browser.

Available in October or November of 1995, the Virtus VRML browser can be found on the Virtus Web site (http://www.virtus.com).

# Creating a Director movie for use with the Shockwave Director Internet Player

*Summary:* *Macromedia's new tool for playing Director movies on the Internet includes a new Player technology that will be integrated into the next release of the Netscape browser.*

The Director Internet Player described in this section is one step on the way to integrating Director's multimedia authoring with Netscape. As a helper application, the new player technology provides sound, animation and interactivity. When the Director Player is integrated into Netscape, movies can be "streamed" directly from the Web into the Player's memory and played before it's entirely received. This means no waiting for downloading!

Director movies created for the Web are created with Macromedia Director's software, but the size must be limited to 200 K. "Preprocessing" a movie with Macromedia's Afterburner software compresses a movie, and the Director Internet Player decompresses the file contents. In this section, artist Curtis Eberhardt (CurtisAE@aol.com) offers tips on how to limit the size of your Director movies

## 1. Import one bit images into Cast.

**a.** Select Cast from the Window pull-down menu. This will open the Cast window.

**b.** Click on the Cast window to select it.

**1a.**

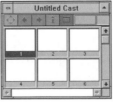

**1b.**

1c.

2a.

2b.

**c.** Select Import from the File pull-down menu. Director will display an Import File dialog box.

**d.** You can either import each cast member one at a time, or click on the Import All button to import several cast members at once.

**e.** Each file format may be imported separately into the Cast window as single cast members or in groups.

**f.** With the cast members imported, you can begin the process of authoring the movie in the Score window.

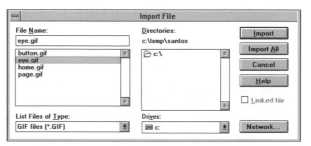

1d.

## 2. Move cast members to the Score window.

**a.** Click on a cast member in the Cast window to select the cast member.

**b.** Press and drag the cast member to a desired cell position in the Score window. (*The mouse pointer will turn into a hand while you drag.*) When the cast member is positioned over the desired cell position, release the mouse button. (*Note: At the same time the cell member fills a cell position, it will also appear on Director's Stage.*)

**c.** The cell where you dropped the cast member will contain an abbreviated number representing the cast member's number from the Cast window. (*Note: Cast members that occupy a cell position are no longer referred to as cast members. When you drag a cast member to the Score, it becomes a "sprite."*)

**d.** To see more information about a particular sprite than what can be seen in a cell, click on a cell to select it. Director will display the contents in the upper-left corner of the Score window.

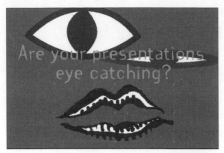

**3a.**

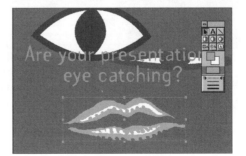

| Window | Cast | Score |
|---|---|---|
| Stage | | Ctrl+1 |
| ✓ Control Panel | | Ctrl+2 |
| ✓ Cast | | Ctrl+3 |
| ✓ Score | | Ctrl+4 |
| Paint | | Ctrl+5 |
| Text | | Ctrl+6 |
| Tools | | Ctrl+7 |
| Color Palettes | | Ctrl+8 |
| Digital Video | | Ctrl+9 |
| Script | | Ctrl+0 |
| Message | | Ctrl+M |
| Tweak | | |
| Markers | | |
| Duplicate Window | | |

**3b.**

## 3. Colorize one-bit cast members.

Limiting the bit-depth of a cast members substantially reduces the file size. One-bit cast members, which are black and white, can be colorized on the Director Stage to conserve on file size.

**a.** Click on an onstage cast member to select it. A bounding box will signify that the cast member is selected.

**b.** Select Tools from the Window pull-down menu.

**c.** With the cast member (or sprite) selected, click on the foreground color in the Tools window to open the palette. Drag to select a color.

**d.** When you release the mouse button, the cast member will take on the color you selected.

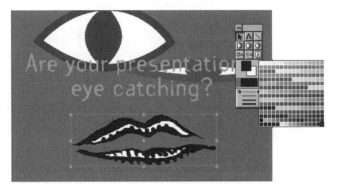

**3c.**

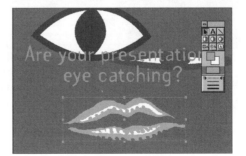

**3d.**

**4a.**

**4b.**

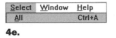

**4c.**

## 4. Use tiles to fill a background or other shape.

Tiles can be used to create a wallpaper effect on the Director stage. Because they are based on one small cast member, tiling is a way to conserve on file size. Use the Fill|Pattern command in Photoshop to experiment with the tile pattern.

**a.** Start by selecting an area of a Photoshop document you would like to see "tiled."

**b.** Select Define Pattern from the Edit menu.

**c.** To test the pattern, open a new document by selecting New from the File pull-down menu.

**d.** Enter 200 pixels in the Width box and 200 pixels in the Height box.

**e.** With the new test document open, select All from the Select pull-down menu.

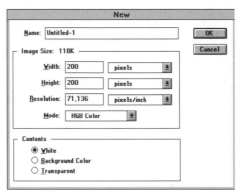

**4d.**

**f.** You'll notice the document is selected when you see a trail of "marching ants" around the perimeter.

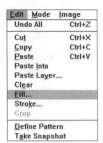

**4g.**

**g.** Select Fill from the Edit pull-down menu.

**h.** Select Pattern from the pop-up menu in the Fill dialog box.

**i.** Your document will be filled with the pattern you're testing.

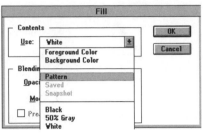

**4h.**

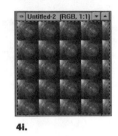

**4i.**

**j.** If you're satisfied with the tile and would like it to be available in Director, import the tile into Director's Cast window. (*See "Import one bit images into the Cast" for instructions on how to import the cast into the Cast window.*)

**k.** Open Director's Paint window by selecting Paint from the Window pull-down menu.

**l.** With the Paint window open, select Tiles from the Paint menu.

**m.** Click on the Cast Member radio button and click on the right and left arrows to locate the cast member you wish to tile.

**n.** Use the Width and Height pop-up menus to pick a size for the tile.

**4k.**

**4l.**

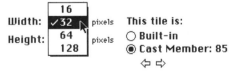

**4m, 4n.**

**4o.**

**o.** A small dotted rectangle will reflect the size of your tile in the tile window. Drag the small dotted outline to the area you would like as your tile.

**p.** Click on OK.

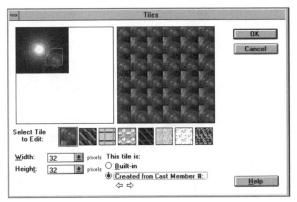

**4p.**

**q.** Your tile will become a pattern on the pattern selector chip at the base of the Tools window.

**4q.**

**r.** To create a tiled background, select the shaded half of rectangle tool from the Tools window.

**s.** Then use the tool's crosshair to drag a rectangle large enough to cover the Stage.

**4r.**

**4s.**

**t.** With the rectangle selected, select the pattern selector chip and drag-selected the new pattern.

**u.** When you let go of the mouse, the new pattern will fill the rectangle.

**4t.**

**4u.**

## 5. Check on cast member size.

The Bitmap Cast Member Info dialog box will provide valuable information about cast member sizes as you are building your movie.

**a.** Click on a cast member in the Cast window.

**b.** Select Cast Member Info from the Cast pull-down menu.

**c.** Notice the size is indicated in the dialog box that opens.

**5a.**

```
 Cast  Score   Text   Help
 Cast Member Info...    Ctrl+I
 Open Script            Ctrl+'
 Edit Cast Member

 Convert to Bitmap
 Transform Bitmap...
 Align Bitmaps

 Cast to Time
 Duplicate Cast Member  Ctrl+D
 Find Cast Members...   Ctrl+;
 Sort Cast Members...
 Cast Window Options...
```

**5b.**

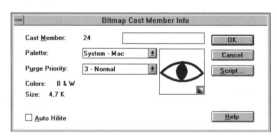

**5c.**

*Tip: For information and instructions on how to upload files to your Internet provider's server, see the Image Map chapter.*

**6a.**

## 6. Try remapping a color cast member.

Director's Transform Bitmap command allows you to alter the bit-depth of a color cast member and as a result, reduce the file size. Since this command cannot be undone, always test the remap on a copy of the cast member.

**a.** Click on a color cast member in the Cast window to select it.

**b.** Select Copy Cast Members from the Edit pull-down menu.

**c.** Click on an empty cast member position in the Cast window.

| Edit | Window | Cast | Score |
|------|--------|------|-------|
| Undo Score | | | Ctrl+Z |
| Cut Cast Members | | | Ctrl+X |
| Copy Cast Members | | | Ctrl+C |
| Paste Bitmap | | | Ctrl+V |
| Clear Cast Members | | | |
| Select All | | | Ctrl+A |
| Play | | | Ctrl+P |
| Stop | | | Ctrl+. |
| Rewind | | | Ctrl+R |
| Step Backward | | | |
| Step Forward | | | |
| Disable Sounds | | | Ctrl+~ |
| √ Loop | | | Ctrl+L |
| Selected Frames Only | | | Ctrl+\ |
| Disable Lingo | | | |
| Lock Frame Durations | | | |

**6b.**

**6c.**

**d.** Select Paste Bitmap from the Edit pull-down menu.

| Edit | Window | Cast | Score |
|------|--------|------|-------|
| Undo Score | | | Ctrl+Z |
| Cut Cast Members | | | Ctrl+X |
| Copy Cast Members | | | Ctrl+C |
| Paste Bitmap | | | Ctrl+V |
| Clear Cast Members | | | |
| Select All | | | Ctrl+A |
| Play | | | Ctrl+P |
| Stop | | | Ctrl+. |
| Rewind | | | Ctrl+R |
| Step Backward | | | |
| Step Forward | | | |
| Disable Sounds | | | Ctrl+~ |
| √ Loop | | | Ctrl+L |
| Selected Frames Only | | | Ctrl+\ |
| Disable Lingo | | | |
| Lock Frame Durations | | | |

**6d.**

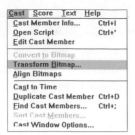

6e.

**e.** With the cast member copy still selected, select Transform Bitmap from the Cast pull-down menu to display the Transform Bitmap dialog box.

**f.** Select a smaller bit-depth from the Color Depth pop-up menu. Click on OK to remap the cast member to a smaller bit-depth.

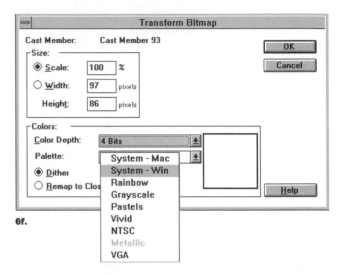

6f.

6g.

**g.** Double click on the cast member to examine the color in Director's Paint window.

**h.** Sometimes the color is acceptable at a smaller bit-depth; other times, it is not.

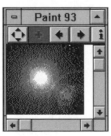

6h.

**7a.**

**7b.**

**7c.**

*Tip: To conserve on file size, try to use sound sampled at 11kHz rather than 22kHz.*

**8a.**

## 7. Use small sound snips and loop one or two.

**a.** Curtis used several small 2 to 4 K sound snips throughout his movie (Figure 7a).

**b.** To loop a sound, start by selecting a sound in the Cast window.

**c.** Select Cast Member Info from the Cast pull-down menu to display the Cast Info dialog box.

**d.** Click to put an X in the box labeled Looped. This will extend a sound without adding to the file size.

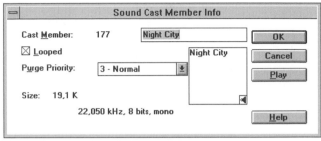

**7d.**

## 8. Use In-Between Linear to duplicate a sprite.

To copy a sprite into a group of contiguous cells, use Director's In-Between command.

**a.** Click on the cell in the Score window that contains a sprite you would like to duplicate. This will select the cell and its contents.

**b.** Drag to select the contiguous group of cells where you would like the sprite to be repeated.

**8b.**

**c.** Select In-Between Linear from the Score pull-down menu to fill the group of contiguous cells with the sprite.

**d.** Director fills the selected cells with duplicates of the original.

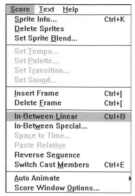

**8c.**

**8d.**

# Setting up a Web server

In this chapter, we will take an in-depth look at setting up and administering a Web server under Windows NT or Windows 95. We will explore O'Reilly's WebSite server software, one of the easiest and most complete server packages available for the Windows platform. A 60-day demo version is available on the CD-ROM included with this book.

# O'Reilly's WebSite software Overview

*Summary:* In this section, we will introduce the O'Reilly WebSite server package and discuss some of its general features.

This chapter focuses mainly on setting up a specific Web server, O'Reilly and Associates' WebSite. There are now many free and commercial Web servers available for both 16- and 32-bit Windows, but WebSite is one of the most complete and easy-to-use packages I've seen. In addition, WebSite is well-documented with a comprehensive manual, superb online help, and HTML pages, which explain recent additions and walk users through testing the server.

We've seen a variety of uses for WebSite, ranging from a full-time Internet-accessible World Wide Web server to an internal Web server on a LAN to a developmental server that is never made accessible to users. Since WebSite has such strong CGI script handling capabilities (discussed later in this chapter) it is ideal for use as a developmental server. Typically, a developmental server is not networked, or is networked only for testing purposes. A user in a developmental environment is usually checking to see how their Web pages run before uploading files to a full-time Internet-connected Web server.

### So what is a Web server, anyway?

A Web server is, perhaps, a much simpler program than you might think. The one requirement for a Web server is that it speak the language of the Web, HTTP (Hypertext Transfer Protocol). A Web server simply takes requests sent from a client (usually a Web browser such as Netscape) and returns the information that was requested. This is a simple client/server scenario, in which one computer requests information from another and the information is returned. Anyone who wants to provide Web documents from their computer must run a Web server so their machine will be able to understand requests made by other computers.

*Tip: You don't necessarily need to run your server locally. You can save a considerable amount of money by renting space from a service provider. And this doesn't have to be* your *service provider, nor does it have to be a provider in your local dialing area. However, do keep in mind that, when you rent space from a provider, you lose some degree of control over the daily operations of your server.*

## 1. 60-day fully functioning demo.

WebSite, which lists for $499 (though street prices may be less), makes setting up and administering a Web server a simple process. A
60-day fully functioning demo of WebSite is available on the CD-ROM that accompanies this book. The demo is also available from WebSite Central, a site that O'Reilly set up to support and market this product. WebSite Central runs off a single processor 90MHz Pentium with 65 MB RAM, Windows NT and the WebSite software. The address for WebSite central is:

`http://website.ora.com/`

## 2. E-mail and telephone support.

One of the many outstanding features that sets WebSite apart is O'Reilly's dedication to supporting this product. In addition to WebSite Central, O'Reilly offers excellent e-mail and telephone support to registered users for the first 90 days. If you would prefer to set up a different Web server, be sure to check what kind of product support is available, you may find yourself without any technical resources to consult should problems occur.

## 3. WebSite vs. Unix Servers.

WebSite is a full 32-bit application, which means, it will only run under Windows 95 or Windows NT. It will not run under Windows 3.11, even with Win32s. WebSite is easy to install and configure and, when run under Windows NT, it can compete with many high-end Unix servers. In fact, WebSite is limited only by a computer's hardware configuration. It also has some advantages over Unix servers such as graphical configuration and the ability to run Windows-based CGI applications.

The WebSite server is Robert Denny's 32-bit port of the popular WinHTTPD Web server package for Windows 3.1, which has been available on the Internet since early 1994 at:

`http://www.city.net/win-httpd/`

EMosaic

4a.

Image Map Editor

4b.

Server Admin

4c.

Web Server

4d.

WebIndex

4e.

WebView

4f.

The WebSite package was created in cooperation with Robert Denny and Enterprise Integration Technologies, Inc. (EIT).

## 4. WebSite's collection of applications.

The full WebSite product comes on two diskettes and installs in only a few minutes. A 350-page book provides complete documentaion. The WebSite package consists of the following applications:

**a. EMosiac.** Enhanced NCSA Mosaic 2.0 Web browser from SpyGlass.

**b. Image Map Editor.** A simple image map editor.

**c. Server Admin.** Graphical configuration tools for WebSite.

**d. Web Server.** The 32-bit Web server for Windows 95 or Windows NT.

**e. Web Index.** A tool used for indexing your HTML documents.

**f. WebView.** A valuable tool that helps you administer and maintain a Web site.

## 5. What you need before installing WebSite.

Since WebSite is a 32-bit Windows application, you must install it on a computer running either Microsoft Windows 95 or Microsoft Windows NT version 3.5 or later. We suggest as a minimal system, a 486 with 12 to 16 MB RAM, 5 MB free space (although you'll need much more for your HTML and graphic files), a VGA display and a 3 1/2" floppy drive. In addition, you must be running a TCP/IP stack, even if you do not plan to allow Internet access to your server. A TCP stack comes standard with both Windows 95 and Windows NT, but you may need to make sure that TCP/IP networking was added during the installation of your operating system.

Running a Web server over the Internet or over an internal network will require a network card or modem to be installed on your machine. You should also have the following information handy:

**a.** The IP address of your machine.

**b.** Your Fully Qualified Domain Name (FQDN), if applicable.

**c.** The e-mail address of the person who will administer the server.

**d.** The IP address of a DNS (Domain Name System) server and a backup DNS server.

If you plan on setting up a World Wide Web server (as opposed to an internal or developmental server), you should also have a dedicated connection to the Internet. While it's possible to run WebSite through an ordinary modem line with a PPP or SLIP connection, even a medium size site will require you to provide more bandwidth than a 28.8 Kbps modem. To obtain this type of connection, speak to an Internet Service Provider (ISP). Some major Internet access providers include Performance Systems International, Inc. (PSI), NETCOM, and AlterNet (UUNET). A large list of providers can be found at:

```
http://www.isp.net/pocia/
```

# Windows 95 or Windows NT?

*Summary:* Should you set up WebSite under Windows 95 or Windows NT? This section describes some of the pros and cons.

You may be wondering at this point whether to set up WebSite under Windows 95 or Windows NT. For a full-time, commercially accessible Internet World Wide Web server, there is little question that Windows NT is a better choice than Windows 95. However, for small-scale servers, and for servers running on an internal network (which is fast becoming known as the "Intranet"), Windows 95 is indeed a viable alternative. Not only are the hardware demands for Windows 95 not as great as they are for Windows NT, but Windows NT also doesn't offer the hardware support that Windows 95 offers. It may be impossible to install Windows NT on a machine that could otherwise function as your Web server.

Windows NT has many advantages over Windows 95, including more robust multithreading and multitasking, and greater security. In addition, Windows NT is capable of supporting more simultaneous users and has a better and more secure file system if you choose to use NTFS—the NT File System. Windows NT can also run on high-end, non-Intel platforms such as MIPS, Alpha and PowerPC as well as being able to take advantage of multiple processors in a single machine (multiprocessing). NT, unlike Windows 95, also has a POSIX component, which makes it possible to run Unix Shell scripts. If you are installing WebSite as a development platform, NT is the only option for testing standard Unix-style CGI scripts.

If you expect even moderate traffic on your Web server and you wish to use Windows 95, we strongly suggest using the computer as a dedicated machine—that is, a computer that functions solely as a Web server. Although Windows 95 is not as robust or secure as Windows NT, you may find that it more than does the job as an internal Web server or as a small, moderate-traffic location on the Internet. Robert Denny, the creator of WinHTTPD and the driving force behind the WebSite package, runs a small Internet site off of a laptop with nothing more than Windows 95, WebSite, and a 14.4 Kbps connection to the Internet. The address is:

```
http://solo.dc3.com/
```

## 1. Windows NT checklist.

If you are thinking about setting up a full-time Internet Web server to run under Windows NT, you should consider the following conditions:

**a.** Your computer's hardware. How much RAM can your system support? Not just how much is installed, because you will probably wish to add more RAM in the future as traffic at your site increases. An important point to remember is that the most stressed components on a server are RAM and the hard disk, not the computer's processor. Most modern processors (486/66 and up) can more than handle the demands of being a network server, but without enough RAM your system will slow to a crawl.

A medium to large size NT server should have 32 MB of RAM and be expandable to 128 MB. This may sound like a lot of RAM (and it is) but an equivalent Unix machine might easily require 64 MB. Also, a full installation of Windows NT can eat up 80 MB of hard disk space, so make sure you will still have room for the rest of your files! We have entered the age of cheap hard drives—get a minimum of a gigabyte for storage. Or better yet, get two!

**b.** Compatibility with Windows NT. Because of its advanced architecture, Windows NT will not support real-mode DOS device drivers. Real mode (as opposed to protected mode) drivers run on Intel CPUs, and usually load hardware devices. Real mode drivers have been in use since the introduction of the 8086 processor, and they require a specific memory address to run in, a fact that can cause conflicts with other programs. By not supporting real mode drivers, NT offers greater security and stability than standard Windows (including Windows 95) systems. Unfortunately, if no protected mode driver is available, there is a very real possibility that Windows NT may not recognize a key component of your system (such as your network card or CD-ROM drive). This makes it especially important to check ahead of time to see if Windows NT will work with your current hardware configuration.

**c.** When running WebSite under Windows NT, you will also want to consider whether to run the Web server as an application or as a service. A service in NT is very similar to a daemon under Unix or a TSR (terminate and stay resident) program in DOS. NT Services run continuously in the background, accepting requests from network clients. The chief advantage to running WebSite as a service is that users don't need to be logged onto the computer in order for the server to run. Of course, the computer must still be turned on for system services to work.

An advantage to running WebSite as an application is that it is easier to start and stop the server. This is especially useful if you are in a developmental environment. When WebSite is running as an application under NT, the minimized icon reflects when the server is busy or idle, which can be useful if you are troubleshooting.

## 2. A word about dynamic IP addresses.

Every computer with a direct or dial-up connection to the Internet has an IP address. An IP address consists of four groups of numbers separated by periods, referred to as a dotted quad. An example would be the IP address 255.255.255.255. Using a registered domain name, users can find your IP address by simply entering the domain name. When someone on the Internet requests your domain

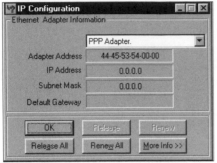

**2.**

name, the request routes to a DNS (Domain Name System) server which, in turn, connects the request to your IP address.

In a developmental environment, you can get a surprising amount of work done without ever connecting to the Internet. Throughout many of the examples in this chapter, we often use the URL syntax http://localhost/. This sends a request to the server without requiring a live connection to the Internet, an especially valuable technique if you do not wish to make your server public right away. You can replace this syntax with your domain name or IP address, but to do so you must be connected to the Internet.

If you are running a PPP (point to point protocol) Internet account and wish to run only a part time or developmental Web server, it is possible to run WebSite with a dynamic IP address. If you want others to connect to your Web through a dynamic IP address, you will need to figure out which IP address you have been assigned. A dynamic IP address changes each time you dial in over a modem PPP or SLIP connection, so keep in mind that if you use this addressing scheme, you will have to update the new address in the Server Admin application each time you reconnect. As the popularity of the Internet increases, more and more providers are adopting the dynamic addressing scheme as the pool of available IP addresses keeps shrinking.

Using dial-up networking in Windows 95, you can determine your IP address by running the WINIPCFG.EXE program located in your C:\WINDOWS directory (see Figure 2). This application is also available for Windows NT users using RAS (remote access services) in the software component of the Windows NT 3.5 Resource Kit, which can be downloaded from Microsoft at:

`http://www.microsoft.com/BackOffice/ntutil.htm`

### 3. Static IP addressing.

If you plan on running a full-time Internet server, a dynamic IP obviously will not meet your needs. You should either speak with your service provider about getting a static (unchanging) IP address or else find another provider. You will also need to request a registered domain name. It is

*Tip:* *If you're using Windows 95 and dial-up networking, a utility like Keep Goin' from Wintronix can automatically redial a dropped phone connection. A demo version is available on the CD-ROM in the back of this book.*

much easier to have users connect to your server with a domain name than it is to have them remember your IP address. In addition, if you change Internet providers or if your IP address changes, you can still have users connect to your new address through your domain name by updating information at the DNS servers.

The table below lists options for telephone connections.

| Connection | Description |
| --- | --- |
| Dial-up PPP | The least expensive option requiring a modem. The connection is made over standard telephone lines and is limited to 28.8 Kbps since phone line noise limits reliable transmissions to 31 Kbps or less. (Note: modem connections may drop; see information about Keep Goin' by Wintronix on this page.) |
| Dedicated SDN | Stepping up to ISDN should be to a dedicated ISDN connection, not to a dial-up ISDN connection. ISDN uses standard telephone lines but provides digital transmission via improved line-switching equipment. It uses two 56 Kbps at once giving a speed of 115 Kbps. It requires a router, which connects computers to phone lines. |
| Frame Relay | May be less expensive than ISDN since it is distance-insensitive. Several businesses share a high speed connection (usually a T1) and the sharing keeps costs down. |
| T1 | An abbreviated reference to a North American T1 Trunk cable, a cabling system that has much higher speeds than standard telephone cables. |
| T3 | Uses fiber optic cables to provide the fastest communication available. |

# Installing WebSite under Windows 95 or Windows NT

***Summary:*** *This section walks you through the individual steps to installing the WebSite server package.*

**1d.**

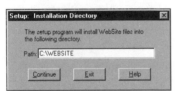

**2a.**

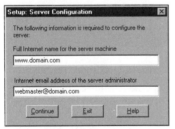

**3.**

Installing WebSite is an easy process that takes only a few minutes. Before beginning the installation process, you should make sure your computer meets the minimum requirements mentioned earlier in this chapter.

## 1. Start the installation.

**a.** Assuming your computer is turned on and Windows 95 or Windows NT is running, insert WebSite Disk 1 into your floppy drive. If you are using Windows NT, you must be logged on as an administrator.

**b.** Select Run from the Start menu on the Windows 95 taskbar. If you are running Windows NT, select File and Run from program manager.

**c.** Assuming your floppy drive is a:, type A:\SETUP then click on the OK button.

**d.** You should be prompted by a WELCOME TO THE WEBSITE SETUP dialog box. Click on the Install button to continue the WebSite installation.

## 2. Select an installation directory.

**a.** A dialog box will now prompt you for an installation directory. We recommend accepting the default C:\WEBSITE directory.

**b.** A dialog box will now prompt you to enter the full Internet name of your computer. You should enter your full domain name here, such as www.domain.com. (Don't enter the http:// portion of your address.) If you don't have a domain name, it is possible to enter your IP address instead. Again, if you are working in a developmental environment and do not plan on maintaining an Internet-accessible server, consider entering "localhost" as the domain name here.

## 3. Enter an e-mail address.

Enter an existing e-mail address where you want mail to be sent, such as webmaster@domain.com and click on the continue button. This entry should be an administrator's address, since WebSite will automatically generate error messages with a mail link to this address for reporting problems.

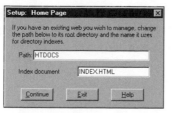

**4.**

**5.**

## 4. Enter the path to your Web.

Setup will now ask you to enter the path for your home page. We suggest using the default directory of HTDOCS, but if you already have an existing home page you should enter the full directory in the path field, such as C:\HOMEPAGE. If your home page is not named INDEX.HTML, you should change the "index document" field to reflect the name of your existing home page such as HOME.HTML or INDEX.HTM.

## 5. Complete the installation.

Insert Disk 2 when prompted, and setup will finish the installation. The WebSite server will automatically launch when the installation is finished.

# Testing the O'Reilly server

*Summary: This section offers suggestions for testing the server to make sure that it is set up correctly.*

*Tip: Once you have determined that the server is functioning properly, you should also try to access it from another computer with an Internet connection using all of these methods.*

**3a.**

**3b.**

O nce you install the WebSite package, you should test the server to make sure it was set up properly. The easiest way to do this is to load a test document installed by WebSite. It is not necessary to be connected to the Internet to run these initial tests.

Web Server

### 1. Start the Web Server.
Load the Web server by selecting the Web Server icon in the WebSite 1.0 program group. The server should appear on the screen for a few seconds and then minimize to your Windows 95 taskbar or NT desktop. Note that the server also starts itself at the end of the installation process, so this step may not be necessary.

### 2. Open a Web browser.
Start a Web browser, such as Netscape or the EMosaic browser, which comes with WebSite.

### 3. Test your IP address.
  **a.** Enter the URL of:

      `http://localhost/`

  and click on OK.

  **b.** If WebSite was installed correctly using all the defaults, typing this address should return the INDEX.HTML document located in the C:\WEBSITE\HTDOCS directory. The heading on the document should read "Your Home Page Goes Here" (see Figure 3b.)

  **c.** Clicking on the *WebSite Readme* link will lead you to several server tests that will ensure that your server is functioning. Take the time to go through these tests to verify that WebSite is set up properly. You don't want to configure the server only to discover later on that something isn't working right and that you need to reinstall the software.

**3d1.**

**3d2.**

**d.** You should also test the server by entering your IP address in the form of http://IPaddress/. You must be connected to the Internet to test your IP address. If your IP address is 255.255.255.255, enter the URL:

```
http://255.255.255.255/
```

If you have a registered domain name, you should also test that address in the form of:

```
http://domain name/
```

For example, if your domain name is www.domain.com, the address to enter would be:

```
http://www.domain.com/
```

Entering any of these addresses should return the same document that was returned using the URL:

```
http://localhost/
```

# Server Administration:
# Configuring your server's general properties

*Summary:* This section introduces the Server Admin utility, WebSite's graphical configuration program.

*Tip:* To access all the property pages in the Server Admin utility, use the arrow buttons on the upper right-hand corner of the application to scroll through the available options.

O ne of the most advanced and appealing features of O'Reilly's WebSite is its ability to configure the server graphically, rather than forcing you to edit configuration files in a text editor. Configuration of the WebSite server is done through the Server Admin program, which is located in the WebSite program group.

Server Admin

## 1. Server administration "property pages."

Server Admin is powerful not only for its graphical setup abilities, but also for its ability to make major changes to your server's configuration without stopping and restarting the Web server. You must, however, exit the Server Admin application before your changes will take effect. Server Admin beeps to let you know when changes have been updated. The Server Admin application has the following "property pages," or tabs, which help you configure the server:

| Property | Purpose |
|---|---|
| General | Configures the general properties of your server |
| Mapping | Configures directory and URL mapping (discussed later in this chapter) |
| Indexing | Configures WebSite's automatic directory indexing feature |
| Users | Sets user security access |
| Groups | Sets group security access |
| Access Control | Sets directory permissions |
| Logging | Configures WebSite's log tracing features |
| CGI | Configures how WebSite handles CGI scripts |

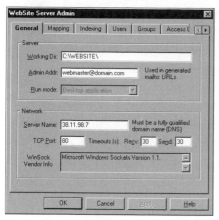

**2.**

*Tip: On a slow connection (such as a 28.8 Kbps modem), I recommend increasing the send/receive timeouts to 60 seconds.*

## 2. General configuration options.

Although the default installation of WebSite is generally enough to set up a simple server quickly, you will probably want to make some changes to the configuration after you have determined that the server is functioning.

The General property page in the Server Admin application (see Figure 2), lets you specify the server's working directory, the server administrator's e-mail address, run mode as an application or service (grayed out unless you are running Windows NT), your server's domain name, the server's TCP port (where requests and responses are routed), send and receive timeouts, and the Windows sockets version information.

In most cases, it will not be necessary to configure much from the General property page, but if you are running Windows NT, the General property page is the best place to change WebSite's run mode as a service or application.

If you are running WebSite on a relatively slow connection, such as a PPP connection, you might want to increase the send and receive timeouts. A timeout simply specifies the amount of time a server spends sending and receiving documents before automatically cutting off the request.

The General property tab also displays information about your Winsock version number, which should read Microsoft Windows Sockets Version 1.1. This information cannot be changed by the Server Admin application.

# Server Administration:

## Configuring MIME content types for your server

*Summary: This section discusses how to configure the server so that it will recognize the various types of files you wish to make available at your Web.*

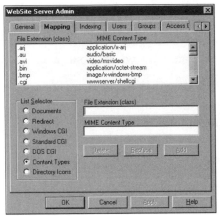

1a, 1b, 1c.

Server Admin

Now that you have a working Web server, one of the first things to consider is what types of files you will be serving. Whether you are serving HTML files, graphics, video or other multimedia files, you need to configure the server to provide information for each file type. Though WebSite comes configured to handle most common file types, you will probably wish to add new types sooner or later. Fortunately, this is an easy process.

The official HTTP specification states that Web servers should include Mime content type information with every document or file returned to a browser. By returning the content type information, a browser can quickly determine whether the file can be viewed directly or whether the browser needs to launch an external viewer or helper application.

Mime stands for Multipurpose Internet Mail Extensions, though it is also referred to as Multimedia Internet Mail Extensions. Mime is simply a standard for sending audio, video, graphics and binary files through the Internet. WebSite comes configured to handle 34 standard MIME types, and you can add or create new content types whenever necessary.

### 1. View WebSite's preconfigured Mime types.

**a.** You can view WebSite's preconfigured Mime types by selecting the Mapping property tab in the Server Admin application.

**b.** Click on the Content Types radio button to display Mime types.

**c.** Check this list carefully. If you are serving files from your Web that are not listed in this section, it will be necessary to add the new file types to your server.

### 2. Add a new Mime content type.

Let's say you've viewed the list of configured content types and want to add Adobe Acrobat files. Acrobat is a file type that users can view through Adobe's free Acrobat reader,

**2b, 2c, 2d, 2e.**

which is available on the CD-ROM that accompanies this book, or at Adobe's Web site at:

`http://www.adobe.com/Acrobat/`

To add this MIME content type, follow these steps:

**a.** From the Mapping property page in the Server Admin utility, select the Content Types radio button.

**b.** Enter the MIME type you wish to add into the File Extension field. If the extension is already mapped, it will highlight itself as you type. MIME types should be entered in the format of a period and the file extension. For example, if you are adding a MIME type for Adobe Acrobat files, you would enter

`.pdf`

in the file extension field, because that is the default extension of Acrobat documents.

**c.** In the MIME Content Type field, add the MIME type and subtype separated by a slash (/) that you want assigned to files with the .pdf extension. The content type must be one of the six types listed in the table below. Using the Acrobat example, you could enter

`application/acrobat file`

as the content type and subtype in this field. Note that the subtype can be any description you want. You could have just as easily have made the subtype "Adobe document."

**d.** Click on the Add button.

**e.** Close the Server Admin application by clicking on the OK button and the changes will take effect.

The following table lists the six content types supported by WebSite, referred to in 2c.

| Type | Description |
|------|-------------|
| **text** | Used to describe plain ASCII text files and HTML files |
| **image** | Used to describe graphic files that are not standard inline graphics, such as BMP (bitmap) files |

*Tip: Make sure you do not use the same document extension for multiple file types. For instance, if you are adding MS Word documents and WordPerfect documents, only one can use the file extension DOC.*

| | |
|---|---|
| **video** | Used to describe video clips such as MPEG and AVI files |
| **audio** | Used to describe audio clips such as AU files and WAV files |
| **application** | Used to describe files that require an external application to run, such as Acrobat or MS Word documents |
| **wwwserver** | A proprietary WebSite content type used for CGI applications |

You can add or delete MIME types from your Web server whenever necessary by simply updating the content type information.

# Server Administration:

## WebSite's Document Mapping

***Summary:*** *This section discusses how to map directories so that the WebSite server can find your files.*

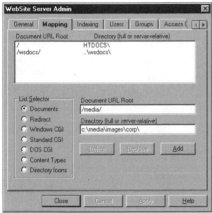

**1.**

Server Admin

If you plan on storing files in directories other than the default C:\WEBSITE\HTDOCS directory, it will be necessary for you to map these directories through WebSite's Document Mapping feature. *Document mapping lets the server know where to find files when a user enters a URL address in their browser.* This concept should make more sense in a few moments.

To understand document mapping, you should first understand how the WebSite server and most HTTP servers handle directories. By default, the WebSite server document root directory is C:\WEBSITE\HTDOCS\. If a user types the http://localhost/ URL the WebSite server returns the INDEX.HTML document contained in this directory. If there is no INDEX.HTML document and automatic directory indexing is enabled, the server returns the contents of the directory, with icons representing each file.

Let's say you have an archive of media clips you would like to make available on your Web site stored in the directory C:\MEDIA\IMAGES\CORP. You could also have files on another physical or network drive, but let's say that your files are located on the C drive. Since this directory is not contained under the server's document root directory, you need to map it so that the server can find your files. An added bonus to doing this is that you may now rename the directory with a more intuitive name, such as Media.

### 1. Map a document directory.
Using the C:\MEDIA\IMAGES\CORP directory, let's use document mapping to redirect the server whenever the URL http://www.domain.com/media/ is entered. Follow these steps:

**a.** Under the Mapping property page in the Server Admin utility, select the Documents radio button.

# WebSite Server

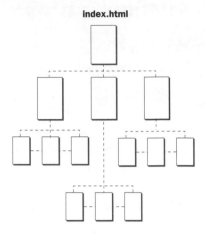

index.html

## c:\media\images\corp
### directory

Through WebSite's Document Mapping, shortened, intuitive names can be used to refer to directories. For example, a directory named: c:\media\images\corp can be shortened to \media\.

(Note: This index.html page is considered a home page since it's the default page for this Web. This page will be returned when Web browser sends a request: www.domain.com/media.)

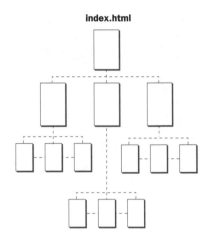

index.html

## c:\HTDOCS
### directory
### (server root)

If you plan on storing files in directories other than the default C:\WEBSITE\HTDOCS directory, it will be necessary to map these directories through WebSite's Document Mapping feature.

(Note: The index.html page in the HTDOCS directory is considered the primary home page.)

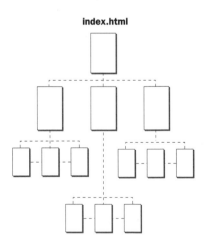

index.html

## c:\media\finance\corp
### directory

If an index.html document exists, the server returns it as a default page, if not, it returns a directory (see *Indexing Overview*).

**2e.**

**b.** In the Document URL Path field, enter the name of the redirected URL path enclosed with a forwardslash (/) on either end. In our example, we will enter

`/media/`

by itself to reflect the path.

**c.** Enter the directory name of your files in the Directory field. Although you can use relative path names, We suggest using the complete pathnames in this field. In our example, you would enter the following:

`C:\MEDIA\IMAGES\CORP\`

Note that you should use the regular DOS backslash (\), not the Unix-style forward slash (/).

**d.** Click on the Add button.

**e.** Now close the Server Admin application by clicking on the OK button. (Note: Remember that changes you make in Server Admin do not take effect until you exit the utility.) You should hear a beep after a few seconds.

**f.** Now, using your Web browser, type in the URL you have redirected. Using our example, type:

`http://localhost/media/`

If no INDEX.HTML document is located in this directory and directory indexing is enabled. (See *Indexing* in the next section—directory indexing is enabled by default), this URL should return the contents of C:\MEDIA\IMAGES\CORP\.

# Server Administration:

# Redirecting Web visitors to other sites

*Summary: This section discusses how to use URL redirection, a useful feature for directing traffic at your Web.*

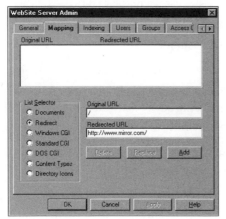

**2.**

Server Admin

With directory mapping, you can create multiple Web sites on the same disk. Let's say you are setting up a Web site for a company with several departments. You can easily create files for each department in their own directory and assign users their own path name. We will discuss this option further in the indexing section of this chapter.

## 1. URL redirection.

You would only use document mapping to redirect the server from one directory to another on your physical site. But what if you want to redirect users to an entirely different site? To do this, you must use URL redirection.

URL redirection is most useful if your site is mirrored on separate servers. Let's say you are revamping your server or you are having problems with your site and don't want users accessing your files, but you also don't want your information to be inaccessible. You could still run the server and use URL redirection to send users to the mirror site.

## 2. Redirect Web visitors to a mirror site.

Let's say that you are making extensive modifications to your site and you want to redirect people to a mirror site that exists at the imaginary URL http://www.mirror.com/. Follow these steps:

**a.** In the Server Admin application, select the Redirect radio button on the Mapping property page.

**b.** In the Original URL field, enter the name of the URL you want to redirect. Do not include any http:// information in this field. In our example, we are redirecting our root URL, and would simply enter:

/

**c.** Now enter the URL where you want to send users in the Redirected URL field. You must include the http:// information in this field. Using our example, you would enter:

```
http://www.mirror.com/
```

*Tip: You can also redirect URLs on a per-document basis by simply entering information in the format of www.domain.com/document.html in the original URL field.*

d. Click on the Add button.

e. Close the Server Admin application by clicking on the OK button. After you hear the beep, you know that the information has been updated.

f. Now test the redirection by typing your URL into your browser. In our case, we would type:

```
http://www.domain.com/
```

The server should redirect to our mirror site, in this case http://www.mirror.com/. You need to be connected to the Internet or network to test URL redirection.

Redirecting URLs is something you would only want to do on a temporary basis. There is little use in running a Web server that only directs traffic to other locations.

# Server Administration: CGI mapping

*Summary: This section discusses CGI mapping.*

**1.**

The same concepts that apply to document and URL mapping apply to standard, Windows, and DOS CGI mapping. Here, however, the server must be told when a program is an executable CGI program or else a user entering the URL containing the CGI executable script, for example:

Server Admin

```
http://www.domain.com/cgi-bin/webfind.exe
```

would be prompted to download the executable file! Therefore, it is necessary to map directories where CGI programs will run. We do not suggest that novice users change these settings, and instead should run CGI programs from the regular CGI directories.

## 1. WebSite directories for CGI applications.
*(Note: The "cgi-bin" directory doesn't exist in the WebSite path, but if you enter this URL, it launches the WebFind CGI program contained in the C:\WEBSITE\CGI-SHL\ directory. This is because WebSite installs with this directory already mapped. We'll discuss the WebFind program later in this chapter.)*

The table below lists default WebSite directories.

| Directory | Pathname |
|---|---|
| C:\WEBSITE\CGI-SHL | Standard CGI and CGI shell scripts |
| C:\WEBSITE\CGI-WIN | Windows CGI programs |
| C:\WEBSITE\CGI-DOS | DOS CGI programs |

# Server Administration:

# Using the Image Map Editor

*Summary: Image maps can add a new level of functionality to your Web site. Here, we explain how image mapping works with the WebSite server.*

*Tip: While the map editor can read BMP files, if you are creating maps to be used on the Internet, you will want to use a standard GIF image.*

**2.**

Image maps are easy to do and, when used tastefully, can add a greater level of functionality to your Web site. For example, let's say you want to direct people from various parts of the country to different areas on your Web

Image Map Editor

site. You could easily incorporate a clickable GIF map of the United States, where a user would click on the area he or she is connecting from and be directed to the appropriate area on your Web.

WebSite comes with a simple utility for creating image maps. It is important to note that WebSite handles image maps differently than most Unix-based servers, in that the information saved in the Image Map Editor program is saved directly into the Windows 95 or Windows NT registry. By entering this information in the registry, rather than in a separate map file, WebSite offers a slight speed advantage in processing image map requests. The next version of WebSite, due out by the end of 1995, should have the ability to process standard NCSA or CERN image map files.

## 1. Open Image Map Editor.
You may be surprised at how simple it is to work with Image Map Editor. To start the program, select the Image Map Editor from the WebSite program group. Image Map Editor launches with a blank screen. *(Note: In order to create a new image map, you should already have an existing GIF image to map and an idea of where you would like clicks on the image to lead.)*

## 2. Select a GIF file.
Select the GIF file you would like to map by opening the Edit menu, and then choosing Select Image. Image Map Editor prompts you with an Open dialog box, which will allow you to browse for the image you would like to map.

## 3. Enter a background URL.
Image Map Editor then prompts you to enter a target URL for your map. The target URL is the address that loads if a

*Tip: Use absolute URLs when mapping an image. Relative URLs do not always process correctly.*

**4a.**

user clicks outside any of the target areas of your image map. You don't have to enter a target URL, but it is generally a good idea, even if it only reloads the current document. You may also enter a description of the URL in the description field. The information entered in the Description field is useful if you need to go back and edit the map later, but this information will not display in your document.

## 4. Map the image.

**a.** Once the background URL is entered, you can start mapping the image. Image Map Editor lets you select regions of your image with a rectangle tool, an ellipses or circle tool, and finally, a freeform polygon tool. Use these tools to map out "hot spots" on your image. *(Note: After drawing a shape with one of these tools, a dialog box will pop up requesting a URL.)*

**b.** Enter the target URLs.

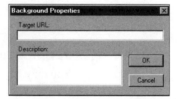

**4b.**

## 5. Save your map.

Choose File then Save As and assign a name to your new image map.

## 6. Create the HTML code.

**a.** Once you have the GIF mapped, you need to enter the HTML code in your document that lets the server know the image loading is an imagemap. This should be done using the following format:

```
<A HREF="/~imagemap/MAPNAME">
<IMG SRC="GIF FILE" ISMAP>
</A>
```

For example, if you named your image map WFC, and your GIF file was named WFC.GIF (it's generally a good idea to give the image map the same name as the map file for tracing purposes) you would enter the following into your HTML document:

```
<A HREF="/~imagemap/WFC">
<IMG SRC="wfc.gif" ISMAP>
</A>
```

The tilde portion of the HTML coding is unique to WebSite. This syntax instructs WebSite to pull image map information out of the Windows registry.

**b.** Once you have coded your document, you should test it to make sure the image map is functioning properly.

# Server Administration:

## Indexing Overview

*Summary: This section discusses the Automatic Directory Indexing feature of WebSite, which allows you to provide an FTP-like environment without installing an FTP server.*

Server Admin

The Indexing property page in the Server Admin application controls WebSites' automatic directory indexing feature. This shouldn't be confused with indexing your site with WebIndex for keyword searching.

WebSite is capable of automatically indexing and displaying whole directories whenever a browser requests a location on your Web that doesn't contain an index document. In short, WebSite can act as a simple FTP (file transfer protocol) server when the automatic indexing feature is enabled. By default, automatic indexing is enabled during installation. You should note that WebSite is limited to acting as an FTP server only, which means that users cannot upload files, they can only download them.

### 1. Automatic indexing adds functionality.

Why would you want to enable FTP services when you can create a fancy Web site? There are several reasons. Let's say, for example, that you are a software developer and release add-in programs or software patches for your users to download every week or so. All your users really need is a very brief description of the file. Any HTML page you created would probably only be a list of links. In addition, the HTML page would have to be recoded every time new files were made available. Using automatic directory indexing, you can have the server take care of creating the links, while still providing some information about the files you are making available. Of course, you should keep in mind that automatic directory indexing can be used in addition to your regular Web pages, so you can offer both the fancy Web site and the more functional FTP services from the same server.

Control of automatic directory indexing is handled on the Indexing property page of the Server Admin application. The most important thing to recognize on the Indexing property page is the "index" field under the Special

**1.**

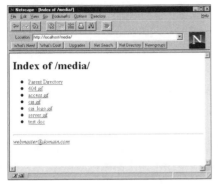

**1a.**

*Above:* Standard directory
*Below:* Extended directory

**2.**

Documents section. This field controls the name of the document that loads as your home page. By default, WebSite tries to load a document named INDEX.HTML every time any directory on your Web is accessed. If a directory does not contain this document, an automatic directory index is generated by the server, displaying all the files contained in the path. If you don't ever want WebSite to reveal directory contents, simply uncheck the Enable Indexing box. If directory indexing is disabled, the server will simply return an error message whenever a directory was incorrectly entered in a URL address.

Of course, you might only want some files in a directory to automatically display. You can prevent specific files from displaying by entering the file type in the Ignore Patterns section of the Indexing property page. For example, many people keep newer and older files in the same directory by renaming the older file's extension to .bak. Let's say we're making a file available on our site named PROGRAM.EXE. This file is replacing an older version that we don't want to lose track of, so we might rename the older file PRO-GRAM.BAK. Then, by entering *.bak in the Ignore Patterns section of the Indexing property page, the server knows not to display any files with the .bak extension.

WebSite supports two types of automatic directory indexing—standard and extended. Standard directory indexing can be used to create a very simple listing of files very quickly. For an example of a regular directory index generated by WebSite, see Figure 1. We think most people will want to use extended directory indexing, however, and extended directory indexing is enabled by default.

## 2. Extended directory indexing.

Extended directory indexing is far more flexible and visually attractive than standard directory indexing. For an example of an extended directory index, see Figure 2.

The server takes care of several things for you when you enable extended directory indexing. While standard directory indexing simply displays the names of files in a directory as a bulleted list, extended directory indexing automatically displays additional file information including the file's name, the date it was last modified, file size, and a file description. This information is separated on the top and bottom of the screen by a horizontal rule. The directory listing also includes icons representing the various recognized MIME types, such as graphics, video and sound files. The icons WebSite uses to signify MIME types are controlled in the Server Admin utility under the Mapping property page.

**c:\media\finance\corp directory**

**If an index.html document exists, the ser returns it as a default page, if not, it retu a directory.**

**index.html**

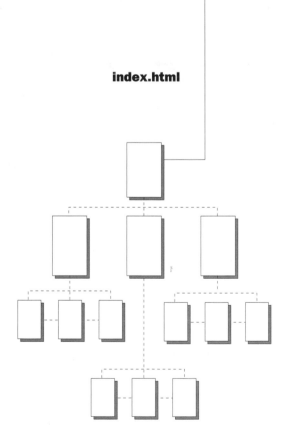

# Server Administration:

# Adding icons for extended directory indexing

***Summary:*** *You can add custom icons for your automatic directory indexes. This section explains how.*

**1.**

***Tip:*** *Be consistent with your MIME types. MIME content types should be entered the same way when configuring directory icons as they were when configuring MIME types.*

L et's say we would like to add an icon to signify when a file is a Microsoft Word document. First, create a small GIF file that you want to represent Word documents and save it into the C:\WEBSITE\ICONS\ directory, which is the directory where the WebSite server looks for icons.

Server Admin

## 1. Identify the file icon.

You can make this new icon available to the server by following these steps:

**a.** Start the Server Admin application and select the Mapping property page.

**b.** Click on the Directory Icons radio button.

**c.** Under the Mime Content Type field, enter the Mime type in the format of type/subtype. If you are adding a new Mime type, you need to enter it in the Content Types field first (see *Add a new Mime content type* later in this chapter) Since Word documents are already a registered MIME type with WebSite, we can enter the information into the MIME Content Type field as simply:

```
application/msword
```

which is also how it appears in the Content Types listing.

**d.** Next, add the name of the GIF file in the Icon File for Directory Listings field. There is no need to enter the path in this field, just the name of the file.

**e.** Click on the Add button.

**f.** Close the Server Admin application by clicking on the OK button. When you hear a beep, your changes have taken effect. (Note: Whenever a file with the registered MIME extension of DOC is located in a directory where an automatic index is generated, the new icon will appear next to the file name.)

# Server Administration:

## Adding header and footer files to directory indexes

*Summary: You can jazz up your automatic directory indexes by including header and footer files that display every time an indexed directory is generated.*

Server Admin

Open the Server Admin application and look at the Indexing property page. Notice that under the Special Documents heading, there are fields that specify Header, Footer, and File Description file names.

### 1. Creating a header file.

By creating these special files, you can include additional information that will display whenever a directory index is created. WebSite looks for these special files with either an HTML or TXT extension. For example, if you create a document named #HEADER.HTML, and place it in the directory that is to be automatically indexed, the server will load this file as a header each time a directory index is generated.

You must follow special HTML coding conventions when creating these files. In the header file, you must include the standard beginning tags, including <HTML>, <HEAD>, </HEAD>, <TITLE>, </TITLE>, <BODY> and any other tags you may wish to include. You should not, however, include the closing </HTML> and </BODY> tags or else the header will not display properly. An example header follows:

```
<HEAD>
<TITLE>Automatic Indexing Example</TITLE>
</HEAD>
<BODY>
<H1>Welcome!</H1>
With WebSite, you can index a variety of files in an FTP-
like environment. Here, several files have been set up
with this default header. Neat, huh?
```

### 2. Creating a footer file.

The footer file works in a similar way, but you should not use the <HTML> or <BODY> start or end tags. A footer file can, in fact, be plain text and it will be formatted by the server. Here is a very simple footer file:

```
Thank you for visiting our site! Be sure to check back
often for new updates.
```

**Header**

**3.**

**Footer**

**File Description**

When saved as #FOOTER.HTML and placed in the directory to be automatically indexed, this footer will display whenever someone accesses the directory through their browser.

### 3. Creating file descriptions.

You can also add custom file descriptions by including a file named #FILEDESC.CTL in the directory you are indexing. This can be helpful if you want to explain the contents of a file the user is downloading.

This file should be saved as a plain text file, and should be written in the format of (file name)|(file description) with an initial entry (which will be used to describe the "back" button) starting with two periods and a vertical bar "|". (*Note: The vertical bar is located over the backslash character on most computer keyboards.*) The easiest way to understand this file is to look at a sample:

```
..|Back to the home page
aroma.wav|<a href="readme.txt">Read me first!</a>
dante-sp.mpg|a sample movie file
u_constr.gif|under construction GIF file
bio.gif|Picture of a scientist
```

Note that this sample includes a hyperlink to another file, in this case README.TXT. You can add hyperlinks like this to your file descriptions if you feel that more information might prove useful to someone downloading from your site. Figure 3 shows the finished directory with a header file and file descriptions.

Automatic directory indexing is a powerful feature of WebSite and has many applications. A good example of an automatically generated directory index can be found at WebSite Central at:

```
http://website.ora.com/software/
```

# Server Administration:
## Limiting access to your Web site

*Summary: WebSite comes with excellent security for controlling who has access to your Web site. This section shows you how to block out certain sections of your site.*

*Tip: If you are interested in learning about the remote administration features of WebSite, take a look at:*

http://website.ora.com/devcorner/
white/remadmin.html

Server Admin

S ooner or later, you will probably find yourself wanting to keep certain users out of portions of your Web site. You may have areas under development that you don't want people to see, or you may be running a server over an internal network that contains sensitive information, such as human resources records. Perhaps you even want to build areas of a public site that are meant only for special customers. This is all easily accomplished.

WebSite comes with built-in security that is compliant with the HTTP standard of Basic Authentication. It is an easy matter to limit access of whole directories to individual users or groups of users. You cannot, however, block out access to individual files. Access control must be applied on a per-directory basis.

### 1. Security concepts.

Before taking steps to make your Web secure, you should understand security concepts as they apply to WebSite. WebSite creates three separate areas that are used to control security, namely Users, Groups and Realms. A User is simply an individual who might try to access your Web site. A Group is a collection of users who share common access privileges. Realms are collections of users and groups. For practical purposes, most users will only need to deal with users and groups.

Two groups are created automatically in WebSite, the Users group and the Administrators group. Everyone is part of the User group by default and this cannot be modified. By having everyone belong to one common account (Users), it is easy to modify security on a global user level, should the need arise.

### 2. Activate the administrator's account.

The first thing you should do if you want to block out certain portions of your Web is to activate the administrator's account, which is simply named Admin. Activating the

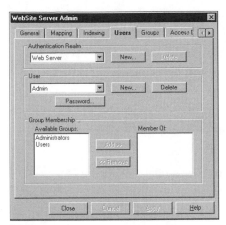

**3a, 3b.**

**3c, 3d.**

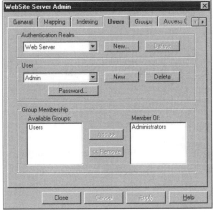

**3e, 3f.**

Admin account will make it easier to restrict URLs, cycle server logs (see the Server Administration: Logging section of this chapter), and is also useful if you plan on using WebSite's remote administration features.

### 3. Activating the Administrator's account.

**a.** In the Server Admin application, click on the Users property page.

**b.** Make sure that Web Server is selected in the pull-down menu in the Authentication Realm field and then click on the User pull-down menu below it and select Admin.

**c.** Click on the password button, and a dialog box will pop up prompting you for a name, password, and password confirmation. By default, the Admin account does not have a password, so skip the Old Password field and tab down to the New Password field.

**d.** Enter your password and then tab to the next field to enter it again (for confirmation). Remember your password for future use.

**e.** Click on the OK button. The Group Membership field should now list Administrators and Users as the available groups to join.

**f.** Click on the Administrators group and then on the Add button.

**g.** Click the Close button to exit the Server Admin utility. You should hear a beep after a few seconds.

You have now activated the Admin account as a member of the Administrators group.

**5a, 5b.**

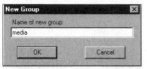

**5c.**

**6a.**

*Tip: If you wish to set directory permissions for individual users instead of groups, you need to enter names as a full text string without spaces. For instance, you could enter a user's name as either Peter or Peter_Pendragon, but not as Peter Pendragon.*

## 4. Simplify server administration with groups.

When protecting access to your Web site, it is best to use a three-step method of creating a group, adding users to the group, then setting security access for the group. While WebSite can set permissions for individual users, it is much easier from an administrative point of view to control access from the group level.

Let's password protect our virtual directory of /media/ so that only people who belong to our Media Group (a group we will create) can have access to the files:

## 5. Create a Group.

**a.** First, you should create a new group for users to join. Start the Server Admin application and select the Groups property page.

**b.** Make sure the Web Server item is selected from the pull-down menu in the Authentication Realm section.

**c.** Next, click on the New button next to the Group pull-down menu and a dialog box will appear where you can type in the name of the group to be created. In this case, we'll name our group Media. Then click on the OK button. You have now created a group named Media with no users.

**d.** Notice that when you click on OK, the Admin name appears in the Non-members area of Group Membership.

## 6. Add users to the group.

**a.** Now select the Users page from the Server Admin application, again making sure that Web Server is selected from the initial pull-down menu under Authentication Realm.

**6b.**

**7a, 7b.**

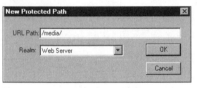

**7c.**

*Tip: Once the server determines that a user has access to a given directory of your Web site, the user is allowed to access the entire protected directory and all its subdirectories without requiring additional password confirmation.*

**b.** Click on the New button in the User section and a small dialog box will prompt you to enter a name, a password, and a password confirmation. Enter this information and click on the OK button. For our example, we'll create the user named Peter, and give him the password "green." Notice that the password does not display as text on the screen so that no one can see the password that is entered.

**c.** If you created the Group item correctly (see step a, Create a group) Media should be listed in the Available Groups section. Select Media and click on the Add button. The group name should move from the Available Groups to the Members Of section.

## 7. Set directory permissions.

Now you have created a user and a group. The next step is to attach either the user or group to a directory. Again, for administrative purposes I suggest controlling access on a group level. Attaching groups to a directory can be accomplished by following these steps:

**a.** Select the Access Control page in the Server Admin application.

**b.** Since we are adding a mapped directory, it will be necessary to add the path manually in the URL Path or Special Function field. Click on the New button in the upper right-hand corner and a dialog box will appear.

**c.** Enter the URL path you wish to restrict and the Realm to attach it to (which should say Web Server, in this case). Type the URL path without the http:// informa-

**7d.**

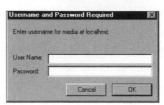

**8.**

tion into the first field. In this case, we want to restrict our media files, so we type in the URL of /media/ and click on the OK button. Remember, the server already knows that /media/ is really:

`C:\MEDIA\IMAGES\CORP`

Make sure that the /media/ directory remains selected and move on to the next step.

**d.** Under the Authorized Users & Groups section, click on the Add button and a list of names should appear with the user and group you created. Highlight either the user or the group and click on the OK button. Groups will appear surrounded in brackets [ ] whereas individual names will appear without brackets. Again, we recommend adding the group so that you won't have to deal with individual user accounts if access privileges change. The name you selected should now appear under Authorized Users & Groups.

**e.** Close the Server Admin utility by clicking on the Close button and your changes will take effect.

## 8. Test access to your server.

Now, try to access the restricted area of your Web from your browser. In the case of our example, we would enter the URL:

`http://www.domain.com/media/`

We should be prompted with a dialog box requesting a password. Enter the user name and password you created and click on OK.

# Server Administration:

## Filtering IP addresses

***Summary:*** *Expanding on the security concepts you learned in the previous section, here I discuss how to control access by a user's IP address.*

***Tip:*** *You can also filter incoming requests by domain name, but this requires the DNS lookup feature to be enabled. We do not recommend enabling this feature since it puts added strain on the server.*

***Tip:*** *The IP address 127.0.0.1 is the default IP address for "localhost" when you are not connected to the Internet, so by entering this IP address you are restricting yourself from your Web site. To give yourself access again, just select the IP number you entered in the Deny Classes section and click on the delete button.*

Server Admin

Y ou may find that you wish to filter out individual IP addresses from accessing your Web. By doing this, you can ensure that users with a specific IP address cannot access your files. When you filter access by IP address, users with the rejected address are completely denied access to your Web. They never see a password confirmation dialogue, the server simply looks at the incoming address and then grants or denies access based on the user's address.

### 1. Restrict access by IP address.

Restricting access by IP address is easy to accomplish. You can even restrict access by partial IP address. Let's restrict our Media directory from users with the IP address of 127.0.0.1.

**a.** In the Server Admin utility, select the Access Control property page.

**b.** Next, select the URL path you want to protect from the pull-down URL Path menu. If the desired path does not appear in the list, you must first add the path by clicking on the New button.

**c.** Once you have the path you want to protect selected, click on "Deny, then Allow" radio button.

**d.** Look under the "...then Allow classes" section. If "All" is listed here, remove it by selecting it and clicking on the Delete button.

**1a, 1b, 1c, 1d.**

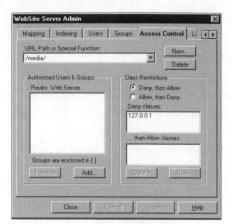

**1e.**

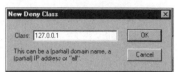

**1f, 1g.**

*Tip: A filtered address may be either a full IP address or a partial address (for example, 127.0 instead of 127.0.0.1), in which case all addresses that begin with the partial numbers of 127.0 will be restricted.*

**2.**

**e.** Now click on the Deny Classes rectangular box. You know this area is selected if it is highlighted in yellow. Click on the New button in the Class Restriction section. A dialog box named New Deny Class will appear, prompting you to enter an address.

**f.** Enter the IP address you wish to block from your site and click on the OK button. In our example, we will enter the IP address:

`127.0.0.1`

**g.** Now click on the Close button to exit the Server Admin application.

## 2. Test IP access.

If we were to enter the URL http://localhost/media/ now, we would get the server response 403, forbidden. You will only get this message if you are not connected to the Internet and do not have an assigned IP address. WebSite records all failed attempts to access your site in the server log files, discussed in the next section.

# Server Administration:
# Logging

*Summary:* As an administrator or Webmaster for a site, you should familiarize yourself with server logs. This section describes some of WebSite's logging features.

*Tip:* VBSTATS is a popular Windows program that analyzes server logs, and is available at WebSite Central at http://website.ora.com/software/.

Certain events that take place on your Web site are stored in server-created event logs, such as access attempts to restricted areas and server-generated error messages. WebSite stores activity in three different log files. The Logging property page in the Server Admin utility controls the way WebSite records activity at your Web site. From here, it is possible to control the name of the files WebSite uses to trace server activity, as well as configuring the types of events you want recorded in the logs.

Server Admin

### 1. WebSite's log files.

The default names of the log files created by WebSite are ACCESS.LOG, SERVER.LOG, and ERROR.LOG, which are all stored in WebSite's log directory, usually located at C:\WEBSITE\LOGS. The files created by the server are plain ASCII text files and can be viewed in any text editor, such as the Windows Notepad. The log files record the following data:

| Log | Description |
| --- | --- |
| ACCESS.LOG | This log records every attempt made to access a URL on your server, and whether it was successful or not. Check this log to determine which areas of your Web are accessed most frequently and by what users. The Access Log uses the common log format defined by NCSA and CERN, so many common log analysis tools can be used to pull information from this file. |
| ERROR.LOG | This log file helps you determine where the problem areas are on your Web site. Perhaps files have been removed from your Web site or URLs have been coded |

**2.**

*Tip: Since the SERVER.LOG file is overwritten every time the server is restarted, be sure to check this log BEFORE exiting the Web server application.*

*Tip: Enabling these options can lead to a huge SERVER.LOG file. Try not to leave logging options enabled for too long, or you may wind up with more data than you can read through.*

incorrectly. This log only records errors, so it should (hopefully!) be fairly small. Failed access attempts are also recorded here, so this would be a good place to look if you want to see who's attempting to access restricted areas of your Web site.

**SERVER.LOG** This log is different from the other two because it is written over every time the server is restarted. This log can be configured to trace the various options listed in the table below. The SERVER.LOG file is used primarily to troubleshoot the WebSite server.

## 2. SERVER.LOG tracing options.

The SERVER.LOG file records error messages and output from the all the tracing options that are enabled on the Logging property page in the Server Admin application. These Tracing Options are useful if you are troubleshooting the server or your CGI scripts. The options you can enable on this page are as follows:

| No. | Server Log | Description |
|-----|------------|-------------|
| 1 | HTTP protocol | Traces incoming requests to the server |
| 2 | Dump Sent Data | Traces the server's response to requests |
| 3 | Image Maps | Traces requests made to the server through an image map |
| 4 | Back-end Exec (CGI) | Traces CGI activity on your server (useful in debugging CGI programs) |
| 5 | Access Control | Useful for making sure access control is functioning properly |
| 6 | Authentication | Traces all authentication attempts made to the server |

| 7 | Thread | Used by O'Reilly technical support |
|---|---|---|
| 8 | Service Threads | Used by O'Reilly technical support |
| 9 | Network I/O | Used by O'Reilly technical support |
| 10 | Network Buffering | Used by O'Reilly technical support |

## 3. General transaction tracing.

*(Note: We won't discuss options 7 through 10, since they are primarily used by O'Reilly technical support.)*

The HTTP Protocol option works in conjunction with the Dump Sent Data option. Together, the two record server requests and responses in detail and write a record of these transactions to the SERVER.LOG file. Enabling these tracing options can generate large logs, but can also give a detailed picture of transactions and transaction errors occurring on your Web site. The Dump Sent Data option records a hex/ASCII dump of every piece of data sent from the server to a browser. The output generated by these options can be quite complex to read through, so for most users we recommend enabling the HTTP Protocol tracing by itself at first.

## 4. Image Map tracing.

Enabling the Image Map tracing option allows the server to record detailed information sent back to a user when an image map on your Web is accessed. If you are having trouble with your image maps, you should enable this feature to get a detailed report of how the server is responding to map requests.

## 5. CGI tracing.

CGI tracing records any activity that takes place when a user executes a CGI program. This is particularly useful if you are debugging CGI programs. CGI execution behavior is also modified if this tracing option is activated. For instance, if you enable CGI tracing, a DOS window opens whenever a standard or DOS CGI program is executed, so you can view line-by-line how the script runs.

## 6. Access control and authentication.

The Access Control and Authentication options merely keep track of all successful and failed attempts made to gain access to restricted areas of your Web site. These options are useful if you are making sure that the security features of the server are functioning properly. They can also be used to see if users without proper access are trying to break into restricted areas of your Web site.

## 7. A sample log entry.

For most users, simply enabling the HTTP Protocol option will be enough to get a good idea of how the server is functioning. A sample log entry with HTTP Protocol tracing enabled might look like this:

```
** REQUEST from 127.0.0.1 **
GET  /wsdocs/book/ch01.htm?HTTP/1.0
Referer: http://localhost/wsdocs/book/contents.htm
Connection: Keep-Alive
User-Agent: Mozilla/2.0b1 (Windows; I; 32bit)
Host: localhost
Accept: image/gif, image/x-xbitmap, image/jpeg,
image/pjpeg, */*
node=C:/WEBSITE/wsdocs/book/ch01.htm: args=
— REPLY —
>>send file C:/WEBSITE/wsdocs/book/ch01.htm args=
>> done <<
```

Note that this log entry records where the request came from, the browser the user accessed your data with, and the server's response. This request succeeded and the server returned the requested document, which in this case was CH01.HTM.

**8a, 8b, 8c.**

Had this request failed, an entry would have been made in the ERROR.LOG file. A sample entry for this log might look like this:

```
[08/Oct/1995:17:35:09 -0500] Access to
C:/WEBSITE/HTDOCS/contents.htm failed for 127.0.0.1, rea-
son: file does not exist
```

Here, the user tried to access the file CONTENTS.HTM, which doesn't exist on the server. The server generated this log entry, recording the time the error occurred, the file the user tried to access, the user's IP address, and the server's response.

Also note the Enable DNS Reverse Lookup checkbox on the Logging property page. Enabling this feature can allow the server to record fully qualified domain name (FQDN) addresses in the server logs instead of IP addresses. We don't recommend enabling this feature, though, because it can put a large strain on both the Web server and the DNS server. You should only enable this feature if you are sure both servers can take the additional strain.

## 8. Cycling the log files.

Since log files have a tendency to grow quickly, you may find it necessary to clear out, or cycle, these files periodically. WebSite provides an easy way to do this, but you must have administrator privileges to cycle the logs. (See the section *Activate the administrator's account* earlier in this chapter.)

**a.** Open the Self Test document included with WebSite in your Web browser. This document is located in the default directory of C:\WEBSITE\WSDOCS\ 32DEMO and is named INDEX.HTML. You can load the document automatically by entering the URL:

```
http://localhost/wsdocs/32DEMO/INDEX.HTML
```

**b.** Scroll all the way down to the Server Administration section at the bottom of this document.

**c.** Click on the button for the log you wish to cycle, either the ACCESS.LOG, the ERROR.LOG, or both logs. Remember, the SERVER.LOG file is automatically erased each time the server starts and thus cannot be cycled from this page.

When the logs are cycled, they are backed up in the same directory as the regular logs, usually C:\WEBSITE\LOGS. The old files are given a numbered extension, such as ACCESS.001. You should periodically delete or archive these files when you feel they will be no longer useful.

As a site administrator, you should frequently check server logs to get an idea of what kind of activity is taking place at your Web site. In the remainder of this chapter, we will talk about additional administration techniques for your Web site.

# Server Administration:
## The CGI property page

*Summary: This section discusses the CGI property page in the Server Admin utility.*

Server Admin

The one property page we haven't talked about in the Server Admin application is the CGI property page. The CGI property page controls the way WebSite handles standard DOS and Windows CGI applications. This page is for advanced users only, so we will not go into the options here in detail and suggest you refrain from changing anything unless you are sure of what you're doing. Any wrong changes you make here may prevent CGI applications from executing properly.

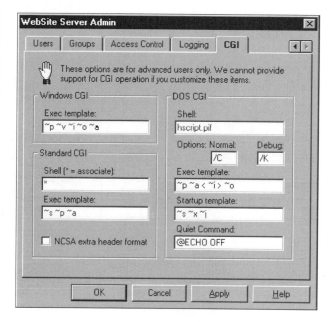

# Server Administration:

# View your Web with the WebView Utility

*Summary:* *The WebView utility is an extremely useful application that simplifies the administration of a Web site.*

1a.

1b.

If you maintain or are Webmaster for a Web site, you will quickly come to appreciate the WebView utility that comes with WebSite. WebView lets you view your Web site in a hierarchical "tree" structure. Even a simple Web can grow to contain hundreds of HTML, GIF, and multimedia files. WebView lets you organize your information in an easy manner and also lets an administrator perform a variety of maintenance tasks, including searching for broken links, viewing access control, performing HTML diagnostics, and viewing general activity on your Web site. It can also be used remotely, if your Web site is running from a server other than the one where WebView is installed, by simply entering your URL. WebView provides information on all the files in your Web site, including links to other files on the Internet.

## 1. Quickstats and Wizards.

WebView contains two mini-applications, QuickStats and Wizards. QuickStats is a program that quickly displays activity at your Web site within the last seven days. It reports the number of requests made to your site, the number of unique hosts making their first access to your site, the total number of HTML file requests served, the total number of non-HTML requests served (such as graphics or audio files), the total number of CGI documents served, the total number of erroneous requests, the average number of requests per hour, the average number of requests per day, and the number of unique hosts that have visited your site. With QuickStats, you can get a fast summary of activity on your site without having to analyze the server logs.

The Wizards included with WebView aid you in very simple HTML authoring for creating a home page and a what's new page. The Wizards function of WebView can help you quickly create these documents, but chances are most people will not be satisfied with the limited functionality of the Wizards. If you use Wizards to create the what's new or home page, you will probably want to go back later with a text editor or HTML editor to enhance these pages.

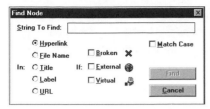

**2.**

This is easy to do, since the WebView application can function as a central "control center" for a site, with the ability to launch files into your HTML editor as well as having the ability to send an HTML document to your favorite browser for previewing. All the components of the WebSite package, with the exception of the server itself, can also be launched directly from WebView. WebIndex, Server Admin, and Image Map Editor can be launched from WebView's Tools menu, as well as the Quick Stats application and the Wizards program.

## 2. Views and searches.

WebView offers five different views and searches of your Web site. WebView also provides icons for links that are broken, external links, links that cannot be verified by WebView, and virtual links (usually links created by a CGI program). Listed below are the five views provided by WebView. You can also search your entire Web using any of these methods:

| Method | Description |
| --- | --- |
| **Hyperlink** | This view displays files by hyperlink in your Web site, including all external links to other sites. |
| **File Names** | This view allows you to view the names and path for every file in your Web site, including graphic files, HTML files, and any other files available for downloading such as video, audio, or other MIME files. |
| **Title** | The title view displays information contained in the <TITLE> tag of each HTML document. |

| | |
|---|---|
| **Label** | This displays document names using the text contained in the ANCHOR tag that accompanies each HREF link. The Label view also displays information found in the ALT tag of an embedded image or the submit button in an online form. |
| **URL** | This view displays the full URL of all physical documents and links in your Web site as well as external links to other Web sites. |

These different views are all accessible from the View menu in the WebView application. You can search using these options by selecting Search from the menu, and then Find Node.

# Server Administration:

# Configuring an alternate browser

*Summary: This section explains how to configure an alternate browser to use with the WebView utility.*

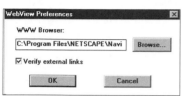

**3.**

Although WebSite comes with Enhanced NCSA Mosaic from Spyglass, you may want to configure a different browser to use for the Browser Preview function. This is a simple process.

### 1. Open Preferences.
In the WebView application, select File then Preferences.

### 2. Enter a Path and Filename.
a. In the WWW Browser field, enter the path and file name for your browser. You can browse for the EXE file if you are not sure of the path. Let's say you would like to configure Netscape Navigator as the default browser for previewing documents. Enter the path to the executable file, in this case NETSCAPE.EXE is located at:

```
C:\PROGRAM FILES\NETSCAPE\NAVIGATOR\
   PROGRAM\NETSCAPE.EXE
```

but it may be different for you, depending on where your browser was installed.

b. Click on the OK button.

### 3. Verify External links.
You also have the option to uncheck the option box for Verify external links. By default, WebView will try to verify every external link in your WebSite. If you are working on a local hard drive or if verifying external links takes too long for your liking (depending on how many external links you have and the speed of your connection, this can be a time-consuming process) uncheck this option. Note that this option must be unchecked each time you start WebView—the verify external link option is not saved.

# Server Administration:

## Diagnosing your HTML files with WebView

***Summary:*** *WebView is capable of diagnosing your HTML files to see that they conform to the official HTML specification. This section explains how to troubleshoot your files.*

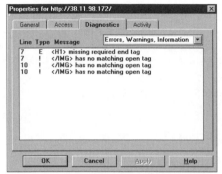

**2.**

WebView also allows you to do simple error checking on your HTML files to see if they are up to HTML coding standards. This can be an easy way to ensure that pages will, for the most part, display properly in the large variety of browsers that are available. To diagnose an individual HTML file, follow these steps.

### 1. Select a file.
Select a file in your Web site from WebView with your mouse and select File|Properties from the menu. A tabbed window should pop up offering options for General, Access, Diagnostics, and Activity. Select Diagnostics from the tabbed menu.

### 2. View the diagnostic information.
The WebView Diagnostics page reports errors, warnings and general information. You can filter errors by using the pull-down menu. Filtering options include viewing errors, warnings and information; errors and warnings only; and errors only.

### 3. Fix file errors.
Click on the OK button and the diagnostics page will close. But you probably want to correct any errors that were reported for the file. The easiest way to do this is to double click on the file in question. By default, WebSite associates files with the HTML extension to the Windows Notepad during installation. If no other programs have altered this file association, double clicking here should launch Notepad and you can correct the errors.

The diagnostics property page reports some HTML 3.0 markup codes as errors, since they are not officially part of the HTML 2.0 specification. Errors reported in your files mean that either the HTML coding in a file is not correct, or that it contains codes that are not a part of the official HTML 2.0 DTD (document type definition). Errors reported by WebView may mean that your document may display incorrectly in a Web browser.

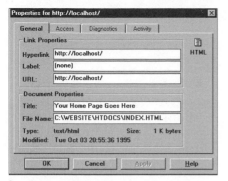

4a.

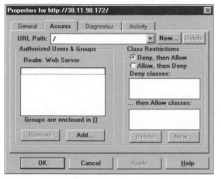

4b.

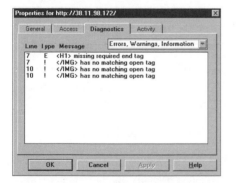

4c.

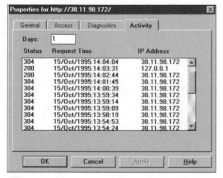

4d.

Warning messages reported by WebView are similar to errors, although not as severe. A warning is given for unknown tags or tags that are not fully HTML 2.0 compliant, such as <CENTER>.

## 4. Other file properties available in WebView.

When you were viewing your file's diagnostics in the previous example, you may have noticed that there were four options to choose from (General, Access, Diagnostics, and Activity). We will now discuss each of these options and what kind of information they offer.

**a.** **General.** This option tells you about link and document information for a selected file. It includes information about hyperlinks, labels, and URLs. It also includes information about the title, path, and file name for a file.

**b.** **Access.** This option allows you to view and modify access control for a directory. Like the Server Admin utility, this property sheet can only set permissions on a per-directory basis. It cannot set access for individual files.

**c.** **Diagnostics.** This option provides HTML 2.0 level error checking on a file. It includes errors, warnings and general information.

**d.** **Activity.** This option reports activity on a file based on the server's access log. It includes the IP address of the user who requested the file, the date and time the file was accessed, and the server response code to the request. Checking the server response code can be helpful in diagnosing how well your server is working. Some common server response codes follow.

| Code | Meaning |
|---|---|
| **Level 200 codes** | Generally mean that the request was received successfully. |
| **Level 300 codes** | Generally mean that some type of server redirection was necessary to fulfill the client request. |
| **Level 400 codes** | Generally mean that there was an error on the client side. |
| **Level 500 codes** | Generally mean that there was an error on the server side. |

The table below lists server response codes.

| Code | Meaning |
|---|---|
| **200: Okay.** | The server returned the document without a problem. |
| **204: No Content.** | The document was served, but contained no content. |
| **400: Bad request.** | The request sent by the client cannot be fulfilled. |
| **403: Forbidden.** | The client was denied access by the server. Additional authorization will not help in retrying the request. |
| **404: Not found.** | The specified URL does not exist on the server. |
| **500: Internal server error.** | The server encountered an unexpected condition which prevented it from fulfilling the request. |

We think that you will find WebView an invaluable tool for administering a Web site. By having the ability to launch editors, configure security, search for broken links, and preview files in your browser, WebView provides an administrator with a sort of "control center" for their Web site.

# Server Administration:

# Using WebIndex

***Summary:*** *WebIndex helps you offer keyword searching from your Web site. This section explains how to index your HTML files.*

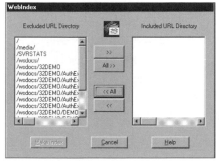

**1, 2, 3.**

***Tip:*** *Remember that WebIndex only indexes HTML documents. If you are serving Word documents or other non-text files, WebFind will not return browser-viewable content.*

***Tip:*** *The larger your Web site is, the longer it will take to create an index.*

WebIndex

A useful feature to provide with your Web site is the ability to search HTML documents for keywords. WebSite comes with a simple search program, WebFind, preconfigured. To allow WebFind to search your site, the only necessary steps are to index your site and then run the WebFind program.

WebIndex is a simple program that indexes your Web site for keyword searching. By indexing your site, WebFind can search all your indexed HTML files and quickly return results. Although they are not as powerful as a commercial search engine, WebIndex and WebFind should prove suitable for most people without modification. Here's how to index your site:

## 1. Open WebIndex.
Start the program by selecting WebIndex from the WebSite program group.

## 2. Select the directories to be indexed.
Select the directories you want indexed in the Excluded URL Directory list. You can do this either by double clicking on the directory entry, or by selecting a directory and then clicking the arrow button pointing toward the Included URL list. If you want to index all the directories, simply click on the All button that points to the Included URL directory.

## 3. Make an index.
When you have chosen the directories you want to index, click on the Make Index button.

The program automatically exits when it finishes creating the index file.

As you can see, WebIndex is an extremely simple program to use. The program creates a file named INDEX.SWISH, which is saved in the WebSite root directory (usually C:\WEBSITE). You should remember that whenever any major changes occur to your Web site, you need to reindex the files. WebSite does not automatically generate search index files, so it is up to you to keep your index file current.

# Server Administration: Using WebFind

**Summary:** *In the previous section, you learned how to index your files for keyword searching. This section explains how to search your indexed files.*

You can search the index file you created by invoking the WebFind program. WebFind is a CGI application frontend used for searching your indexed HTML files. You can invoke the WebFind application by entering the following URL in your browser:

```
http://localhost/cgi-bin/webfind.exe
```

WebFind creates a simple form for searching that allows you to use "and/or" keywords (see the figure below) and allows you to search through every file that was indexed by WebIndex. It returns links that a user can click on to go right to the document he or she searched for.

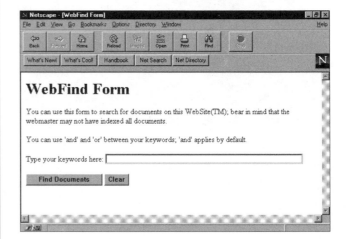

# Locating a good HTML Editor to use with WebSite

*Summary:* *A good HTML editor can make the creation of Web pages a simple process.*

Hot Dog!

The only obvious item missing from the WebSite package is a good HTML editor. Although many people prefer to use a simple text editor to edit HTML files, and there is no substitute for knowing the HTML specification, a good editor can really make the job of creating HTML documents faster and easier.

Fortunately, there are an abundance of good HTML editors available on the Internet for just about every imaginable computer platform, many of which are free or carry a nominal registration fee. One of our personal favorites is the Hot Dog editor from Sausage Software (included on the CD-ROM that accompanies this book). It is also available for downloading at:

`http://www.sausage.com/`

Hot Dog supports many HTML 3.0-level tags and has many features that make creating Web pages a breeze.

A comprehensive list of HTML editors can also be found in the Yahoo Internet directory at:

`http://www.yahoo.com/Computers/World_Wide_Web/HTML_Editors/`

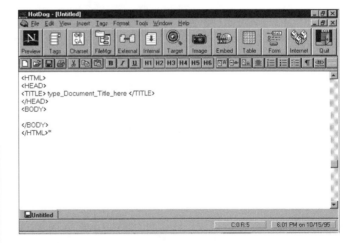

# A note on CGI under WebSite

***Summary:*** *This section offers a general overview of CGI applications under WebSite.*

C GI (Common Gateway Interface) scripts are simple programs that run through a Web server and extend the Web in a way that standalone HTML pages cannot. The most common use of CGI scripts is to process online forms.

Every online form on the Web is processed through some sort of CGI script. People use forms for a variety of purposes, including requesting visitor feedback, placing product orders, surveying guests at your site, or just for sending mail. Generally, CGI scripts are written in programming or scripting languages such as C++ or PERL.

## 1. Avoiding Unix.

One of the truly unique features of WebSite is its CGI handling capabilities. WebSite allows you to run three different types of CGI applications, including standard CGI (such as PERL scripts), DOS CGI applications (usually DOS batch files) and, most interestingly, Windows CGI applications. The fact that WebSite runs many standard CGI programs that also run under Unix (if you're using Windows NT) makes WebSite an ideal development environment to use when building applications that will later be uploaded to a Unix server. *Most standard Unix CGI scripts will run in the Windows NT POSIX environment without modification.*

While a tutorial on writing CGI applications is beyond the scope of this book, there are many outstanding CGI resources available on the Internet (see the end of this chapter for a few such locations). In addition, the 350-page manual that comes with WebSite includes four chapters on writing and testing CGI applications.

## 2. Types of CGI.

WebSite can run a variety of standard CGI scripts. Standard CGI scripts include PERL scripts, and shell scripts, such as scripts written for the Unix Bourne or Korn Shell. When running WebSite under Windows NT, you can run virtually any Unix programming language that has an NT interpreter (another example would be TCL, the Tool Control Language, which has an interpreter that runs under NT). To run Unix Bourne/Korn Shell scripts, it will be necessary to

*Tip: To run PERL scripts, you will also need a PERL interpreter. One is available for both Windows 95 and NT at WebSite Central at:*

`http://website.ora.com/software/`

install the software component of the Windows NT Resource Kit. The program files for the Resource Kit are available for downloading from Microsoft at:

`http://www.microsoft.com/BackOffice/ntutil.htm`

To run PERL scripts, you will also need a PERL interpreter. One is available for both Windows 95 and NT at WebSite Central at:

`http://website.ora.com/software/`

We won't say much about DOS CGI programs under WebSite other than that it allows you to run DOS batch (.bat) files. The DOS CGI interface is not as flexible or powerful as the standard or Windows CGI interface, but it may still prove useful for some users. Remember that DOS CGI cannot return HTML content to a browser the way that standard and Windows CGI can, it can only return ASCII text content.

### 3. Windows CGI.

Windows CGI is one of the most exciting features of WebSite. Windows CGI can handle 16- or 32-bit applications. By having the ability to run Windows CGI applications, WebSite can take advantage of some of the many outstanding Windows development tools that are available, such as Visual Basic and Visual C++. With Windows CGI, you can also link to information from Windows-based databases and spreadsheets. The server can pull new information from these databases as they are updated.

Though we can't go into Windows CGI in detail, the WebSite manual provides an excellent treatment of the subject and additional information is also available at:

`http://www.city.net/win-httpd/httpddoc/wincgi.htm`

You should also read the WINDOWS-CGI.HTML document located in the C:\WEBSITE\WSDOCS\32DEMO directory.

# Troubleshooting

**Summary:** *Here are some general tips to help you troubleshoot the WebSite server as well as some additional resources available on the Internet.*

WebSite generally installs and operates without much of a hassle. Like all software, however, there is a chance that something may end up not functioning properly. We've included some troubleshooting tips here that we hope you'll find useful.

## 1. The http://localhost/ URL doesn't work.

Sometimes the WebSite server is finicky about whether the browser is started first or the server is started first, especially under Windows 95. Under Windows 95, the server seems to prefer that the browser is started first and then the server, but try it both ways. Also, make sure your TCP/IP Windows sockets are open. If you are in doubt, simply make a connection to the Internet.

## 2. Check WebSite Central at http://website .ora.com/

O'Reilly does not provide technical support for the demo version of WebSite, but many answers to common questions are available at WebSite Central. There's also a FAQ (frequently asked questions) and even an IAQ (infrequently asked questions).

## 3. Run the server self-test.

Run the server self-test to make sure everything is functioning properly. It is well worth your time to run through the server self-test during installation. You may find out later that some aspect of the server is not functioning properly. For instance, you may not want to implement security at your Web site right away, but you might want to add it later on. Make sure these features are functioning correctly from the beginning so you don't need to reinstall the server software after you have your whole Web up and running.

## 4. No one can connect to your server.

Networking issues are complex, to say the least. As a general suggestion, try pinging your IP address and domain name from a remote computer to make sure your Internet connection is functioning. Both Windows NT and Windows 95 have built-in command line ping utilities. Simply start a

**5.**

*Warning! Uninstalling the WebSite server will wipe out your whole Web if you're not careful! Be sure to remove any documents you wish to preserve from the WebSite directory and sub-directories.*

DOS session and type ping followed by your domain name. For example:

```
ping www.domain.com
```

Then try pinging your IP address.

## 5. Nothing else seems to work!

Sometimes, reinstalling the WebSite software can work wonders when you're experiencing problems. WebSite comes with an uninstall option. (Don't you wish all your programs came with one?) Simply run the setup program again. Setup will detect that WebSite has already been installed and will offer the option of uninstalling.

Uninstall can delete the WebSite software, the Windows registry keys and the WebSite service (under Windows NT). After uninstalling, try to reinstall the WebSite software.

If you are interested in purchasing the full version of WebSite, it is distributed in most software and bookstores. You can also call O'Reilly directly at (800) 998-9938, or send an email message to order@ora.com. WebSite Central also has an online form if you would prefer to order directly from the Internet. For product questions, send an email message to website@ora.com.

If you would like to know more about Windows-based Web servers, there are many resources available on the Internet. We suggest looking into the following:

| Resource | Description |
| --- | --- |
| comp.os.ms-windows. nt.setup | newsgroup |
| comp.os.ms-windows. nt.setup.hardware | newsgroup |
| comp.os.ms-windows. win95.misc | newsgroup |

*Tip:* O'Reilly recently set up a mailing list, WebSite-talk, for users interested in the WebSite product. The list is open to everyone. For information on joining, send an e-mail message to listproc@online.ora.com with no subject line and the body of the message simply reading "info website-talk."

*Tip:* Registered users of WebSite are automatically subscribed to the WebSite-news list, which was created to notify users of updates, bug fixes, and other general announcements.

| | |
|---|---|
| comp.os.ms-windows.win95.setup | newsgroup |
| http://www.bhs.com/winnt/ | The Windows NT Resource Center |
| http://mfginfo.com/htm/website.htm | Resource Guide For Windows 3.5 NT Server Websites |

The table below lists resources for setting up and running a Web server.

| Resource | Description |
|---|---|
| comp.infosystems.www.servers.ms-windows | newsgroup |
| comp.os.ms-windows.nt.admin.networking | newsgroup |

The table below lists CGI References.

| Resource | Description |
|---|---|
| http://hoohoo.ncsa.uiuc.edu/cgi/ | General CGI |
| http://www.city.net/win-httpd/httpddoc/wincgi.htm | Windows CGI |
| http://www.stars.com/Vlib/Providers/CGI.html | General CGI |
| http://www.halcyon.com/hedlund/cgi-faq/faq-general.html | CGI FAQ |
| comp.infosystems.www.authoring.cgi | newsgroup |

The World Wide Web FAQ, a listing of frequently asked questions, is located at: http://sunsite.unc.edu/~boutell/faq/

# Creating Web Pages with HTML 3

# Appendix

As you probably know, HTML is the formatting language used by the World Wide Web. The acronym *HTML* stands for *Hypertext Markup Language*. The hypertext part means that an HTML document can contain references to other documents. This is why HTML makes a great platform for developing interactive multimedia applications. You can design HTML documents to link to other HTML documents or video, sound, and animation files.

The HTML that we use in this book to create our Web documents is actually a subset of a language called *SGML*, which stands for *Standard Generalized Markup Language*. SGML was designed as a typesetting language for documents that were created using a computer. The "markup" part of its name comes from the days when book and magazine editors made special marks on the authors' manuscripts to instruct typesetters how to format the text. Although HTML evolved from the markup typesetting codes used in SGML, HTML was created specifically for displaying graphics on the Internet and for creating links between different Internet addresses.

We discussed some of the basic features of HTML as we presented our design projects, but covered only a few of the many HTML tags that are available. This appendix provides a useful guide to most of the HTML features supported by leading Web browsers such as Netscape. You'll want to use this guide as you create HTML documents to design your Web pages.

## HTML—The Language of the Web

HTML commands are enclosed in angle brackets, <like this>. Most commands come in pairs that mark the beginning and end of a part of text. The end command is often identical to the start command, except that it includes a forward slash between the opening bracket and the command name. For example, the title of an HTML document called "Web Design Guide" would look like this:

```
<TITLE>Web Design Guide/TITLE>
```

*Tip: You can use a custom HTML editor like WebEdit to help automate the process of creating Web pages.*

Similarly, a word or phrase that you want to display in bold type would be indicated like this:

```
<B>Display this phrase in bold</B>
```

It's not too hard to mark up your text, but all the bracketed tags can make your source text hard to read and proofread. No one has created a true "Web processor," a WYSIWYG word processor that happens to read and write HTML files, but we're bound to see one soon. For now, we have to use word processors, text editors, or simple HTML editors that display the tags, not their effects.

It's our belief that the best way to learn HTML is to type in the commands using a text editor like Notepad. That way, you'll get plenty of reinforcement to help you commit the language to memory.

### Using an HTML Editor

But many experienced Web page designers prefer using an HTML editor over a word processor like Microsoft Word or a simple text editor like Windows Notepad. In fact, we've included some handy HTML editors on the companion CD-ROM, including WebEdit and HTMLAssistant. It is easier to start writing HTML with an HTML editor than with a basic text editor, because most HTML editors offer some sort of menu of tags. This can help you get acquainted with the HTML tag set.

The other advantage of an HTML editor is that when it inserts tags for you, it inserts both the start and the end tags. This feature greatly reduces the chance that your whole document will end up in the <H1> (first level header) style, or that a bold word will become three bold paragraphs.

## HTML Basics

All HTML files consist of a mixture of text to be displayed and HTML tags that describe how the text should be displayed. Normally, extra whitespace (spaces, tabs, and line breaks) is ignored, and text is displayed with a single space between each word. Text is always wrapped to fit within a browser's window in the reader's choice of fonts. Line

*Tip: Some begin tags can take parameters, which come between the tag name and the closing bracket like this: <DL COMPACT>. Others, like description lists, have optional parameters. Still others, such as anchors and images, require certain parameters and can also take optional parameters.*

breaks in the HTML source are treated as any other whitespace, that is, they're ignored—and a paragraph break must be marked with a <P> tag.

Tags are always set off from the surrounding text by angle brackets, the less-than and greater-than signs. Most tags come in begin and end pairs, for example, <I> ... </I>. The end tag includes a slash between the opening bracket and the tag name. There are a few tags that require only a start tag; we'll point out these tags as they come up.

HTML is case insensitive: <HTML> is the same as <html> or <hTmL>. However, many Web servers run on Unix systems, which are case sensitive. This will never affect HTML interpretation, but will affect your hyperlinks: My.gif is not the same file as my.gif or MY.GIF.

## The Structure of an HTML Document

All HTML documents have a certain standard structure, but Netscape and most other Web browsers will treat any file that ends in .HTML (.HTM on PCs) as an HTML file, even if it contains no HTML tags. All HTML text and tags should be contained within this tag pair:

```
<HTML> ... </HTML>
```

### <HEAD> ... </HEAD> Tag

All HTML documents are divided into a header that contains the title and other information about the document, and a body that contains the actual document text.

While you should not place display text outside the body section, this is currently optional since most Web browsers and HTML readers will format and display any text that's not in a tag. Also, while you can get away with not using the <HEAD> tag pair, we recommend you use it.

### <BODY> ... </BODY> Tag

The tags that appear within the body of an HTML document do not separate the document into sections. Rather, they're either special parts of the text, like images or forms, or they're tags that say something about the text they enclose, like character attributes or paragraph styles.

## Headings and Paragraphs

In some ways, HTML text is a series of paragraphs. Within a paragraph, the text will be wrapped to fit the reader's screen. In most cases, any line breaks that appear in the source file are totally ignored.

Paragraphs are separated either by an explicit paragraph break tag, <P>, or by paragraph style commands. The paragraph style determines both the font used for the paragraph and any special indenting. Paragraph styles include several levels of section headers, five types of lists, three different block formats, and the normal, or default, paragraph style. Any text outside of an explicit paragraph style command will be displayed in the normal style.

## <ADDRESS> ... </ADDRESS> Tag

The last part of the document body should be an <ADDRESS> tag pair, which contains information about the author and, often, the document's copyright date and revision history. While the address block is not a required part of the document in the same way that the header or the body is, official style guides urge that all documents have one. In current practice, while most documents use the <HTML>, <HEAD>, and <BODY> tag pairs, almost all documents have address blocks—perhaps because the address block is visible.

The format for using the <ADDRESS> tag is as follows:

```
<ADDRESS>Address text goes here</ADDRESS>
```

## Comments

Comments can be placed in your HTML documents using a special tag as shown:

```
<!-Comment text goes here->
```

Everything between the <> will be ignored by a browser when the document is displayed.

## Header Elements

The elements used in the header of an HTML document include a title section and internal indexing information.

*In Netscape, the text placed between the <TITLE> tag pair appers in the window title bar.*

## <TITLE> ... </TITLE> Tag

Every document should have a title. The manner in which a title is displayed varies from system to system and browser to browser. The title could be displayed as a window title, or it may appear in a pane within the window. The title should be short—64 characters or less—and should contain just text.

The title should appear in the header section, marked off with a <TITLE> tag pair; for example, <TITLE>Explore the Grand Canyon</TITLE>. Some Web browsers like Netscape are quite easy-going and will let you place the title anywhere in the document, even after the </HTML> tag, but future browsers might not be quite so accommodating. Including a title is important because many Web search engines will use the title to locate a document.

The format for using the <TITLE> tag is as follows:

```
<TITLE>Title text goes here</TITLE>
```

## Other <HEAD> Elements

There are a few optional elements that may only appear in the document's header (<HEAD> tag pair). The header elements that browsers use are the <BASE> and <ISINDEX> tags. Both are empty or solitary tags that do not have a closing </...> tag and thus do not enclose any text.

The <BASE> tag contains the current document's *URL,* or *Uniform Resource Locator*; browsers can use it to find local URLs.

The <ISINDEX> tag tells browsers that this document is an index document, which means that the server can support keyword searches based on the document's URL. Searches are passed back to the Web server by concatenating a question mark and one or more keywords to the document URL and then requesting this extended URL. This is very similar to one of the ways that form data is returned. (See the section *Form Action and Method Attributes* for more information.)

HTML includes other header elements, such as <NEXTID> and <LINK>, which are included in HTML for the benefit of editing and cataloging software. They have no visible effect; browsers simply ignore them.

# Normal Text

Most HTML documents are composed of plain, or normal, text. Any text not appearing between format tag pairs is displayed as normal text.

Normal text, like every other type of paragraph style except the preformatted style, is wrapped at display time to fit in the reader's window. A larger or smaller font or window size will result in a totally different number of words on each line, so don't try to change the wording of a sentence to make the line breaks come at appropriate places. It won't work.

### <BR> Tag

If line breaks are important, as in postal addresses or poetry, you can use the <BR> command to insert a line break. Subsequent text will appear one line down, on the left margin.

The general format for this tag is:

```
<BR CLEAR=[Left|Right]>
```

The section listed between the [] is optional. This is a feature introduced as an HTML enhancement and supported by newer versions of Netscape.

Let's look at an example of how <BR> is used. To keep

```
Coriolis Group Books
7339 East Acoma Drive, Suite 7
Scottsdale, Arizona 85260-6912
```

from coming out as

```
Coriolis Group Books 7339 East Acoma Drive, Suite 7
Scottsdale, Arizona 85260-6912
```

you would write:

```
Coriolis Group Books<BR>
7339 East Acoma Drive, Suite 7<BR>
Scottsdale, Arizona 85260-6912<BR>
```

The extended form of the <BR> tag allows you to control how text is wrapped. The CLEAR argument allows text to be broken so that it can flow to the right or to the left around an image. For example, this tag shows how text can be broken to flow to the left:

```
This text will be broken here.<BR CLEAR=Left>
```

This line will flow around to the right of an image that can be displayed with the IMG tag.

### <NOBR> Tag

This tag stands for No Break. This is another HTML extension supported by Netscape. To keep text from breaking, you can include the <NOBR> tag at the beginning of the text you want to keep together.

### <WBR> Tag

This tag stands for Word Break. If you use the <NOBR> tag to define a section of text without breaks, you can force a line break at any location by inserting the <WBR> tag followed by the <BR> tag.

### <P> Tag

The <BR> tag causes a line break within a paragraph, but more often we want to separate one paragraph from another. We can do this by enclosing each paragraph in a <P> tag pair, starting the paragraph with <P> and ending it with </P>. The actual appearance of the paragraphs will depend on your reader's Web browser: Paragraph breaks may be shown with an extra line or half line of spacing, a leading indent, or both.

The </P> tag is optional; most people include a single <P> at the beginning of each paragraph, at the end, or alone on a line between two paragraphs.

## Physical and Logical Attributes

Character attribute tags let you emphasize words or phrases within a paragraph. HTML supports two different types of character attributes: *physical* and *logical*. Physical attributes include the familiar bold, italic, and underline, as well as a tty attribute for monospaced text.

Logical attributes are different. In keeping with the SGML philosophy of using tags to describe content and not the actual formatting, logical attributes let you describe what sort of emphasis you want to put on a word or phrase, but leave the actual formatting up to the browser. That is, where a word marked with a physical attribute like <B>bold</B> will always appear in bold type, a word marked with <EM>emphasized</EM> may be italicized, underlined, bolded, or displayed in color.

Web style guides suggest that you use logical attributes whenever you can, but there's a slight problem: Some current browsers only support some physical attributes, and few or no logical attributes. Since Web browsers simply ignore any HTML tag that they don't understand, when you use logical tags, you run the risk that your readers will not see any formatting at all! The following table shows a list of physical attributes.

| Attribute | Tag | Sample | Effect |
|-----------|-----|--------|--------|
| Bold | <B> | Some <B>bold</B> text | Some **bold** text |
| Italic | <I> | Some <I>italicized</I> text | Some *italicized* text |
| Underline | <U> | Some <U>underlined</U> text | Some <u>underline</u> text |
| TTY | <TT> | <TT>monospaced </TT> text | Some `monospaced` text |

The standard format for using any of the physical attribute tags is as follows:

```
<tag>text goes here</tag>
```

You can nest attributes, although the results will vary from browser to browser. For example, some browsers can display bold italic text, while others will only display the innermost attribute. (That is, <B><I>bold italic</I></B> may show up as bold italic.) If you use nested attributes, be sure to place the end tags in reverse order of the start tags; don't write something like <B><I>bold italic</B></I>! This may work with some Web browsers, but may cause problems with others.

The table on the following page shows a list of logical attributes.

| Attribute | Tag | Use or Interpretation | Typical Rendering |
|---|---|---|---|
| Citation | \<CITE\> | Titles of books and films | Italic |
| Code | \<CODE\> | Source code fragments | Monospaced |
| Definition | \<DFN\> | A word being defined | Italic |
| Emphasis | \<EM\> | Emphasize a word or phrase | Italic |
| PRE | \<PRE\> | Used for tables and text | Preformatted text |
| Keyboard | \<KBD\> | Something the user should type, word-for-word | Bold monospaced |
| Sample | \<SAMP\> | Computer status messages | Monospaced |
| Strong | \<STRONG\> | Strong emphasis | Bold |
| Variable | \<VAR\> | A description of something the user should type, like \<filename\> | Italic |

*Inappropriate use of the BLINKTAG (http://www.meat.com/netscape_hos.html)*

Keep in mind that even if current browsers arbitrarily decide that \<EM\> text will be displayed as italic and \<KBD\> text will be displayed as Courier, future browsers will probably defer these attributes to a setting controlled by the user.

### \<BLINK\> ... \</BLINK\>

This is a new enhanced tag supported by Netscape. Text placed between this pair will blink on the screen. This feature is useful for attention-grabbing, but using it too much could get rather annoying. The format for this tag is:

```
<BLINK>This text will blink</BLINK>
```

### \<CENTER\> ... \</CENTER\>

This HTML enhancement makes some Web page authors feel like they've died and gone to heaven. Any text (or images) placed between this pair is centered between the left and right margins of a page. The format for this tag is:

```
<CENTER>This text will be centered between the left and
right margins</CENTER>
```

### \<FONT\> ... \</FONT\>

This HTML enhancement allows you to control the sizes of the fonts displayed in your documents. The format for this tag is:

```
<FONT SIZE=font-size>text goes here</FONT>
```

where font-size must be a number from 1 to 7. A size of 1 produces the smallest font. The default font size is 3. Once the font size has been changed, it will remain in effect until the font size is changed by using another tag.

### <BASEFONT>

To give you even greater control over font sizing, a new HTML tag has been added so that you can set the base font for all text displayed in a document. The format for this tag is:

```
<BASEFONT SIZE=font-size>
```

Again, font-size must be a number from 1 to 7. A size of 1 produces the smallest font. The default font size is 3. Once the base font size has been defined, you can display text in larger or smaller fonts using the + or - sign with the <FONT> tag. Here's an example of how this works:

```
<BASEFONT SIZE=4>
This text will be displayed as size 4 text.
<FONT SIZE=+2>
This text will be displayed as size 6.
</FONT>
This text will return to the base font size—size 4.
```

## Headings

HTML provides six levels of section headers, <H1> through <H6>. While these are typically short phrases that fit on a line or two, the various headers are actually full-fledged paragraph types. They can even contain line and paragraph break commands.

You are not required to use a <H1> before you use a <H2>, or to make sure that a <H4> follows a <H3> or another <H4>.

The standard format for using one of the six heading tags is illustrated by this sample:

```
<H1>Text Goes Here</H1>
```

## Lists

HTML supports five different list types. All five types can be thought of as a sort of paragraph type. The first four list types share a common syntax, and differ only in how they format their list elements. The fifth type, the description list, is unique in that each list element has two parts—a tag and a description of the tag.

All five list types display an element marker—whether it be a number, a bullet, or a few words—on the left margin. The marker is followed by the actual list elements, which appear indented. List elements do not have to fit on a single line or consist of a single paragraph—they may contain <P> and <BR> tags.

Lists can be nested, but the appearance of a nested list depends on the browser. For example, some browsers use different bullets for inner lists than for outer lists, and some browsers do not indent nested lists. However, Netscape and Lynx, which are probably the most common graphical and text mode browsers, do indent nested lists; the tags of a nested list align with the elements of the outer list, and the elements of the nested list are further indented. For example,

```
·   This is the first element of the main bulleted list.
            ·This is the first element of a nested list.
            ·This is the second element of the nested list.
·   This is the second element of the main bulleted list.
```

The four list types that provide simple list elements use the list item tag, <LI>, to mark the start of each list element. The <LI> tag always appears at the start of a list element.

Thus, all simple lists look something like this:

```
<ListType>

<LI>
There isn't really any ListType list, however the OL, UL,
DIR, and MENU lists all follow this format.
<LI>
Since whitespace is ignored, you can keep your source legible
by putting blank lines between your list elements. Sometimes,
we like to put the &lt;li&gt; tags on their own lines, too.
<LI>
(If we hadn't used the ampersand quotes in the previous
list element, the "&lt;li&gt;" would have been interpreted
as the start of a new list element.)
</ListType>
```

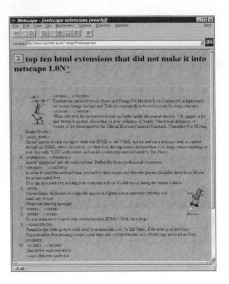

*For a little humor try this site that lists the top ten HTML extensions that didn't make it into Netscape.*

## Numbered List

In HTML, numbered lists are referred to as ordered lists. The list type tag is <OL>. Numbered lists can be nested, but some browsers get confused by the close of a nested list, and start numbering the subsequent elements of the outer list from 1.

## Bulleted List

If a numbered list is an ordered list, what else could an unnumbered, bulleted list be but an unordered list? The tag for an unordered (bulleted) list is <UL>. While bulleted lists can be nested, you should keep in mind that the list nesting may not be visible; some browsers indent nested lists; some don't. Some use multiple bullet types; others don't.

## Netscape List Extensions

Netscape has added a useful feature called TYPE that can be included with unordered and ordered lists. This feature allows you to specify the type of bullet or number that you use for the different levels of indentation in a list.

## Unordered List with Extensions

When Netscape displays the different levels of indentation in an unordered list, it uses a solid disk (level 1) followed by a bullet (level 2) followed by a square (level 3). You can use the TYPE feature with the <UL> tag to override this sequence of bullets. Here's the format:

```
<UL TYPE=Disc|Circle|Square>
```

For example, here's a list defined to use circles as the bullet symbol:

```
<UL TYPE=Circle>
<LI>This is item 1
<LI>This is item 2
<LI>This is item 3
</UL>
```

## Ordered List with Extensions

When Netscape displays ordered (numbered) lists, it numbers each list item using a numeric sequence—1, 2, 3, and so on. You can change this setting by using the TYPE modifier with the <OL> tag. Here's how this feature is used with numbered lists:

```
<OL TYPE=A|a|I|i|1>
```

where TYPE can be assigned to any one of these values:

    A  Mark list items with capital letters
    a  Mark list items with lowercase letters
    I  Mark list items with large roman numerals
    i  Mark list items with small roman numerals
    1  Mark list items with numbers (default)

Wait, there's more. You can also start numbering list items with a number other than 1. To do this, you use the START modifier as shown:

```
<OL START=starting-number>
```

where starting-number specifies the first number used. You can use the feature with the TYPE tag. For example, the tag

```
<OL TYPE=A START=4>
```

would start the numbered list with the roman numeral IV.

## Using Modifiers with List Elements

In addition to supporting the TYPE modifier with the <UL> and <OL> tags, Netscape allows you to use this modifier with the <LI> tag to define list elements for ordered and unordered lists. Here's an example of how it can be used with an unordered list:

```
<H2>Useful Publishing Resources</H2>
<UL TYPE=Disc>
<LI>HTML Tips
<LI>Web Page Samples
<LI TYPE=Square>Images
<LI TYPE=Disc>Templates
</UL>
```

In this case, all the list items will have a disc symbol as the bullet, except the third item, Images, which will be displayed with a square bullet.

The TYPE modifier can be assigned the same values as those used to define lists with the <UL> and <OL> tags.

Once it is used to define a style for a list item, all subsequent items in the list will be changed, unless another TYPE modifier is used.

If you are defining <LI> list elements for ordered lists <OL>, you can also use a new modifier named VALUE to change the numeric value of a list item. Here's an example:

```
<H2>Useful Publishing Resources</H2>
<OL>
<LI>HTML Tips
<LI>Web Page Samples
<LI VALUE=4>Images
<LI>Templates
</UL>
```

In this list, the third item would be assigned the number 4 and the fourth item would be assigned the number 5.

## Directory and Menu Lists

The directory and menu lists are special types of unordered lists. The menu list, <MENU>, is meant to be visually more compact than a standard unordered list; menu list items should all fit on a single line. The directory list, <DIR>, is supposed to be even more compact; all list items should be less than 20 characters long, so that the list can be displayed in three (or more) columns.

We're not sure if we've ever actually seen these lists in use, and their implementation is still spotty; current versions of Netscape do not create multiple columns for a <DIR> list, and while they let you choose a directory list font and a menu list font, they do not actually use these fonts.

## Description List

The description list, or <DL>, does not use the <LI> tag the way other lists do. Each description list element has two parts, a tag and its description. Each tag begins with a <DT> tag, and each description with a <DD> tag. These appear at the start of the list element, and are not paired with </DT> or </DD> tags.

The description list looks a lot like any other list, except that instead of a bullet or a number, the list tag consists of your text. Description lists are intended to be used for creating

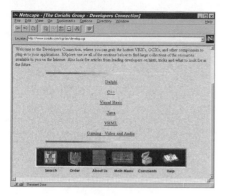

*Here is an example of how to use inline images to look like an image map without the headache of using CGI.*

formats like a glossary entry, where a short tag is followed by an indented definition, but the format is fairly flexible. For example, a long tag will wrap, just like any other paragraph, although it should not contain line or paragraph breaks. (Netscape will indent any <DT> text after a line or paragraph, as if it were the <DD> text.) Further, you needn't actually supply any tag text; <DT><DD> will produce an indented paragraph.

### Compact and Standard Lists

Normally, a description list puts the tags on one line, and starts the indented descriptions on the next:

```
Tag 1
Description 1.
Tag 2
Description 2.
```

For a tighter look, you can use a <DL COMPACT>. If the tags are very short, some browsers will start the descriptions on the same line as the tags:

```
Tag 1              Description 1
Tag 2              Description 2
```

However, most browsers do not support the compact attribute, and will simply ignore it. For example, with current versions of Windows Netscape, a <DL COMPACT> will always look like a <DL>, even if the tags are very short.

## Inline Images

Using only text attributes, section headers, and lists, you can build attractive-looking documents. The next step is to add pictures.

```
<IMG ...> Tag
```

The <IMG> tag is a very useful HTML feature. It lets you insert inline images into your text. This tag is rather different from the tags we've seen so far. Not only is it an empty tag that always appears alone, it has a number of parameters between the opening <IMG and the closing >. Some of the parameters include the image file name and some optional modifiers. The basic format for this tag is:

*Tip: When you define an image, you can specify that the image be loaded from any URL. However, if you want to ensure that your images always load, you should store them on the same server used to store your HTML files.*

```
<IMG SRC="URL" ALT="text"
    ALIGN=top|middle|bottom
    ISMAP>
```

Since HTML 3 has emerged and additional Netscape extensions have been added, this tag has expanded more than any other HTML feature. Here is the complete format for the latest and greatest version of the <IMG> tag:

```
<IMG SRC="URL" ALT="text"
    ALIGN=left|right|top|texttop|middle|absmiddle|
        baseline|bottom|absbottom
    WIDTH=pixels
    HEIGHT=pixels
    BORDER=pixels
    VSPACE=pixels
    HSPACE=pixels
    ISMAP>
```

The extended version allows you to specify the size of an image, better control image and text alignment, and specify the size of an image's border.

Every <IMG> tag must have a SRC= parameter. This specifies a URL, or Uniform Resource Locator, which points to a GIF or JPEG bitmap file. When the bitmap file is in the same directory as the HTML document, the file name is an adequate URL. For example, <IMG SRC=MySmilingFace.gif> would insert a picture of a smiling face.

Some people turn off inline images because they have a slow connection to the Web. This replaces all images, no matter what size, with a standard graphic. This isn't so bad if the picture is ancillary to your text, but if you've used small inline images as bullets in a list or as section dividers, the placeholder graphic will usually make your page look rather strange. For this reason, some people avoid using graphics as structural elements; others simply don't worry about people with slow connections; still others include a note at the top of the page saying that all the images on the page are small, and invite people with inline images off to turn them on and reload the page.

Keep in mind that some people use text-only browsers, like Lynx, to navigate the Web. If you include a short description of your image with the ALT= parameter, text-only browsers can show something in place of your graphic. For example, <IMG SRC=MySmilingFace.gif could be supplemented by the code: ALT="A picture of the author">, so that no one feels left out.

Since the the value assigned to the ALT parameter has spaces in it, we have to put it within quotation marks. In general, you can put any parameter value in quotation marks, but you need to do so only if it includes spaces.

# Mixing Images and Text

You can mix text and images within a paragraph; an image does not constitute a paragraph break. However, some Web browsers, like earlier versions of Netscape, did not wrap paragraphs around images; they displayed a single line of text to the left or right of an image. Normally, any text in the same paragraph as an image would be lined up with the bottom of the image, and would wrap normally below the image. This works well if the text is essentially a caption for the image, or if the image is a decoration at the start of a paragraph. However, when the image is a part of a header, you may want the text to be centered vertically in the image, or to be lined up with the top of the image. In these cases, you can use the optional ALIGN= parameter to specify ALIGN=top, ALIGN=middle, or ALIGN=bottom.

## Using Floating Images

With the extended version of the <IMG> tag, you can now create "floating" images that will align to the left or right margin of a Web page. Text that is displayed after the image will either wrap around the right-hand or left-hand side of the image. Here's an example of how an image can be displayed at the left margin with text that wraps to the right of the image:

```
<IMG SRC="limage.gif" ALIGN=left>
```

Text will be displayed to the right of the image.

## Specifying Spacing for Floating Images

When you use floating images with wrap-around text, you can specify the spacing between the text and the image by using the VSPACE and HSPACE modifiers. VSPACE defines the amount of spacing in units of pixels between the top and bottom of the image and the text. HSPACE defines the spacing between the left or right edge of the image and the text that wraps.

### Sizing Images

Another useful feature that has been added to the <IMG> tag is image sizing. The WIDTH and HEIGHT modifiers are used to specify the width and height for an image in pixels. Here's an example:

```
<IMG SRC="logo.gif" WIDTH=250 HEIGHT=310>
```

When a browser like Netscape displays an image, it needs to determine the size of the image before it can display a placeholder or bounding box for the image. If you include the image's size using WIDTH and HEIGHT, a Web page can be built much faster. If the values you specify for WIDTH and HEIGHT differ from the image's actual width and height, the image will be scaled to fit.

### Using Multiple Images per Line

Since an image is treated like a single (rather large) character, you can have more than one image on a single line. In fact, you can have as many images on a line as will fit in your reader's window! If you put too many images on a line, the browser will wrap the line and your images will appear on multiple lines. If you don't want images to appear on the same line, place a <BR> or <P> between them.

### Defining an Image's Border

Typically, an image is displayed with a border around it. This is the border that is set to the color blue when the image is part of an anchor. Using the BORDER modifier, you can specify a border width for any image you display. Here's an example that displays an image with a five pixel border:

```
<IMG SRC="logo.gif" BORDER=5>
```

The following table shows the summary of <IMG> parameters.

| Parameter | Required? | Settings |
|-----------|-----------|----------|
| SRC | Yes | URL |
| ALT | No | A text string |
| ALIGN | No | top, middle, bottom left, right, texttop, absmiddle, baseline, absbottom |
| HEIGHT | No | Pixel setting |
| WIDTH | No | Pixel setting |
| BORDER | No | Pixel setting |
| VSPACE | No | Pixel setting |
| HSPACE | No | Pixel setting |
| ISMAP | No | None |

## IsMap Parameter

The optional ISMAP parameter allows you to place hyperlinks to other documents in a bitmapped image. This technique is used to turn an image into a clickable map. (See the section *Using Many Anchors in an Image* for more detail.)

## Horizontal Rules

The <HR> tag draws a horizontal rule, or line, across the screen. It's fairly common to put a rule before and after a form, to help set off the user entry areas from the normal text.

Many people use small inline images for decoration and separation, instead of rules. Although using images in this manner lets you customize your pages, it also takes longer for them to load—and it may make them look horrible when inline images are turned off.

The original <HR> tag simply displayed an engraved rule across a Web page. A newer version of the tag has been extended to add additional features including sizing, alignment, and shading. The format for the extended version of <HR> is:

```
<HR SIZE=pixels
   WIDTH=pixels|percent
   ALIGN=left|right|center
   NOSHADE>
```

The SIZE modifier sets the width (thickness) of the line in pixel units. The WIDTH modifier specifies the length of the line in actual pixel units or a percentage of the width of the page. The ALIGN modifier specifies the alignment for the line (the default is center) and the NOSHADE modifier allows you to display a solid line.

As an example of how some of these new features are used, the following tag displays a solid line, five pixels thick. The line is left justified and spans 80 percent of the width of the page:

```
<HR SIZE=5 WIDTH=80% ALIGN="left" NOSHADE>
```

# Hypermedia Links

The ability to add links to other HTML documents or to entirely different sorts of documents is what makes the HTML-driven readers so powerful. The special sort of highlight that your reader clicks on to traverse a hypermedia link is called an anchor, and all links are created with the anchor tag, <A>. The basic format for this tag is:

```
<A HREF="URL"
   NAME="text"
   REL=next|previous|parent|made
   REV=next|previous|parent|made
   TITLE="text">

text</A>
```

### Links to Other Documents

While you can define a link to another point within the current page, most links are to other documents. Links to points within a document are very similar to links to other documents, but are slightly more complicated, so we will talk about them later. (See the section *Links to Anchors*.)

Each link has two parts: The visible part, or anchor, which the user clicks on, and the invisible part, which tells the browser where to go. The anchor is the text between the <A> and </A> tags of the <A> tag pair, while the actual link data appears in the <A> tag.

Just as the <IMG> tag has a SRC= parameter that specifies an image file, so does the <A> tag have an HREF= parameter that specifies the hypermedia reference. Thus, <A HREF=SomeFile.Type>click here</A> is a link to somefile.type with the visible anchor click here.

Browsers will generally use the linked document's filename extension to decide how to display the linked document. For example, HTML or HTM files will be interpreted and displayed as HTML, whether they come from an http server, an FTP server, or a gopher site. Conversely, a link can be to any sort of file—a large bitmap, sound file, or movie.

### Images as Hotspots

Since inline images are in many ways just big characters, there's no problem with using an image in an anchor. The anchor can include text on either side of the image, or the image can be an anchor by itself. Most browsers show an image anchor by drawing a blue border around the image (or around the placeholder graphic). The image anchor may be a picture of what is being linked to, or for reasons we'll explain shortly, it may even just point to another copy of itself:

```
<A HREF=image.gif><IMG SRC=image.gif></A>.
```

### Thumbnail Images

One sort of picture of the link is called a thumbnail image. This is a tiny image, perhaps 100 pixels in the smaller dimension, which is either a condensed version of a larger image or a section of the image. Thumbnail images can be transmitted quickly, even via slow communication lines, leaving it up to the reader to decide which larger images to request. A secondary issue is aesthetic: Large images take up a lot of screen space, smaller images don't.

### Linking an Image to Itself

Many people turn off inline images to improve performance over a slow network link. If the inline image is an anchor for itself, these people can then click on the placeholder graphic to see what they missed.

*Image maps allow for some pretty cool interface designs. (http://www.indirect.com)*

## Using Many Anchors in an Image

The <IMG> tag's optional ISMAP parameter allows you to turn rectangular regions of a bitmap image into clickable anchors. Clicking on these parts of the image will activate an appropriate URL. (A default URL is also usually provided for when the user clicks on an area outside of one of the pre-defined regions.) While forms let you do this a bit more flexibly, the ISMAP approach doesn't require any custom programming—just a simple text file that defines the rectangles and their URLs—and this technique may work with browsers that do not support forms. An example of how to do this can be found on the Web site at:

```
http://wintermute.ncsc.uiuc.edu:8080/map-tutorial/
imagemaps.html
```

## Links to Anchors

When an HREF parameter specifies a filename, the link is to the whole document. If the document is an HTML file, it will replace the current document and the reader will be placed at the top of the new document. Often this is just what you want. But sometimes you'd rather have a link take the reader to a specific section of a document. Doing this requires two anchor tags: one that defines an anchor name for a location, and one that points to that name. These two tags can be in the same document or in different documents.

## Defining an Anchor Name

To define an anchor name, you need to use the NAME parameter: <A NAME=AnchorName>. You can attach this name to a phrase, not just a single point, by following the <A> tag with a </A> tag.

## Linking to an Anchor in the Current Document

To then use this name, simply insert an <A HREF=...> tag as usual, except that instead of a filename, use a # followed by an anchor name. For example, <A HREF=#AnchorName> refers to the example in the previous paragraph.

Names do not have to be defined before they are used; it's actually fairly common for lengthy documents to have a table of contents with links to names defined later in the document. It's also worth noting that while tag and parameter names are not case sensitive, anchor names are; <AHREF=#anchorname> will not take you to the AnchorName example.

### Linking to an Anchor in a Different Document

You can also link to specific places in any other HTML document, anywhere in the world—provided, of course, that it contains named anchors. To do this, you simply add the # and the anchor name after the URL that tells where the document can be found. For example, to plant a link to the anchor named "Section 1" in a file named complex.html in the same directory as the current file, you could use <A HREF= "Complex.html#Section 1">. Similarly, if the named anchor was in http://www.another.org/Complex.html, you'd use <A HREF="http://www.another.org/Complex.html#Section 1">.

## Using URLs

Just as a complete DOS file name starts with a drive letter followed by a colon, so a full URL starts with a resource type—HTTP, FTP, GOPHER, and so on—followed by a colon. If the name doesn't have a colon in it, it's assumed to be a local reference, which is a file name on the same file system as the current document. Thus, <A HREF=Another.html> refers to the file "Another.html" in the same directory as the current file, while <A HREF=/html/File.html> refers to the file "File.html" in the top-level directory html. One thing to note here is that a URL always uses "/" (the Unix-style forward slash) as a directory separator, even when the files are on a Windows machine, which would normally use "\", the DOS-style backslash.

Local URLs can be very convenient when you have several HTML files with links to each other, or when you have a large number of inline images. If you ever have to move them all to another directory, or to another machine, you don't have to change all the URLs.

### <BASE> Tag

One drawback of local URLs is that if someone makes a copy of your document, the local URLs will no longer work.

Adding the optional <BASE> tag to the <HEAD> section of your document will help eliminate this problem. While many browsers do not yet support it, the intent of the <BASE> tag is precisely to provide a context for local URLs.

The <BASE> tag is like the <IMG> tag, in that it's a so-called empty tag. It requires an HREF parameter—for example, <BASE HREF=http://www.imaginary.org/index.html>— which should contain the URL of the document itself. When a browser that supports the <BASE> tag encounters a URL that doesn't contain a protocol and path, it will look for it relative to the base URL, instead of relative to the location from which it actually loaded the document. The format for the <BASE> tag is:

```
<BASE HREF="URL">
```

The following table summarizes the <A> Tag Syntax.

| To: | Use: |
| --- | --- |
| Link to another document | <A HREF="URL">highlighted anchor text</A> |
| Name an anchor | <A NAME="Anchor Name">normal text</A> |
| Link to a named anchor in this document | <A href="#Anchor Name">highlighted anchor text</A> |
| Link to a named anchor in another document | <A href="URL#Anchor Name">highlighted anchor text</A> |

## Reading and Constructing URLs

Where a local URL is just a file name, a global URL specifies an instance of one of several resource types, which may be located on any Internet machine in the world. The wide variety of resources is reflected in a complex URL syntax. For example, while most URLs consist of a resource type followed by a colon, two forward slashes, a machine name, another forward slash, and a resource name, others consist only of a resource type, a colon, and the resource name.

The resource-type://machine-name/resource-name URL form is used with centralized resources, where there's a single server that supplies the document to the rest of the net, using a particular protocol. Thus, a URL that reads "http://www.another.org/Complex.html" means "use the

Hypertext Transfer Protocol to get file complex.html from the main www directory on the machine www.another.org", while "ftp://foo.bar.net/pub/www/editors/README" means "use the File Transfer Protocol to get the file /pub/www/editors/README from the machine foo.bar.net".

Conversely, many resource types are distributed. We don't all get our news or mail from the same central server, but from the nearest one of many news and mail servers. URLs for distributed resources use the simpler form resource-type:resource-name. For example, "news:comp.infosystems.www.providers" refers to the Usenet newsgroup comp.infosystems.www.providers, which, by the way, is a good place to look for further information about writing HTML.

The following table shows a partial table of URL resource types.

| Resource | Interpretation | Format |
| --- | --- | --- |
| HTTP | Hypertext Transfer Protocol | http://machine-name/file-name |
| FTP | File Transfer Protocol | ftp://machine-name/file-name |
| GOPHER | Gopher | gopher://machine-name/file-name |
| NEWS | Internet News | news:group-name |
| TELNET | Log on to a remote system | telnet://machine-name |
| MAILTO | Normal Internet e-mail | mailto:user-name@machine-name |

### Using www and Actual Machine Names

In the HTTP domain, you'll often see "machine names" like "www.coriolis.com". This usually does not mean there's a machine named www.coriolis.com that you can FTP or Telnet to; "www" is an alias that a Webmaster can set up when he or she registers the server. Using the www alias makes sense, because machines come and go, but sites (and, we hope, the Web) last for quite a while. If URLs refer to www at the site and not to a specific machine, the server and all the HTML files can be moved to a new machine simply by changing the www alias, without having to update all the URLs.

*Tip: Here's a quick way to locate many vendors on the Web. Start the URL with www, type the "." separator, type the company name, type another "." separator, then end the URL with com, as in:*

```
www.microsoft.com
```

*Not all Web vendors use this address format, but many do.*

# Using Special Characters

Since < and > have special meanings in HTML, there must be a way to represent characters like these as part of text. While the default character set for the Web is ISO Latin-1, which includes European language characters like _ and § in the range from 128 to 255, it's not uncommon to pass around snippets of HTML in 7-bit email, or to edit them on dumb terminals, so HTML also needs a way to specify high-bit characters using only 7-bit characters.

### Two Forms: Numeric and Symbolic

There are two ways to specify an arbitrary character: numeric and symbolic. To include the copyright symbol, ©, which is character number 169, you can use &#169;. That is, &#, then the number of the character you want to include, and a closing semicolon. The numeric method is very general, but not easy to read.

The symbolic form is much easier to read, but its use is restricted to the four low-bit characters with special meaning in HTML. To use the other symbols in the ISO Latin-1 character set, like ® and the various currency symbols, you have to use the numeric form. The symbolic escape is like the numeric escape, except there's no #. For example, to insert é, you would use &eacute;, or &, the character name, and a closing semicolon. You should be aware that symbol names are case sensitive: &Eacute; is É, not é, while &EAcute; is no character at all, and will show up in your text as &EAcute;!

# Preformatted and Other Special Paragraph Types

HTML supports three special "block" formats. Any normal text within a block format is supposed to appear in a distinctive font.

### <BLOCKQUOTE> ... </BLOCKQUOTE> Tag

The block quote sets an extended quotation off from normal text. That is, a <BLOCKQUOTE> tag pair does not imply indented, single-spaced, and italicized; rather, it's just meant to change the default, plain text font. The format for this tag is:

```
<BLOCKQUOTE>text</BLOCKQUOTE>
```

### &lt;PRE&gt; ... &lt;/PRE&gt; Tag

Everything in a preformatted block will appear in a mono-spaced font. The &lt;PRE&gt; tag pair is also the only HTML element that pays any attention to the line breaks in the source file; any line break in a preformatted block will be treated just as a &lt;BR&gt; elsewhere. Since HTML tags can be used within a preformatted block, you can have anchors as well as bold or italic monospaced text. The format for this tag is:

```
<PRE WIDTH=value>text</PRE>
```

The initial &lt;PRE&gt; tag has an optional WIDTH= parameter. Browsers won't trim lines to this length; the intent is to allow the browser to select a monospaced font that will allow the maximum line length to fit in the browser window.

### &lt;ADDRESS&gt; ... &lt;/ADDRESS&gt; Tag

The third block format is the address format: &lt;ADDRESS&gt;. This is generally displayed in italics, and is intended for displaying information about a document, such as creation date, revision history, and how to contact the author. Official style guides say that every document should provide an address block. The format for this tag is:

```
<ADDRESS>text</ADDRESS>
```

Many people put a horizontal rule, &lt;HR&gt;, between the body of the document and the address block. If you include a link to your home page or to a page that lets the reader send mail to you, you won't have to include a lot of information on each individual page.

## Using Tables

Features like lists are great for organizing data; however, sometimes you need a more compact way of grouping related data. Fortunately, some of the newer browsers like Netscape have implemented the proposed HTML 3 specification for tables. Tables can contain a heading and row and column data. Each unit of a table is called a cell and cell data can be text and images.

*Nice use of a table.*

*(http://www.coriolis.com)*

*Using a table that doesn't look like a table.*

*(http://www.yahoo.com)*

## `<TABLE > ... </TABLE>` Tag

This tag is used to define a new table. All of the table-specific tags must be placed within the pair <TABLE> ... </TABLE>, otherwise they will be ignored. The format for the <TABLE> tag is:

```
<TABLE BORDER>table text</TABLE>
```

Leaving out the BORDER modifier will display the table without a border.

## Creating a Table Title

Creating a title or caption for a table is easy with the <CAPTION> tag. This tag must be placed within the <TABLE> ... </TABLE> tags. Here is its general format:

```
<CAPTION ALIGN=top|bottom>caption text</CAPTION>
```

Notice that you can display the caption at the top or bottom of the table. By default, the caption will be displayed at the top of the table.

## Creating Table Rows

Every table you create will have one or more rows. (Otherwise it won't be much of a table!) The simple tag for creating a row is:

```
<TR>text</TR>
```

For each row that you want to add, you must place the <TR> tag inside the body of the table, between the <TABLE> ... </TABLE> tags.

## Defining Table Data Cells

Within each <TR> ... </TR> tag pair come one or more <TD> tags to define the table cell data. You can think of the cell data as the column definitions for the table. Here is the format for a <TD> tag:

```
<TD ALIGN=left|center|right
    VALIGN=top|middle|bottom|baseline
    NOWRAP
    COLSPAN=number
    ROWSPAN=number>
text</TD>
```

The size for each cell is determined by the width or height of the data that is displayed. The ALIGN parameter can be used to center or left- or right-justify the data displayed in the cell. The VALIGN parameter, on the other hand, specifies how the data will align vertically. If you don't want the text to wrap within the cell, you can include the NOWRAP modifier.

When defining a cell, you can manually override the width and height of the cell by using the COLSPAN and ROWSPAN parameters. COLSPAN specifies the number of columns the table cell will span and ROWSPAN specifies the number of rows to span. The default setting for each of these parameters is 1.

### Defining Headings for Cells

In addition to displaying a table caption, you can include headings for a table's data cells. The tag for defining a heading looks very similar to the <TD> tag:

```
<TH ALIGN=left|center|right
    VALIGN=top|middle|bottom|baseline
    NOWRAP
    COLSPAN=number
    ROWSPAN=number>
text</TH>
```

## Using Forms

The HTML features presented so far correspond with traditional publishing practices: You create a hypermedia document, and others read it. With HTML forms, however, you can do much more. You can create a form that lets your readers search a database using any criteria they like. Or you can create a form that lets them critique your Web pages. Or—and this is what excites business people—you can use forms to sell things over the Internet.

Forms are easy to create. However, to use them, you'll need a program that runs on your Web server to process the information that the user's client sends back to you. For simple things like a "comments page," you can probably use an existing program. For anything more complex, you'll probably need a custom program. While we will briefly describe the way form data looks to the receiving program, any discussion of form programming is beyond this book's scope.

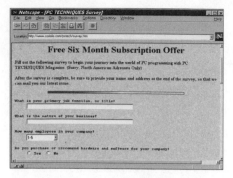

*One of the increasingly popular use of forms is to encourage people to order products or services or to fill in marketing surveys.*

*Search engines often use forms to allow users to define different search criteria.*

## <FORM> ... </FORM> Tag

All input widgets—text boxes, check boxes, and radio buttons—must appear within a <FORM> tag pair. When a user clicks on a submit button or an image map, the contents of all the widgets in the form will be sent to the program that you specify in the <FORM> tag. HTML widgets include single- and multi-line text boxes, radio buttons and check boxes, pull-down lists, image maps, a couple of standard buttons, and a hidden widget that might be used to identify the form to a program that can process several forms.

Within your form, you can use any other HTML elements, including headers, images, rules, and lists. This gives you a fair amount of control over your form's appearance, but you should always remember that the user's screen size and font choices will affect the actual appearance of your form.

While you can have more than one form on a page, you cannot nest one form within another.

The basic format for the <FORM> tag is as follows:

```
<FORM ACTION="URL"
    METHOD=get|post>
text</FORM>
```

Notice that text can be included as part of the form definition.

## Form Action and Method Attributes

Nothing gets sent to your Web server until the user presses a Submit button or clicks on an image map. What happens then depends on the ACTION, METHOD, and ENCTYPE parameters of the <FORM> tag.

The ACTION parameter specifies which URL the form data should be sent to for further processing. This is most commonly in the cgi-bin directory of a Web server. If you do not specify an action parameter, the contents will be sent to the current document's URL.

The METHOD parameter tells how to send the form's contents. There are two possibilities here: Get and Post. If you do not specify a method, Get will be used. Get and Post both format the form's data identically; they differ only in how they pass the form's data to the program that uses that data.

Get and Post both send the forms contents as a single long text vector consisting of a list of WidgetName=WidgetValue pairs, each separated from its successor by an ampersand. For example:

```
"NAME=Tony Potts&Address=aapotts@coriolis.com"
```

(Any & or = sign in a widget name or value will be quoted using the standard ampersand escape; any bare "&" and any "=" sign can therefore be taken as a separator.) You will not necessarily get a name and value for every widget in the form; while empty text is explicitly sent as a WidgetName= with an empty value, unselected radio buttons and check boxes don't send even their name.

Where Get and Post differ is that the Get method creates a "query URL," which consists of the action URL, a question mark, and the formatted form data. The Post method, on the other hand, sends the formatted form data to the action URL in a special data block. The Web server parses the query URL that a Get method creates and passes the form data to the form processing program as a command line parameter. This creates a limitation on form data length that the Post method does not.

Currently, all form data is sent in plain text. This creates a security problem. The optional ENCTYPE parameter offers a possible solution, which only allows you to ratify the plain text default. In the future, however, values may be provided that call for an encrypted transmission.

## Widgets

From a users' point of view, there are seven types of Web widgets; all of them are generated by one of three HTML tags. Except for the standard buttons, all widgets must be given a name.

### <INPUT> Tag

The <INPUT> tag is the most versatile, and the most complex. It can create single-line text boxes, radio buttons, check boxes, image maps, the two standard buttons, and the hidden widget. It's somewhat like the <IMG> tag in that it appears by itself, not as part of a tag pair, and has some optional parameters. Of these, the TYPE= parameter determines both the widget type and the meaning of the other parameters. If no other parameters are provided, the <INPUT> tag generates a text box.

The format for the <INPUT> tag is:

```
<INPUT TYPE="text"|"password"|"checkbox"|"radio"|"sub-
mit"|"reset"|"hidden"|"image"
        NAME="name"
        VALUE="value"
        SIZE="number"
        MAXLENGTH="number"
        CHECKED>
```

The TYPE parameter can be set to one of eight values. We'll look at each of these options shortly. Each input must contain a unique name defined with NAME. The VALUE parameter specifies the initial value of the input. This value is optional. The SIZE parameter defines the size of a text line and MAXLENGTH is the maximum size allowed for the returned text.

The following table shows the syntax of the text and password input types.

| Attribute | Required? | Format | Meaning |
| --- | --- | --- | --- |
| TYPE | No | TYPE="text" or TYPE="password" | Determines what type of widget this will be. Default is "text". |
| NAME | Yes | NAME="WidgetName" | Identifies the widget. |
| VALUE | No | VALUE="Default text" | You supply default value. Cannot contain HTML commands. |
| SIZE | No | SIZE=Cols | Width (in characters) of a single line text area. Default is 20. |
| SIZE | No | SIZE=Cols,Rows | Height and width (in characters) of a multi-li text area. |
| MAXLENGTH | No | MAXLENGTH=Chars | Longest value a single line text area can return. Default unlimited. |

## Text Boxes

If the TYPE= parameter is set to text (or no parameter is used), the input widget will be a text box. The password input type is just like the text type, except that the value shows only as a series of asterisks. All text areas must have a name. Text areas always report their value, even if it is empty.

## Check Boxes and Radio Buttons

Check boxes and radio buttons are created by an <INPUT> tag with a checkbox or radio type. Both must have a name and a value parameter, and may be initially checked. The name parameter is the widget's symbolic name, used in returning a value to your Web server, not its onscreen tag. For that, you use normal HTML text next to the <INPUT> tag. Since the display tag is not part of the <INPUT> tag, Netscape check boxes and radio buttons operate differently from their dialog box kin; you cannot toggle a widget by clicking on its text, you have to click on the widget itself.

Radio buttons are grouped by having identical names. Only one (or none) of the group can be checked at any one time; clicking on a radio button will turn off whichever button in the name group was previously on.

Check boxes and radio buttons return their value only if they are checked.

The following table shows the syntax of the check box and radio types.

| Attribute | Required? | Format | Meaning |
|---|---|---|---|
| TYPE | Yes | TYPE=checkbox or TYPE=radio | Determines what type of widget this will be. Default is "text". |
| NAME | Yes | NAME="WidgetName" | A unique identifier for a checkbox; a group identifier for radio buttons. |
| VALUE | Yes checked. | VALUE="WidgetValue" | The value is sent if the widget is |
| CHECKED | No get | CHECKED | If this attribute is present, the wid- |

## Image Maps

Image maps are created with the TYPE="image" code. They return their name and a pair of numbers that represents the position that the user clicked on; the form handling program is responsible for interpreting this pair of numbers. Since this program can do anything you want with the click position, you are not restricted to rectangular anchors, as with <IMG ISMAP>.

Clicking on an image map, like clicking on a Submit button, will send all form data to the Web server.

## Submit/Reset Buttons

The submit and reset types let you create one of the two standard buttons. Clicking on a Submit button, like clicking on an image map, will send all form data to the Web server. Clicking on a Reset button resets all widgets in the form to their default values. These buttons are the only widgets that don't need to have names. By default, they will be labeled Submit and Reset; you can specify the button text by supplying a VALUE parameter.

The following table shows the syntax of the image type.

| Attribute | Required? | Format | Meaning |
|---|---|---|---|
| TYPE | Yes | TYPE=image | Determines what type of widge this will be. Default is "text". |
| NAME | Yes | NAME="WidgetName" | Identifies the widget. |
| SRC | Yes | SRC="URL" | The URL of a bitmapped image to display. |

The next table shows the syntax of the submit and reset types.

| Attribute | Required? | Format | Meaning |
|---|---|---|---|
| TYPE | Yes | TYPE=submit or TYPE=reset | Determines what type of widge this will be. Default is "text". |
| NAME | No | NAME="WidgetName" | The buttons never return their values, so a name will never be used. |
| VALUE | No | VALUE="WidgetValue" | The button text. Default is Submit or Reset, respectively |

### Hidden Fields

A hidden type creates an invisible widget. This widget won't appear onscreen, but its name and value are included in the form's contents when the user presses the Submit button or clicks on an image map. This feature might be used to identify the form to a program that processes several different forms.

### <TextArea> ... </TextArea> Tag

The <TEXTAREA> tag pair is similar to a multi-line text input widget. The primary difference is that you always use a <TextArea> tag pair and put any default text between the <TEXTAREA> and </TEXTAREA> tags. As with <PRE> blocks, any line breaks in the source file are honored, which lets you include line breaks in the default text. The ability to have a long, multi-line default text is the only functional difference between a TEXTAREA and a multi-line input widget.

The format for the <TEXTAREA> tag is:

```
<TEXTAREA NAME="name"
          ROWS="rows"
          COLS="cols"> </TEXTAREA>
```

The following table shows the syntax of the hidden type.

| Attribute | Required? | Format | Meaning |
|-----------|-----------|--------|---------|
| TYPE | Yes | TYPE=hidden | Determines what type of widge this will be. Default is "text". |
| NAME | Yes | NAME="WidgetName" | Identifies the widget. |
| VALUE | Yes | VALUE="WidgetValue" | Whatever constant data you might want to include with the form. |

The next table shows the syntax of the <TEXTAREA> tag.

| Attribute | Required? | Format | Meaning |
|-----------|-----------|--------|---------|
| NAME | Yes | NAME="WidgetName" | Identifies the widget. |
| ROWS | No | ROWS=Rows | TextArea height, in characters. |
| COLS | No | COLS=Cols | TextArea width, in characters. Default is 20. |

## <SELECT> ... </SELECT> Tag.

The <SELECT> tag pair allows you to present your users with a set of choices. This is not unlike a set of check boxes, yet it takes less room on the screen.

Just as you can use check boxes for 0 to N selections, or radio buttons for 0 or 1 selection, you can specify the cardinality of selection behavior. Normally, select widgets act like a set of radio buttons; your users can only select zero or one of the options. However, if you specify the multiple option, the select widget will act like a set of check boxes, and your users may select any or all of the options.

The format for the <SELECT> tag is:

```
<SELECT NAME="name"
        SIZE="rows"
        MULTIPLE>text/option list</SELECT>
```

Within the <SELECT> tag pair is a series of <OPTION> statements, followed by the option text. These are similar to <LI> list items, except that <OPTION> text may not include any HTML markup. The <OPTION> tag may include an optional selected attribute; more than one option may be selected if and only if the <SELECT> tag includes the MULTIPLE option.

The following table displays the syntax of the <SELECT> tag.

| Attribute | Required? | Format | Meaning |
|-----------|-----------|--------|---------|
| NAME | Yes | NAME="WidgetName" | Identifies the widget. |
| SIZE | No | SIZE=Rows | This is the widget height, in character rows. If the size is 1, you get a pull down list. If the size is greater than 1, you get a scrolling list. Default is 1. |
| MULTIPLE | No | MULTIPLE | Allows more than one option to be selected. |

For example:

```
Which Web browsers do you use?
<SELECT NAME="Web Browsers" MULTIPLE>
<OPTION>Netscape
<OPTION>Lynx
```

```
<OPTION>WinWeb
<OPTION>Cello
</SELECT>
```

For more information on creating HTML documents, go to
the following World Wide Web sites:

### A Beginner's Guide to HTML

```
http://www.ncsa.uiuc.edu/General/Internet/WWW/HTMLPrimer.
html
```

### The HTML Quick Reference Guide

```
http://kuhttp.cc.ukans.edu/lynx_help/HTML_quick.html
```

### Information on the Different Versions of HTML

```
http://www.w3.org/hypertext/WWW/MarkUp/MarkUp.html
```

### Composing Good HTML

```
http://www/willamette.edu/html-composition/strict-
html.html
```

### HTML+ Specifications

```
http://info.cern.ch/hypertext/WWW/MarkUp/HTMLPlus/htmlplu
s_1.html
```

### HTML Specification Version 3.0

```
http://www.hpl.hp.co.uk/people/dsr/html3/CoverPage.html
```

### HTML Editors

```
http://akebono.stanford.edu/yahoo/Computers/World_Wide_We
b/HTML_Editors/
```

### Resources for Converting Documents to HTML

```
http://info.cern.ch/hypertext/WWW/Tools/Filters.html
```

### An Archive of Useful HTML Translators

```
ftp://src.doc.ic.ac.uk/computing/information-
systems/www/tools/translators/
```

# Using the Companion CD-ROM

The companion CD-ROM to this book is packed with applications, clip art, and resources that will help you design and build great Web pages.

Keep in mind that most of the software on this disk is either shareware or freeware. Shareware means that the author or authors of the software are allowing you to try out the software with the expectation that if you like it, you will pay them for it or upgrade to a commercial version. Freeware means that you can use the software as much as you want with no charge, but there is usually a more advanced version available for a price. Check for a README or LICENSE file with each of the applications you use to see what restrictions the author has placed on the software and its distribution and use.

Here is a description of what the four main directories on the CD contain:

| | |
|---|---|
| **\BOOKSTUF** | Sample images and videos from the book |
| **\CLIPART** | Thousands of images, videos, and sound files you can use |
| **\HELPERS** | Helper applications that work really well with Web browsers |
| **\TOOLS** | Great selection of Web page building tools and accessories |

Now, let's take a look at some of the more useful applications on the CD-ROM. Don't be afraid to experiment a little and play with all the different types of software. Most of the software is described in this guide, but for those programs that aren't, just check in the applications directory for more information.

**Application:** Clipart

**Where on CD:**

```
\CLIPART
```

**Where Online:**

```
http://www.lycos.com (Lycos search for "CLIPART
     ARCHIVES")
http://sunsite.nus.sg/ftpmultimedia.html
http://seidel.ncsa.uiuc.edu/ClipArt/funet.html
```

**Description:** This collection of clipart was gathered from many different places. You can find images here that can really spice up your Web pages. Check out the collections in \CLIPART\ART\COHEN and \CLIPART\ART\FUNET to see some really impressive line art pieces. There are also many images that can be used as separator bars and custom list bullets. Why stick to what Netscape has to offer you? Use custom images to give your page a unique style. But, be careful. Too many images can really slow things down!

**Application:** Adobe Acrobat Reader

**Where on CD**: \HELPERS\ACROBAT

**Where Online**:

```
http://www.adobe.com/Software/Acrobat/
```

**Description:** Adobe Acrobat lets you create electronic documents from a wide range of authoring tools for sharing across different computer platforms. Simply "print" files to the Adobe Portable Document Format (PDF). Now you can distribute your documents over the broadest selection of electronic media, including the World Wide Web, email, Lotus Notes(R), corporate networks, CD-ROMs, and print-on-demand systems. Adobe is pushing the PDF format as a replacement for HTML. It's advantages are unlimited options for layout, and what you design is what others see, which does not always happen with HTML.

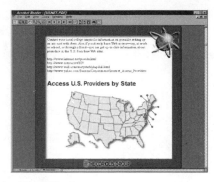

*Adobe Acrobat for Windows*

**Application:** Paint Shop Pro V3.1

**Where on CD:** \HELPERS\PSP3

**Where On-line:**

http://www.winternet.com/~jasc/index.html

**Description:** The complete Windows graphics program
for image creation, viewing, and manipulation. Features
include: painting, photo retouching, image enhancement and editing, color enhancement, image browser,
batch conversion, and TWAIN scanner support. Also
included are 20 standard image processing filters and 12
deformations. Supports Adobe-style image processing
plug-in filters. Over 30 file formats are supported,
including JPEG, Kodak Photo-CD, PBM, and GIF. This
is one graphics package you won't want to be without. It
has many of the features of much more expensive
graphics programs at a fraction of the cost. If you have
never bought a shareware package in your life, this may
be the first!

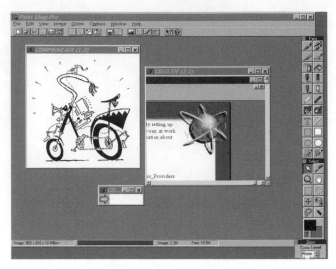

*Paint Shop Pro version 3.1 from JASC, Inc.*

**Application:** MPEG Movie Players

**Where on CD:**

VIDEO\MPEG\WINDOWS\MPEGWIN

**Where Online:**

http://www-plateau.cs.berkeley.edu/mpeg/mpegptr.html

**Description:** MPEG (Moving Pictures Experts Group) is a group that meets under ISO (the International Standards Organization) to generate standards for digital video (sequences of images in time) and audio compression. In particular, they define a compressed bit stream, which implicitly defines a decompressor. However, the compression algorithms are up to the individual manufacturers, and that is where proprietary advantage is obtained within the scope of a publicly available international standard. MPEG itself is a nickname. The official name is: ISO/IEC JTC1 SC29 WG11. MPEG is quickly becoming the standard for video playback for games because it is one of the few protocols that supports full-screen playback at 30-frames per second. The applications on the CD are very easy to use and offer many options for playback.

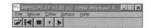

*MPEGWin, a Windows MPEG animation player*

**Application:** QuickTime Player from Apple

**Where on CD:**

\HELPERS\QUIKTIME

**Where On-line:**

http://quicktime.apple.com/

**Description:** Although QuickTime has been a Macintosh
standard for years, it is just beginning to catch on with
Windows users. It offers a few features that Video for
Windows does not have yet and some of the new technologies being developed for it are amazing. Check out
the QuickTime Web page for the latest and greatest versions and watch out for the QuickTime VR players and
editors that are beginning to appear. Note: There is a
QuickTime VR player now available for Windows.
Head up to the QuickTime Web site to download it.

**Application:** Video for Windows 1.1e

**Where on CD:**

\HELPERS\VFW11E

**Description:** Video for Windows (VfW) was originally an
add-on product for Windows 3.1. It has since been
upgraded continuously and is now in its fifth generation, which includes support for 32-bit compression and
decompression. With the release of Windows 95,
Microsoft has finally integrated VfW into the operating
system itself. For people still using Windows 3.11 or
older versions, here is the latest version of VfW.

**Application:** ViewSpace from Caligari

**Where on CD:**

\HELPERS\VIEWSPAC

**Where Online:**

http://www.caligari.com/

**Description:** ViewSpace is an impressive 3D rendering package that is being marketed as a VRML viewer for the Web. The current version allows you to load compatible files and navigate around in a real-time rendered 3D world. You will need a pretty fast computer to really enjoy this one, but it gives you an idea of some of the new technology that will be commonplace in a year or so.

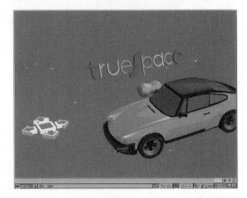

*ViewSpace with a model loaded.*

**Application:** Wham

**Where on CD:**

\TOOLS\SOUND\WHAM

**Where On-Line:**

http://www.netscape.com/MCOM/tricks_docs/helper_docs/

**Description:** WHAM (Waveform Hold and Modify) is a 16-bit application for manipulating digitized sound. It can read and write WAVE files, raw eight-bit digitized sound files, and files of several other formats (of which more may be added). It can also perform various operations on this sound. WHAM can handle sounds of any size, restricted only by memory.

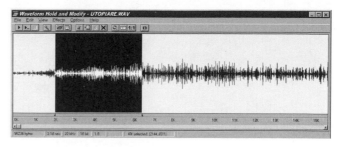

*Wham manipulating a sound file.*

**Application:** WinJammer

**Where on CD:**

\HELPERS\WINJAMR

**Where Online:**

http://www.netscape.com/MCOM/tricks_docs/helper_docs/

**Description:** WinJammer is a fully featured MIDI sequencer. It uses standard MIDI files, giving you access to a huge number of songs. WinJammer also contains a companion program called WinJammer Player, which is used to play MIDI song files in the background.

Major features of WinJammer include:

• imports Adlib ROL files

• supports up to 64 tracks

• runs in *all* Windows modes (including enhanced mode)

• provides very powerful editing commands

• features unique piano roll style notation for editing

• includes full online help

• supports standard MIDI files

• supports MIDI system exclusive bulk dumps

• supports Windows Multimedia Extensions

Major features of WinJammer Player include:

• supports standard MIDI files

• supports up to 64 tracks

• runs in ALL Windows modes (including enhanced mode)

- runs in enhanced mode, and will even play while in DOS
- provides full online help
- builds albums of songs to play (forever if desired)
- supports Windows Multimedia Extensions

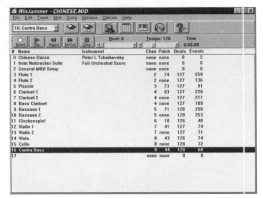

*WinJammer editing a MIDI song track.*

*WinJammer Player playing an album of MIDI songs.*

**Application:** WPlayAny

**Where on CD:**

\HELPERS\WPLAYANY

**Where Online:**

http://burgoyne.com/vaudio/netsound.html

**Description:** WPLAYANY is a compact utility that will detect and play almost any sound file you will run into on the Web. Use the Wham application to create and edit audio. You can also use it as a helper program with your Web browser. The proper drivers for your sound card (or PC speaker) must be loaded prior to using WPlayAny. This program does not have an interface, it simply plays files that it is sent by your browser.

Currently supported sound types include:

- SoundBlaster .VOC
- Sun/NeXT/DEC .AU
- Windows .WAV
- Sounder/Soundtools .SND
- Amiga .8SVX .IFF

**Application:** McAfee Virus Scanner

**Where on CD:**

`\TOOLS\ANTIVRUS\WSCAN`

**Where Online:**

`http://www.mcafee.com/`

**Description:** Hopefully you will never have bugs (yeah, right!). But if you do, McAfee makes some of the best anti-virus software. Check their Web site frequently for updates since new viruses are being found every day.

*McAfee's Wscan searching for viruses on a hard drive.*

**Application:** WinZip V5.6

**Where on CD:**

`\TOOLS\COMPRESS\WINZIP`

**Where On-Line:**

`http://www.winzip.com/winzip/`

**Description:** WinZip brings the convenience of Windows to the use of ZIP files without requiring PKZIP and

PKUNZIP. It features an intuitive point-and-click drag-and-drop interface for viewing, running, extracting, adding, deleting, and testing files in archives. ARJ, LZH, and ARC files are supported via external programs. WinZip also interfaces to most virus scanners so that you can check your compressed files before you run them. New in WinZip 5.6 is built-in support for popular Internet file formats: TAR, gzip, and Unix compress. Now you can use WinZip to access almost all the compressed files you download from the Internet.

*The WinZip interface.*

**Application:** Color Manipulation Device

**Where on CD:**

`\TOOLS\GRAPHICS\CMD`

**Where On-line:**

`http://www.meat.com/software/cmd.html`

**Description:** This simple application takes the guess work out of picking colors and graphics for your Web page backgrounds. If you have ever gotten confused by all the hexadecimal mumbo jumbo, this tool will make life easier for you. Simply pick colors for backgrounds and text and click on COPY. Then, paste the text into your Web page editor and you're done! Very handy and easy to use.

*The Color Manipulation Device.*

**Application:** WebImage

**Where on CD:**

\TOOLS\GRAPHICS\WEBIMAGE

**Where Online:**

http://www.group42.com/webimage.htm

**Description:** WebImage is the next generation of Internet media tools created by Group 42. It is an easy-to-use product that consolidates all of the special requirements needed for Web/Internet images. WebImage includes features for:

• Visually defining and viewing transparent GIF regions

• Easily creating and editing NCSA and CERN compliant Image Map files

• Creating interlaced GIF and PNG files

• Optimizing images based on color content, and compression

• Using high-quality color reduction methods to optimize images

• Turning images into buttons, adding text, or creating new images

• WebImage can even encode or decode files for easy Internet use

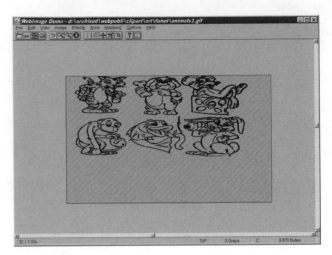

*WebImage*

**Application:** Image'n Bits

**Where on CD:**

\TOOLS\GRAPHICS\IMA

**Where Online:**

http://ios.com:80/~banana/

**Description:** Image 'N Bits is another handy image
manipulation program that you can use. It is designed
for people who are creating images for the Web.
Image 'n Bits v2.0 is an imaging, file conversion, and
screen capture program based on OLE technology.
Although Image'n Bits is fully functional as a stand-
alone application, it really comes to life when it is
used as a "component" of another application. Images
and image documents, stored in the file formats supported by Image 'n Bits, can be embedded or linked
into any OLE-compliant application. In other words,
this package works best as an add-on to another imaging system you may be using that does not have all the
options you want.

*Image 'N Bits.*

**Application:** Eudora

**Where on CD:**

\TOOLS\INTERNET\EMAIL\EUDORA

**Where Online:**

http://www.qualcomm.com/ProdTech/quest/

**Description:** Eudora is one of the most popular email programs in use. It is very easy to set up and use, and there
are plenty of options you can customize. The freeware
version of Eudora for Windows is included on the CD-
ROM. A commercial version of Eudora called Eudora
by QUALCOMM (Version 2.0 and above) is also available. If you would like information about the commercial version, a brief description is provided in the Help
menu of the freeware version. Select About Commercial
Eudora to display this dialog.

*Eudora e-mail package.*

**Application:** Pegasus Mail

**Where on CD:**

\TOOLS\INTERNET\EMAIL\EUDORA

**Where Online:**

http://www.cuslm.ca/pegasus/

**Description:** Pegasus Mail is another Internet email system with a ton of options. Actually, Pegasus Mail has more features than Eudora, including automatic distribution, NetWare compatibility, and automatic abbreviations. Try both programs and see which one suits you best.

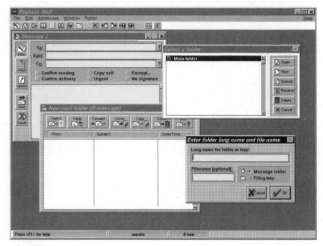

*Pegasus Mail*

**Application:** WS-FTP

**Where on CD:**

\TOOLS\INTERNET\FTP\WS_FTP16
\TOOLS\INTERNET\FTP\WS_FTP32

**Where On-Line:**

http://cwsapps.texas.net/ftp.html

**Description:** FTP is one of the most widely used Internet applications, and WS-FTP makes this often-used protocol quick and painless. Configurability options include several alternative screen layouts, the ability to associate remote files with local programs, automatic logging, and quick screen sizing. WS-FTP also comes pre-configured with an extensive array of ftp sites to check out. Multiple copies of the program can be launched to download multiple files at the same time. WS-FTP comes in two varieties: a 16-bit app and a 32-bit app. The only features missing are drag 'n' drop capabilities between local and remote file listings. WS-FTP is another of the must-have Internet applications.

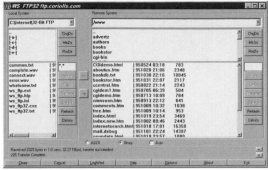

*WS-FTP*

**Application:** CuteFTP

**Where on CD:**

\TOOLS\INTERNET\FTP\CUTEFTP

**Where Online:**

http://papa.indstate.edu:8888/CuteFTP/

**Description:** CuteFTP is another stand-alone FTP program that expands on some of the features of WS_FTP. One of the best features of CuteFTP is its robust STOP command, similar in nature to the stop button found on many Web browsers. This command allows a user to stop any operation in progress while still maintaining the connection. Beyond the STOP command, CuteFTP also integrates the file listing process with file descriptions obtained from the index files found at many anonymous FTP sites (extremely helpful for deciphering the cryptic file names found at many FTP sites). Caching of recently visited directories is another distinctive feature found in CuteFTP. In addition to fixing many bugs, the newer releases of CuteFTP have implemented WS-FTP's File Manageresque approach to listing both remote and local directories side-by-side, comprehensive login listings, selectable file viewers, and selectable colors, the ability to recursively download directory trees, and the ability to easily send multiple files at once.

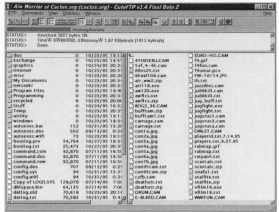

CuteFTP

**Application:** Home Page Creator

**Where on CD:**

\TOOLS\INTERNET\HTML\HPC

**Description:** HomePage Creator is a new tool designed to help you automatically create your own Web pages. It's not just another HTML editor, however. It allows you to insert a picture, text, and links to your favorite sites on the Web and then does the dirty work of generating HTML tags for you. The installation procedure for HomePage Creator is easy: Just run the SETUP.EXE program in the directory \TOOLS\HPC. You'll need to specify the directory where you want to install the HomePage Creator program. The developer of this program, Demetris Kafas, is currently developing a more feature-rich version of HomePage Creator that you'll be able to purchase in the future.

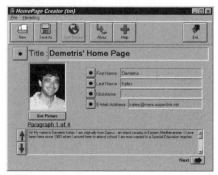

Home Page Creator

**Application:** HTMLed

**Where on CD:**

\TOOLS\INTERNET\HTML\HTMLED

**Where Online:**

http://www.ist.ca/

**Description:** HTMLed incorporates many advanced features into a program that is extremely easy to use. Intelligent tag insertion, tag removal, automatic saving with or without HTML tags, word wrap, and configurable floating toolbars are just a few of HTMLed's advanced features. In addition, the task of creating background images and identifying colors for your Web pages is made easy with HTMLed. HTMLed also makes good use of right mouse button functionality.

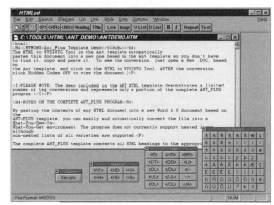

HTMLed

**Application:** Programmer's File Editor

**Where on CD:**

\TOOLS\INTERNET\HTML\PFE

**Where Online:**

http://www.lancs.ac.uk/people/cpaap/pfe/

**Description:** Programmer's File Editor (PFE) is a large-capacity, multi-file editor that runs on Windows 95, Windows 3.1x, and Windows NT 3.51 on Intel and PowerPC platforms. Although it's primarily oriented toward program developers and contains features like the ability to run compilers and development applications, it also makes a very good general purpose editor for any function at all, like HTML editing.

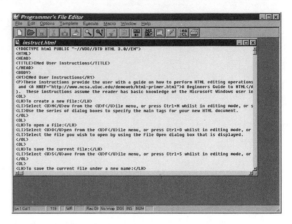

*Programmers File Editor*

**Application:** Mapedit

**Where on CD:**

\TOOLS\INTERNET\HTML\MAPEDIT

**Where Online:**

http://sunsite.unc.edu/boutell/mapedit/mapedit.html

**Description:** A graphical editor for World Wide Web image maps (clickable imagemaps). It does not magically make it possible for you to "serve" the maps; you need a real Web server for that. However, this application makes the production of MAP files very easy. Check with your provider to find out what to do with the MAP files.

*Mapedit image map file creation software*

**Application:** HotJava Browser

**Where on CD:**

\TOOLS\INTERNET\JAVA

**Where Online:**

http://java.sun.com

**Description:** HotJava is a new type of browser that you'll need to experiment with to realize its potential. This is a beta release so it's a little buggy, and Netscape's Navigator now supports the Java language also. Check out Sun's Web site for all the details.

**Application:** WinVN News Reader

**Where on CD:**

`\TOOLS\INTERNET\NEWS\WINVN`

**Where On-Line:**

`http://www.ksc.nasa.gov/software/winvn/winvn.html`

**Description:** WinVN is a Windows 95, and Windows NT based news reader. Its name stands for Windows Visual Newsreader. Like other news readers, it can be used to select, view, write, sort, and print Usenet News articles. Articles can be saved locally, cut into the Windows Clipboard or forwarded to other individuals via Electronic Mail. WinVN offers a more visual approach to Usenet News than earlier news readers. WinVN also allows the user to easily navigate between newsgroups and articles via its point-and-click interface. It allows multiple articles to be viewed simultaneously and on multi-tasking operating systems like Windows NT. It even allows multiple simultaneous news server connections.

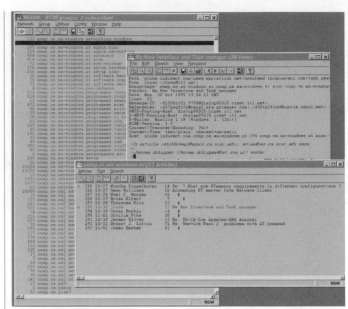

*WinVN Newsreader*

**Application:** HotMetal HTML Editor

**Where on CD:**

`\TOOLS\INTERNET\HTML\HOTMETAL`

**Where Online:**

`http://www.sq.com/products/hotmetal/hmp-org.htm`

**Description:** HotMetal is a Windows-based HTML editor
from SoftQuad. HotMetal has several elements that
make it a good choice for beginning HTML publishers.
It sticks to the basic, standard features of HTML, so you
won't be overwhelmed by dozens of different tags. In
fact, selecting Hide Tags from the View menu lets you
ignore the tags altogether.HotMetal comes with 14 tem-
plates for typical documents like home pages, customer
registration forms, and hotlists. Just choose File|Open
Template, pick the appropriate one from the list, type
your text between the tags, save your work as an HTM
file, and voila!—instant HTML. Be sure to start with
readme3.htm—a template that describes the other tem-
plates. If you don't like to use HTML coding, and you
want an application that will insert all the tags for you,
then give this one a try!

**Application:** VocalTec Internet Phone

**Where on CD:**

\TOOLS\INTERNET\PHONE

**Where Online:**

http://www.vocaltec.com/

**Description:** With Internet Phone, you can use the Internet to speak with any other user, from any point in the world! Real-time voice conversations over the Internet, at the price of a local phone call or even less! All you need is Internet Phone, a TCP/IP Internet connection and a Windows-compatible audio device. Plug in a microphone and speaker, run Internet Phone, and, by clicking a button, get in touch with Internet users all over the world who are using the same software. A friendly graphical user interface and a Voice-Activation feature make conversation easy. VocalTec's sophisticated voice compression and voice transfer technology makes sure your voice gets across in a flash, using only a fraction of the available bandwidth. Internet Phone now also supports Full Duplex audio: It lets you speak and listen at the same time.This software is getting better all the time. Look for some hot stuff from VocalTec and other companies in the near future.

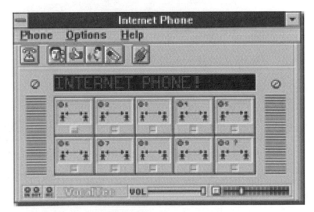

*VocalTec's Internet Phone*

**Application:** WebSpace VRML Browser

**Where on CD:**

`\TOOLS\INTERNET\VRML\WEBSPACE`

**Where Online:**

`http://webspace.sgi.com/`

**Description:** Many people think that software like this is the wave of the future for online navigation. The current version of the software needs some pretty powerful computer equipment to run well, but as software gets better and machines get faster, everyone will be using some sort of 3D browser. If you can afford it, buy an SGI machine and use SGI's VRML editor to create your own worlds. You will only need about $50,000 to get started! Oh well, for the rest of us, we will just have to tinker and dream for the time being.

*WebSpace VRML Browser*

**Application:** AdHoc 3D Studio to VRML Converter

**Where on CD:**

`\TOOLS\INTERNET\VRML\3DTOVRML`

**Where On-line:**

`http://www.best.com/~adhoc/html/vrml.html`

**Description:** While we are on the subject of VRML, this handy little utility will take 3DS files created in Autodesk's 3D Studio and convert them into VRML files. It is very handy if you use 3D Studio.

**Application:** Trumpet Winsock

**Where on CD:**

`\TOOLS\INTERNET\TRUMPET`

**Where Online:**

`Http://www.webcom.com/~llarrow/trouble.html`

**Description:** Trumpet Winsock is probably one of the most widely used shareware programs ever written. Why? Because it's simple and reliable. Trumpet can be used as a TCP/IP stack for internal or external use. It other words, it works over a LAN or a phone line. Trumpet is usually used over a phone line to connect to a service provider. The documentation that comes with Trumpet tells you everything you need to know about using it, so we recommend looking at the INSTALL.DOC file for help setting it up.

# Index

## F

## G

## X

X Files, The, 235

## Y

Yahoo search engine, 27, 69, 84-85
Yang, Jerry, 27, 84

## Z

Zima Web site, 227, 229-230